HONG KONG

HONG KONG

A CULTURAL HISTORY

Michael Ingham

OXFORD
UNIVERSITY PRESS

2007

OXFORD
UNIVERSITY PRESS

Oxford University Press, Inc., publishes works that further
Oxford University's objective of excellence
in research, scholarship, and education.

Oxford   New York
Auckland   Cape Town   Dar es Salaam   Hong Kong   Karachi
Kuala Lumpur   Madrid   Melbourne   Mexico City   Nairobi
New Delhi   Shanghai   Taipei   Toronto

With offices in
Argentina   Austria   Brazil   Chile   Czech Republic   France   Greece
Guatemala   Hungary   Italy   Japan   Poland   Portugal   Singapore
South Korea   Switzerland   Thailand   Turkey   Ukraine   Vietnam

Copyright © 2007 by Michael Ingham

Foreword © 2007 by Xu Xi

Foreword © 2007 by Lord Patten

Published by Oxford University Press, Inc.
198 Madison Avenue, New York, New York 10016

www.oup.com

Oxford is a registered trademark of Oxford University Press

Co-published in Great Britain by Signal Books

Library of Congress Cataloging-in-Publication Data
Ingham, Michael.
Hong Kong : a cultural history / Michael Ingham.
p. cm. — (Cityscapes)
Includes bibliographical references and index.
ISBN 978-0-19-531496-0; 978-0-19-431497-7 (pbk.)
1. Hong Kong (China)—History. 2. Hong Kong (China)—Civilization.
3. Hong Kong (China)—Description and travel. I. Title.
DS796.H757I54 2007
951.25—dc22   2007001938

9 8 7 6 5 4 3 2 1

Printed in the United States of America
on acid-free paper

Foreword

Hong Kong is an exciting city for many reasons.

First, it is one of the greatest maritime cities in the world—in the same league as Sydney, New York, San Francisco and Shanghai.

Second, it provides an extraordinary mix of colonial history and Chinese energy.

Third, Hong Kong is both literally and figuratively at the cross roads of the Asian and Western worlds. Stir all these ingredients together and you have an urban mix which has excited and delighted travellers and writers for over a century.

I am not entirely convinced that the writing has always been as entertaining as the City itself though the great travel memoir by Jan Morris does the business. But Michael Ingham, in this entertaining and original book, gives us a lot of good reasons why Hong Kong should stir our imagination and inspire a suitable response.

No-one who ever visits Hong Kong could ever be bored by the experience. Michael Ingham gives ample reason why this should always have been so.

Lord Patten

Finally.
What a pleasure, and relief, it is to be able to say of a Hong Kong visitor's guidebook: *finally*, one that does our city justice. Of course, this is not the typical guidebook, merely detailing places to stay, eat, shop, sightsee, but rather, one that takes the reader inside the city's soul. "Guidebook" is therefore a misnomer for this volume, because even a local reader will discover Hong Kong as the *imagined city*, which is what any great city becomes in the world.

When in its history can a city be said to exist in the global consciousness? Hong Kong arguably has long been a part of that collective imagination. Our significance in trade and finance, tourism, even the peculiar history that is Hong Kong have all contributed to our city's stature worldwide. Meanwhile, martial arts films, fashion, Canto-pop, TV shows, and increasingly, high quality "made in Hong Kong" brands make their mark on popular culture.

But how and why does a city enter the *world's artistic and cultural consciousness?*

Michael Ingham answers this very question in the pages that follow with insight, wit and yes, imagination. His gaze is that of the "inside outsider", the newcomer who stays and stays and stays so long he becomes one with the city, as Ingham does, this "foreigner" who is now "local". This is a heartfelt perspective, because he pays his adopted city homage, evidenced in his deep respect for local artistic endeavours, in the way he details Hong Kong's cultural maturation. This homage is admirable, because it emerges from a critical gaze and excellent research. This homage is infectious, because it is genuine, enthusiastic, personal. This homage is long overdue to a city that offers the world not just shopping, dining, entertainment, fashion, but also thoughtful films, artistic excellence in all the performing arts, a diverse and stunning cityscape and landscape, good literature, contemporary visual art in many mediums, a peculiarly unique history… all this from a place that ignites and invests the imagination with multiple expressive returns.

Come to Hong Kong, he says, but don't for god's sake come just for Disney ("beware low-flying giant mice" is the message he imagines for the advertisement near the airport) or merely another five-star global experience. Come and peer into this amazing city's soul *and discover your own connection to the humanity of this one-time barren rock.*

I first experienced the *raison d'être* of Ingham's imagined city in the summer of 2001, over curry and beer in London. I was passing through on my way to a writer's residency in Norway; he was doing his annual theatre field trip with his English literature students from Lingnan University. We were in the process of co-editing *City Voices,* the anthology of Hong Kong English writing that brought us together, and were still new colleagues then and did not know each other well. The Tate Modern was already closed—my afternoon ranneth over and I had missed this corner of my imagined London, which I hadn't visited for at least seven or eight years. And here was this Englishman, by then resident in my home city for about a dozen years, telling me all about Hong Kong's literary and cultural consciousness. Was he, as they say in American vernacular, "teaching a grandma to suck eggs?"

"It was the way their eyes lit up," he said of his Hong Kong students, "as the words they studied came to life during their first visit to England," where he brought them to theatre, ferried them along the byways of culture and history, showed them unexpected connections between the words they read in their New Territories classrooms to their own lives, and helped them understand the importance of imagination. Listening to him talk about his students—the abiding faith he had in their abilities to rise above second language limitations and lack of cultural exposure—it struck me that this foreigner to my city placed great value on the intrinsic power of the ordinary person's imaginative abilities. Lingnan is one of the newer universities, certainly not a venerable institution like the University of Hong Kong (which he describes in these pages) and its students are not the privileged elite of the older and more established tertiary institutes. Yet here was this graduate of elite Oxford, believing that Hong Kong students, regardless of their backgrounds and circumstances, would be inspired if given the opportunity to experience arts and culture first hand. What a refreshing perspective, I thought, to hear someone speak of the possibilities of an artistic soul for my city, tired as I was of the old clichés—"Hong Kong is a cultural desert that only cares about money and business"—that much of the local privileged elite, especially, seems too fond of repeating.

As I read this book, I was reminded of our London meeting. Ingham's enlightened perspective is perhaps best summed up in his musings on the high-quality fake antiques that abound in Hong Kong, which visitors are nonetheless drawn to purchase. "After all, value," he writes, "might well be said to reside principally in the belief systems of the imagination." So to all readers I say, *caveat emptor,* those without imagination need not enter here.

Sometimes it takes an outsider to see the true beauty of a place, because locals often become too jaded. Ingham brings an educator's zeal to this volume which instructs yet entertains, informs yet also delights. He roves across a broad spectrum with an open and democratic eye and has penned an astonishing "word album". There are tantalizing historical snapshots (the oft maligned Charles Elliot's viewpoint presages that of Chris Patten, the last British governor); geographical anomalies (early Tsimshatsui streets were originally named after those in Central, with "little thought for the confusion this was likely to cause to posterity"); unexpected connections (Sun Yat-sen juxtaposed with George Bernard Shaw segues to the Canto-pop lyricist James Wong).

But it is the array of cultural expressions he collects and examines, allowing a panoramic view of a clever, contrary, quirky artistic soul, that most delights. This soul continually strives for meaning, significance, identity, excellence, all of which Ingham accords Hong Kong in this highly original and finely detailed collage. He quotes from works of writers passing through who appropriate the city as locale, like Somerset Maugham from England or Eileen Chang (Chang Ai Ling) from Shanghai, as well as from home-grown authors such as P. K. Leung, Xi Xi, Louis Dung (Dung Kai-cheung) and Agnes Lam. He shows us the city on screen, as imagined by numerous directors, Wong Kar-wai certainly, but also Johnnie To, Evans Chan, Ann Hui *et al.* He takes us to live performances by Hong Kong's many theatre companies, to dance and music, Chinese operas. And he guides us through art spaces of all kinds, introducing us to painters, commenting on art installations, photo exhibits. In short, he gives us the imagined city as artists have expressed it, mapping the byways down the roads less and more travelled in order that we may engage with the city as fully as possible before departure. Refreshed, informed, enlightened. Finally.

Xu Xi
June 2006

Preface

It always seems more than a touch presumptuous for a non-indigenous writer to hold forth on the cultural heritage of a city without really belonging to that city. Although I have lived in Hong Kong since 1989 and consider the city my home, I cannot claim to "belong" to the place in the way that those who are born here do. However, many of their parents and grandparents were not "authentic" Hong Kongers. Like me, they made the place their home, even if at first it appeared to them merely a transit point in their lives.

The gulf of language and culture between the Chinese and the average Westerner is enormous, despite the "twin cities" of Hong Kong and Macau representing a unique cultural bridge between East Asia and the West. I have tried my best to cross that bridge from my side, but of course we must recognize that it is usually Chinese people who make the greatest effort to do so from theirs in terms of linguistic and cultural meeting of minds. In this respect I must point out that I have deliberately angled the book toward the reader, who has little or no knowledge of Chinese, which means inevitably that much about Hong Kong that cannot easily be translated is not included.

With reference to language, it is worth pointing out that most of the transliterations used in the book are based on Cantonese pronunciation, rather than Mandarin, the expression *fung shui* being a case in point. In my citations of writers who prefer the *pinyin* Mandarin Chinese version, *feng shui*, I have deliberately retained their spelling for the sake of literal accuracy. However, in general I have chosen to employ the Yale System of Cantonese transliteration as my standard romanization, without wishing to imply that it is the only—or necessarily the most recognized—method of rendering the aurally challenging nature of the Cantonese tonal system. In the case of street and place names in Hong Kong there exist officially recognised transliterations, which I have considered it sensible to follow. A further linguistic note to bear in mind is that a significant number of citations that appear in this book are English translations of the Chinese originals, and that the translators' names can be found in the bibliography. For reasons that should be obvious I have used the English names of films (most of which can be obtained with ease from retailers in Hong Kong or on the internet) and printed works of fiction. In most cases there is only one available translation of the work of fiction or anthology. Readers may be interested to know that standard written Chinese is common to all the various dialects of the spoken language, although Hong Kong employs traditional, non-simplified script, in contrast to the simplified characters characteristic to the mainland, which were introduced as part of the literacy drive of the post-1949 communist government.

My aim has not been to write a travel guide, although I hope the final product is useful to the traveller, keen to penetrate beyond the bland surface of the conveniently packaged experience of the global city. Neither has it been to write an end-of-empire eulogy, drawing the line under the 156 years of colonial rule. That has been done by others, and I have absolutely no desire to repeat what has been said. In any case Hong Kong, Britain and China have all changed dramatically and irrevocably in the nine years since the Territory was "returned" to China. As far as China was concerned Hong Kong had never gone away! One can therefore understand the reference to Hong Kong as "a borrowed place living on borrowed time." Stated simply, my intention has been to convey Hong Kong's genuine claim to be "a city of the imagination", and to correct its clichéd image as purely a temple of mammon. In doing so, I have sought to evoke its perverse but compelling cultural mosaic and its surprisingly rich literary and artistic heritage, as well as it its eventful and under-explored history. I make no apologies for my ideological positions, which are not, I hope, inflicted too heavy-handedly on the reader. Being non-committal and dryly factual throughout would make for anodyne prose in a book such as this, and would in any case be inappropriate in the context of such a vibrant city-with-attitude as Hong Kong undoubtedly is.

My heartfelt thanks and appreciation go to Colin Day, Xu Xi, Jessica Yeung and James Ferguson, who read the manuscript at various stages of preparation, and to Heidi Chun for help with proof reading and indexing, as well as to Devdan Sen and James Ferguson for typesetting and design. Their critical insights and practical suggestions have proved invaluable, and I feel fortunate to have been able to call on their kind services in providing information and corrective feedback at various points of the project. Any errors or omissions apparent to the reader are mine rather than theirs. My sincere thanks are also due to Matt Fung, whose original and expressive photographs of his native city have enriched my prose considerably, and whose research assistance I valued highly.

I would also point out that what seems to be an imbalance in the book's structure—four of the seven chapters dealing exclusively with Hong Kong Island itself—is justified by the cultural-imaginary perspective of the present series. Put simply, there is far more significant material to write about in connection with Hong Kong Island, at least from a non-local viewpoint. I apologize however to Kowloon and New Territories residents (among whom I count myself!) and to historians of this much larger part of present-day Hong Kong for necessarily compressing their place of abode into the last two chapters.

Unusually, this book is dedicated to more than one person: my mother, Peggy, sister, Fiona and brother, Richard, all of whom were captivated by Hong Kong's idiosyncratic character during their visits here, and to my aunt Rita and Uncle Anthony, whose interest in Hong Kong depended on my own oral accounts as well as the images I have sent them of the city, since neither of them were able to see the place for themselves. The penultimate "dedicatee" is my wife, Jessica, who has enabled me to see Hong Kong through a borrowed "local" lens. Without her help I would still be dealing with surfaces. Lastly I dedicate the book to the resilient spirit of the people of Hong Kong, who—unlike their Chief Executive—are prepared to stand up for the universal suffrage they know is their right.

Contents

Chapter Four: "The Great Learning": Pokfulam, Hong Kong University and Western District 95

Chapter Five: A Floating World: The Peak, Aberdeen, Stanley and Repulse Bay 131

Chapter Six: Across the Fragrant Harbour: the Nine Dragons 159

Introduction

Hong Kong is situated slightly south of the Tropic of Cancer on the south-east coast of China. It is the generic name used to refer to an archipelago of 235 islands and the small slice of the China mainland on the peninsula, around which these islands are clustered. Contemporary Hong Kong comprises four distinct sectors: Hong Kong Island, from which the place gets its name; Kowloon, the crowded tip of the Chinese mainland narrowly separated from Hong Kong Island by Victoria Harbour; The New Territories to the north of Kowloon, a more extensive area bordering on China proper; and the scattered Outlying Islands, the biggest of which are inhabited but many of which are not. The total area of the Territory, or Special Administrative Region of Hong Kong, is 425 square miles, roughly double the size of Singapore. Hong Kong Island itself accounts for only thirty square miles of this total.

Hong Kong's climate is sub-tropical with the warm south-west Monsoon giving hot, humid summers between the months of May and October. Typhoons are not uncommon in this summer period, and in the past some have wreaked havoc on the city's infrastructure, although modern Hong Kong is built to withstand the exceptionally high winds. On the opposite western side of the Pearl River, at the mouth of which Hong Kong is located, stands the "sister-city" of Macau. From the sixteenth century onwards Macau had been a flourishing trading enclave under the Portuguese when Hong Kong was entirely undeveloped and sparsely populated. Seventy-five miles upriver is southern China's capital, Guangzhou (formerly known as Canton), which had been the corresponding trading port for the European and American companies prior to 1841, when the opium traders were summarily ejected from the city.

Ever since Captain Charles Elliot's famous (or infamous, depending on one's perspective) landing in Hong Kong in 1841 and Viscount Palmerston's oft-quoted description of Britain's almost accidental territorial acquisition as a "barren rock", a huge leap both of faith and imagination has always been required to envisage what Hong Kong might be, as opposed to the prosaic reality of what was actually beheld. The territory

International Finance Centre (IFC2), Central

is surprisingly rich in myth and legend in the Chinese cultural conscious too. The last emperor of the Sung Dynasty, still a young boy, is reputed to have plunged to his death in the arms of his last remaining advisor at the tip of Kowloon peninsula. As it was, too, for refugees from the 1949 revolution and later the excesses of the Cultural Revolution, there was simply nowhere further to run. This eleventh-century historical event seems, rather like the officially un-commemorated exploit of Captain Elliot, to have receded into the realms of the mythical and the imaginary. If that is not already the case also with the horrors of the Japanese military occupation between late 1941 and 1945, in a few more generations the facts of those events, too, may become clouded in the mists of ideological discourse amid the pragmatism of fast-growing cultural and commercial regional ties.

Hong Kong is in many ways an anomaly. At the time of writing the population numbers approximately 6.9 million. Roughly 97 per cent of them are Cantonese speakers and of Chinese ethnicity. Hong Kong people are diverse in their origins and most families are not indigenous to Hong Kong itself, but from somewhere across the border in Guangdong or further north. Like the European administrators, soldiers, merchants and businessmen who arrived from mid-nineteenth century onwards, most of the Chinese and other nationalities who made their home here previously regarded the place as a temporary haven from persecution and political instability, or as a glorified gold-rush town, a place to get rich and then leave for good. Very few, apart from the small indigenous population, would have seriously thought of Hong Kong as home.

Today that feeling of impermanence, which adds spice to life in any city, is no doubt experienced by expatriates of many nationalities. But the difference now is that while residents of earlier eras, whether from Shanghai or from Chicago, would have found the designation *heung gong yan*, or Hong Konger, bizarre or laughable, in today's Hong Kong there is a sophisticated and increasingly well-educated population who think of the city as home. Indeed, Hong Kong is becoming more and more a young person's metropolis. The rapid economic progress of the 1970s and 1980s and the change whereby younger generations had never lived in mainland China, coupled with the turbulence and insecurity of the Cultural Revolution, produced a population in whose imagination Hong Kong was no longer a transit point on the way to a better future, but the place where the dreams and ambitions of their lives could be realized.

Trilingual and biliterate, which means that many of them, especially the younger generation, can speak Cantonese, Mandarin and English and write English and Chinese, many regard themselves as primarily Hong Kong people before referring to themselves as Chinese. Until 1975 English had been the only official language, after which Cantonese gained equal status to be followed relatively recently by the official recognition of Mandarin. While many older Hong Kong people speak Cantonese and perhaps the Chinese dialect of their native region of China, the younger, more highly educated generations tend to appreciate the growing importance of Mandarin, in addition to the cool cachet and economy of code-mixing between English and Cantonese. The latter vernacular can provoke frowns of disapproval amongst purists, but it seems set to feature in Hong Kong's cultural soundscape for the foreseeable future.

The old clichés of "shopping paradise" and "pearl of the Orient" persist in publicity material, though prices do not always match the hyperbole. Yet there is no denying that Hong Kong has developed from the most humble and inauspicious origins into a vibrant and virtual non-stop metropolis over the course of the last one hundred and fifty years. The city is the eighth biggest trading economy and the third biggest financial centre on the planet, with world-class facilities and institutions and a highly sophisticated cultural life. This is a far cry from as little as thirty years ago, when it was contemptuously dismissed as a cultural desert. Hong Kong people have responded to the opportunities of the past fifty years and transformed the city into what might be termed—rather like the post-war reconstruction of Germany—an economic miracle.

It is said that travellers and especially merchant seamen who revisit a port after thirty of forty years are nowhere more baffled than they are coming back to Hong Kong because the shoreline of the Fragrant Harbour (a now highly misleading translation of the Cantonese name *Heung Gong*) is unrecognizable. Even so, the Star Ferry, the cheapest tourist attraction in the world according to the folklore, has retained its distinctive squat, green appearance and chugs endlessly back and forth between Hong Kong Island and Tsim Sha Tsui on the China mainland peninsula, continuing to stir the imagination of tourist and resident alike by the inspiration of its magical seven-minute respite from the hurly-burly of the city.

The shape of the Hong Kong Peak would still be recognizable to a Kipling, a Coward, a Chaplin or a George Bernard Shaw, or even to the mid-nineteenth-century artist and architect Thomas Allom. Allom's paintings and sketches of South China in general and Hong Kong harbour in particular, with its striking blend of Royal Navy frigates and Chinese junks and sampans set against the steep peaks of the island, were the most famous pictorial representations of the era for a fascinated European public. All of the above luminaries at one time sailed into Hong Kong's busy harbour, though not all of them stayed very long—perhaps through a combination of a tight schedule and foggy weather, as in Chaplin's case. The Peak continues to be virtually invisible at times shrouded in heavy mist, though nowadays pollution is just as likely a culprit as an adverse weather front.

We make our buildings and then they make us, according to Winston Churchill's dictum. This is nowhere as true as in Hong Kong. The overwhelming influx of refugees from the communist victory, or liberation, of China in the years after 1949 had two contrasting effects. One was to produce the misery of squalid squatter camps and the other was to increase dramatically the pool of talent in Hong Kong. Rapid expansion and building including government housing estates, prompted by the disastrous squatter area fire of Christmas 1953, transformed the sleepy colonial outpost into firstly a fiercely competitive industrial zone and subsequently one of the foremost financial powerhouses in the world. In the process Hong Kong's now familiar skyline of towering glass and metal structures gradually emerged along the northern shoreline of Hong Kong Island and increasingly on the Kowloon peninsula.

The latest giant addition, and one which has utterly transformed the panorama, positioned as it is on the foreshore of the business centre, Central, and in front of Hong Kong Peak, is known simply as the IFC (International Finance Centre). The fifth tallest building in the world and a leisure-and-shopping centre as well as a financial building, the sheer dominance of the 88-storey IFC and its sister buildings, bestriding the horizon like so many colossi, is breathtaking. Just opposite on the other side of the harbour in West Kowloon, the 108-storey International

Commerce Centre is springing up and is scheduled to be completed in 2008. The ICC, the Kowloon-side counterpart to the IFC, is being designed as a "Vertical City" dedicated to offices, shops and hotels. If nothing else, it will play an important part in redressing the skyline balance of Hong Kong's famous harbour-front. Plans to link the two harbour-fronts with an audacious 2,500-foot cross-harbour bridge have remained on the drawing-board, as have those for a London-Eye-style giant Ferris wheel on the Kowloon side of the harbour. Such infrastructure projects—whether in conception or reality—are testimony to the boldly imaginative, can-do spirit one often encounters in Hong Kong

Since the 1997 transfer of sovereignty from London to Beijing the pace of rapid economic development experienced by China, which began in the southern special economic zones in close proximity to Hong Kong, can in retrospect be partly attributed to the influence of Hong Kong's entrepreneurial flair. Patriarch Deng Xiaoping, who died only a few months before the return of Hong Kong to Chinese control, was proud of his imaginative solution to the difficulties of assimilating a capitalistic community within a communist system. Deng referred to it as "one country two systems", although he could not have foreseen the huge and rapid changes within China itself, generated by his own programme of reform, which have brought the respective economic systems, at least, much closer together. In theory there will be no change to the one country-two systems policy before 2047. By that time convergence is supposed to have been achieved. The way things are going, it is the mainland that will become like Hong Kong, rather than the other was round (although this view is, in some quarters, heretical).

Interestingly, the harbour is still called after Victoria, despite the colonial associations. Indeed, many of the emblems of the colonial era have remained in place, including the many streets and other public amenities that bear the names of past governors—with the notable exception of the last governor, Chris Patten, and of course Captain Charles Elliot. The old statue of Queen Victoria, which formerly dominated Statue Square in Central, was moved to Victoria Park in Causeway Bay. Now, perhaps fittingly, only the statue of nineteenth-century Hong Kong and Shanghai Bank chairman Thomas Jackson remains. The Prince of Wales Building, at the heart of the old HMS Tamar site, which served as the Headquarters of British Forces during the colonial period, became the central barracks for the first People's Liberation Army contingent in Hong Kong after the Handover. The PLA maintained a very low profile when they arrived due to the controversial nature of their being deployed so close to the central district of the city. This careful low profile combined with good public relations appears to have earned them a degree of local respect and trust. For several years however, possibly on account of their low profile, they obviously failed to spot the royal insignia and name of the Prince of Wales Building boldly and incongruously displayed for all to see on the Central-facing side of their new acquisition.

Incongruity, though, is nothing new. Hong Kong's new emblem, its hybrid flower known as the bauhinia which adorns its red flag, but is distinct from the Chinese flag, was originally named after the predatory late nineteenth-century governor, Henry Blake. As writer and historian Arthur Hacker humorously points out, "it would seem that Hong Kong is doomed to have its flag, coins and banknotes decorated with the image of a sterile hybrid, named after an arch-colonial Irish vandal."

Now that Hong Kong is no longer a British territory, it remains a place of myth and exotically distorted perception for the casual Western observer, partly through its frequently unreliable media depictions, partly through its self-representation for the tourist industry. The alarmist reporting of the 2003 SARS crisis (Severe Acute Respiratory Syndrome, and nothing to do with the city's designation as a SAR, a Special Administrative Region, of China) in certain quarters of the Western media gave readers the impression that here was an Asian pandemic—a new Yellow Peril—of horrifying proportions from which nobody recovered. The successful search for the source of the virus and a vaccine, the very small numbers of people infected, the fact that the vast majority of them recovered and the bravery of the hospital staff were not deemed worthy of mention by the sensation-hungry propagators of news. Admittedly the lack of transparency about the origins of the virus across the border in Guangdong was worrying, if predictable, and the Hong Kong government's inept initial response hardly inspired confidence. However, Hong Kong and South China's social and economic recovery from the deleterious effects of the virus has been nothing short of miraculous.

Landing in Hong Kong is no longer the hair-raising experience it once was, but if one is sitting in the window-seat, one can get a much more encompassing view of its unique topography. Before the 1998 opening of Chek Lap Kok, the impressive, award-winning international airport, planes used to fly in low over the apartments of Kowloon City and passengers had interesting glimpses into the denizens' living quarters. It was reputedly one of the most difficult landings in the world. Today, by contrast, the traveller arrives in the smoothly run modern airport built mainly on reclaimed land just off Lantau Island (the biggest of the Outlying Islands). The next step for many is to take the Airport Express shuttle train into the heart of Central (journey time, 23 minutes). Formerly the Victorian colonial city of Victoria, Central is a sensible place to start the Hong Kong tour. For this reason it is also an ideal place to begin our exploration of the modern city in Chapter Two, having learnt about its chequered colonial history in more detail in Chapter One. Central is a good location in which to feel the business and leisure pulse of Hong Kong, and it is even more spectacular at night, lit up by dazzling lights and by the virtual "fireworks" display of laser light emanating from the skyscrapers. We can get an atmospheric overview of Hong Kong from the public viewing platform on the 55th floor of the IFC spire (Note: ID required for entry permit). Alternatively, there is a rather different impression of Central and the immediate area to be had from the Peak Tram funicular railway, as it climbs steadily away from Central towards its Peak destination, 1,400 feet above sea level.

Chapters Three, Four and Five keep us on Hong Kong-side, which is the way residents refer to the Hong Kong Island-Kowloon split. The north side of Hong Kong Island is well served by both its modern Mass Transit Railway and its venerable tram system, and Central is at the centre of this axis. Chapter Three takes us eastwards toward the bustling entertainment and shopping areas of Wan Chai and Causeway Bay, while Chapter Four explores the older, more traditional western districts of Sheung Wan, Sai Ying Pun and Pokfulam. We climb the famous Peak in the hilly centre of the island in Chapter Five and enjoy its commanding views over Hong Kong Island and Kowloon, then descend to the pleasant southern shores of Repulse Bay and Stanley, where the last resistance to the Japanese invasion in December 1941 took place.

Chapters Six and Seven take us across the harbour to Kowloon and the New Territories. Tsim Sha Tsui, Kowloon's equivalent to Central but a locality with a more culturally varied feel, is the most eye-catching and stimulating of Kowloon's eight designated districts. The site of the famous Walled City, which exists only as a memorial park today, is east of here and close to the old airport of Kai Tak. In this chapter we also look at the colourful and historically rich areas of Yau Ma Tei and Mong Kok. Finally in Chapter Seven we continue north beyond the distinctive Lion Rock and investigate the abundant cultural and historical heritage of the misleadingly named New Territories. This part of Hong Kong is where the first major settlements of the Han and later Tang Dynasties were located and is in many ways the cradle of Hong Kong's Chinese identity. Western influences in the satellite towns of the New Territories such as Sha Tin, directly north of Kowloon City, and Tuen Mun and Yuen Long, to the west and north-west respectively, co-exist alongside more traditional Chinese practices.

Chapter Seven leaves the visitor, appropriately enough, on the Outlying Islands—though unfortunately not on the right one from which to catch the departing flight! A relatively short ferry ride, however, will suffice to take the reader back to Aberdeen on Hong Kong Island, and from there the return journey to Chek Lap Kok is also a return to the fast pace of city life after the more leisurely allure of the rural New Territories and Islands. Only now does one appreciate how it is possible for more than sixty per cent of Hong Kong to consist of country parks and open terrain. As we take off—on a clear day of course—there is a superb vista of sea, islands and skyward-thrusting buildings that is singularly and memorably characteristic of the crossroads of trade, culture and historical development that is Hong Kong.

> *"So if I wish to describe Hong Kong to you, sticking to what I personally saw and experienced, I should have to tell you that it is a colourless city, without character, planted there at random. But this would not be true either. At certain hours, in certain places, along the street, you see opening before you the hint of something unmistakable, rare, perhaps Magnificent; you would like to say what it is, but everything said of Hong Kong before imprisons your words and obliges you to repeat rather than say. Therefore the people of Hong Kong still believe they live in a Hong Kong which grows only with the name Hong Kong, and they do not notice the Hong Kong that grows on the ground."*
>
> *Evans Chan, To Liv(e),*
> *adapted from Invisible Cities by Italo Calvino*

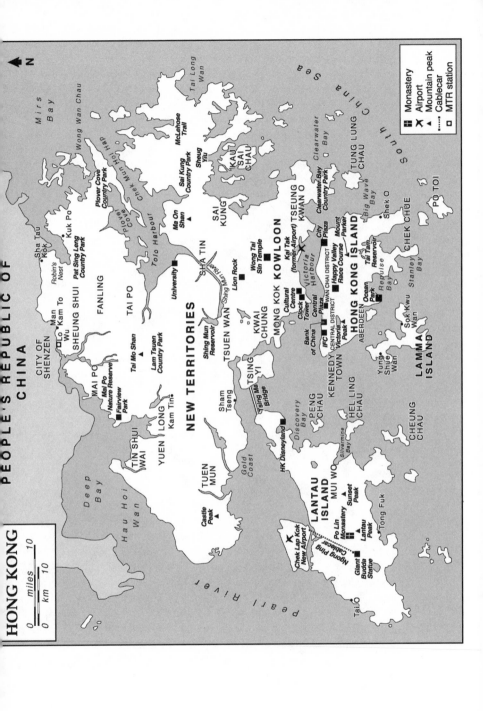

Engraved by M. J. Starling.

HONG KONG

chapter one

THE PEARL RIVER AND THE BARREN ISLAND: THE STORY OF HONG KONG

"The river succours and impedes native and foreigner alike; it limits and enables, it isolates and joins."
Timothy Mo, *An Insular Possession*, 1986

Ancient and Chinese Imperial Hong Kong

Bai-yu Shan, a twelfth-century Chinese mystical poet, presciently wrote of a big city emerging on the south coast of China at the mouth of the Pearl River "lit by a host of stars in the deep night and ten thousand ships passing to and fro within the harbour." Looking at the dazzlingly spectacular modern-day city of Hong Kong, one can only speculate which emotion, a sense of wonder or a sense of vindication, would be uppermost in the poet's mind, if he could witness the results of his literary clairvoyance. Reincarnated, he would doubtless feel confident about heading for one of the popular racecourses in today's Special Administrative Region or SAR—the new designation of the former Crown Colony of Hong Kong—for a flutter on the horses. It would be a pity to waste such impressive powers of prognostication, after all. Historically speaking though, Bai-yu Shan (a pen name meaning "White Jade Mountain" and possibly also a reference to the Baiyue tribe, who were indigenous to the area in Neolithic times) was not the first Chinese poet to evoke mental images of the area in deathless and prophetic verse.

His eighth-century forerunner, Han Yu in the Tang Dynasty, during a period of exile to what was considered then to be a remote and barbarous region, composed an almost epigrammatic couplet. The poem is included in his collected works and a four character reference (meaning "The Finest High Mountain") can be seen inscribed on a big granite tablet at Castle Peak, in what many centuries later became known as The New Territories. The couplet refers to the Tang army's fortress at Tunmen—then a fast-developing port for Indian and Persian traders—being pounded by the waves during a tropical storm, and runs thus: "They say that Tunmen is a high mountain, but even these waves will swallow it up." This is a case of poetic license, of course, because Tunmen or Tuen Mun, as it is now known, did not suffer an Atlantis-like fate and is very much alive and well in the form of a teeming satellite town playing host to about one-sixth of Hong Kong's near seven million-population. The effects of global warming, however, may yet prove Han Yu as prescient a poet as Bai-yu Shan. Indeed, the sea level on the South China coast is believed to have risen dramatically in the prehistoric period between the fifth and fourth millennia BC, so there are historical precedents.

A few centuries before Han Yu's time, in the era of the southern Han rulers, Hong Kong was known as Meichuan, and formed an integral part of the larger Xinan County, with its administrative seat in Nantou, north of the present border with China. Meichuan became important as a centre for pearl-fishing. The emperors and the ruling classes prized the pearl as a decorative ornament not just for their persons, but also for the furnishing and decorations of their palaces. Less fortunate were the specially recruited pearl fishers themselves for whom the treasure hunt meant diving to an extremely hazardous depth in the eponymous Pearl River with frequent loss of life. At the same time, fishing continued to be practised by the inhabitants of the Pearl River delta, many of whom operated from the shelter of the archipelago, now known generically as Hong Kong.

Hong Kong Island itself had been home to a self-sufficient fishing and maritime community going right back to its aboriginal residents, the Yue (or Yao) tribe. These hardy, stocky seafaring people descended from the earliest Neolithic period inhabitants. In their turn the modern-day boat people of Hong Kong, the Tanka, have derived their maritime and fishing cultural traditions from this long lineage. Little is known about the Yue, but some archaeological evidence gathered from Bronze Age rock carvings at Big Wave Bay and Wong Chuk Hang, as well as excavations on the islands of Lantau, Lamma and Cheung Chau, suggests that there was a thriving community supported primarily by mariculture. Stone and bronze tools and weapons, pottery and ceramics, skilfully crafted quartz rings and other ornaments, as well as coins, have also been excavated, pointing to an imaginative and resourceful indigenous population.

Later on, after the unification of China following the Emperor Qin's conquests in the second century BC, Hong Kong, now integrated into the Donguan county of Guangdong province, started to be colonized or settled by non-indigenous peoples from further north. This pattern was to continue until the incursions from the west by the Portuguese and subsequently the British. Interestingly, the endemic racial discrimination, which was to represent a significant blight on the more positive aspects of British imperialism, had its counterpart in the short-lived Qin and subsequent more lasting Dynasties. The Yue and latterly the Tanka (boat people who may have originated in Vietnam) were prohibited from building dwellings on land, as well as from intermarriage with the Han interlopers or being employed as civil servants. Although the rule forbidding building onshore accommodation was relaxed in the seventeenth century, the tradition of the Tanka living on their boats and being treated as social inferiors had already taken root, and has regrettably endured in the city's collective psyche. The influx of new settlers during and after this period from both southern and northern regions was a far more gradual and manageable affair than the wave of economic and political migrants that shook, and ultimately shaped, the colony in the mid-twentieth century. One advantage of the remoteness of Hong Kong in this period and the relative peace and independence enjoyed by its inhabitants is reflected in the common Chinese proverb: "Heaven is high and the Emperor far away."

At this point in its development, of course, not even the fertile imagination of a Chinese poet could have envisaged the statue of Queen Victoria sitting in state on Hong Kong Island, looking highly amused at her acquisition of the territory and her sudden elevation to the putative title of Princess of Hong Kong. The existence of the Western barbarians had not as yet come to the attention of the busy, nation-building Chinese. But two events during the Sung Dynasty brought Hong Kong into the ambit of national affairs, and could be said to presage its transformation from sleepy fishing outpost to player on the world stage at the end of the same millennium. The first and more minor was the arrival of a Sung princess (as opposed to a British one), seeking refuge from the Mongol attackers who had captured the Sung emperor and the rest of his family. She was fortunate enough to be rescued by the powerful Tang clan, who were *de facto* rulers of Hong Kong at this point, and to remain concealed in Kam Tin in the present-day New Territories. She married one of the Tang clan sons and eventually went with him to court after the emperor regained his throne following a truce with the Mongols. (This historical event serves to illustrate the smart Hong Konger's eye for the main chance and willingness to take a gamble.) Initially unimpressed with his new son-in-law, the emperor learned to accept his southern ways. Even so, the princess was said to have pined so much for the fragrant harbour and the rustic delights of life in Kam Tin that the emperor had no option but to allow the couple to return to the deep-south, and lose her once more.

The second royal visitation was in 1277, considerably predating the fleeting visits of various Princes of Wales in the nineteenth and twentieth centuries, and was to prove even more dramatic. Fleeing south with a small army and pursued by the rampant Mongols, the last two Sung emperors, pre-teenage boys who were the only survivors of the Mongol depredations, set up court at Mui Wo (Silvermine Bay) on Lantau Island and later in Kowloon City. Their implacable foes were not to be long delayed in their imperial designs on the Sung throne. After the elder of the two, Yi Wong (also known as Di Zheng), had succumbed to disease, he was succeeded by his seven-year-old brother, Wei Wong (or Di Bing). Both brothers denied the Mongols the satisfaction of capturing their quarry. After definitive defeat for the Sung navy in a sea battle of Hong Kong, the boy emperor is reputed to have leapt to his death by drowning in the waters off Kowloon Peak in the arms of his loyal mentor.

This story could be apocryphal, since, according to other sources, he is supposed to have drowned attempting escape. What is certain is that the Sung-era rock carving in a small park in Sung Wong Toi Park near the old Kai Tak airport still bears witness today to these heady events. The giant boulder under which the boy emperor remained in hiding became known as the Sung Emperor's (*Sung Wong* in Cantonese) Rock, and a terrace and balustrade around the sacred site were constructed in later times and preserved under the terms of the 1898 lease between the Chinese and the British. They survived until the Japanese Occupation in the 1940s, when they were broken up and the stone used for extending the airport at Kai Tak. The part of the smashed rock bearing the inscription survives, however, to this day in the otherwise nondescript park in Ma Tau Chung Road.

The Sung boy emperor's rock, Kowloon

Another Hong Kong legend, connected with the distinctive topography of the territory, can be traced back to this poignant end-of-era event. The boy emperor remarked that the eight hills he could see around him in Kowloon were dragons, a lucky and royal omen, at which his glib retainer, in the knowledge that shoe-shining (the Cantonese equivalent of flattery) could get him everywhere, promptly replied, "No, nine dragons, your majesty. Your sacred majesty is the ninth." This legend accounts for the name of Kowloon, which means "nine dragons" in Cantonese. The man's descendants are almost certain to have become high-ranking civil servants in colonial and post-colonial Hong Kong administrations. It is certainly not difficult to forgive the poetic license and envisage the dragon-like appearance of these suggestively undulating hills, which retain their magic even in the urban landscape of today's Hong Kong. The other official, the loyal one who jumped with the boy emperor in his arms, gave his name to one of Hong Kong's most revered local deities, Hau Wong.

The dislike of Hong Kong people for the Mongol Yuan Dynasty that followed has endured, but perhaps only in the cultural subconscious, in the form of September's Mid-Autumn Festival. Traditionally, Chinese people celebrate this festival with cholesterol-packed sweetmeats known as moon-cakes. The rebellion which succeeded in toppling the Yuan Dynasty in 1368 was instigated by secret messages passed to conspirators in moon-cakes. Hong Kong people exhibit great relish in selling and buying these patriotically evocative delicacies. The sceptical *gweilo* (Westerner—literally *faan gweilo* or foreign devil) who remains unconvinced of the dubious pleasure of eating moon-cake may well surmise that the moon-cakes in 1368 probably tasted better for the added paper ingredient. Another ambivalent heirloom that the Sung presence bequeathed Hong Kong in the shape of its walled garrison was its famous—or infamous, depending on one's point of view—Kowloon Walled City, which as a Chinese imperial enclave in the heart of the ceded territory, was to become a thorn in the side of successive colonial administrations. Without doubt the most valuable legacy of the royal visit was the innovative dish known as *poon choi*, invented out of desperation to serve the boy emperor and his retinue. It is a sort of stew or mixed-pot composed of layers of different types of food including bean curd and vegetables, and topped with chicken and pork. This royal fare, ingeniously concocted out of necessity, has lived on as the special menu for important village celebrations.

It is difficult to estimate the population of Hong Kong during these centuries of dynastic change. It clearly fluctuated in response to the vicissitudes of the various emperors and their courts. However, one disastrous chain of events for Hong Kong in the seventeenth century was triggered by the cataclysmic fall of the cultivated and hitherto stable Ming Dynasty. The notorious pirate, Zheng Chenggong, or Koxinga as he was known, operated with impunity in the waters around Hong Kong, defying the authority of the Manchu emperor of the newly established Qing Dynasty under the guise of loyalty to the late Ming emperor. Unable to deal effectively with Koxinga's impressive fleet of rebel pirate ships, the Manchu authorities decided to simply abandon Hong Kong and other southern coastal regions by means of a radical policy of forced exile. The wretched inhabitants of Hong Kong were coerced into leaving everything behind and migrating at least seventeen miles inland. Although two rare honest advisors to the emperor eventually managed to persuade him to reverse the policy five years later, irreparable damage had already been done to Hong Kong's ecology.

About 16,000 people were forced to leave in the Great Clearance of 1661-2. Of this number only a paltry 1,600, a tenth of the original Tang Punti population (Hong Kong's aboriginal inhabitants), gradually returned to a land laid waste. Many of those who made their way back turned to piracy for their livelihood. Present and future administrations will do well to learn from the lessons of history when contemplating the irreversible effects of benighted policy on the environment of Hong Kong. A visiting magistrate reported seeing piles of dead old people and children in the abandoned streets. Hong Kong was so seriously depopulated by this disaster that even the policy of importing Hakka workers from northern China had only a limited impact.

A Subtle Change of Empire
By the time the British arrived in the South China delta in the seventeenth century hard on the heels of the Portuguese explorers and merchants, who had been initially resisted but subsequently permitted by the Celestial Emperor to settle in Macao, Hong Kong's regular population was a mere three and half thousand, with perhaps a couple of thousand Tanka boat-people augmenting the number. The strait-laced, self-disciplined Manchus, strongly disapproving of the lax, cultivated and, to them, hedonistic lifestyle of the Ming Chinese, instituted a number of reforms, one of which in 1730 aimed to suppress the habit of gambling prevalent in Guangdong (Canton Province), including, of course, Hong Kong. The records attest to their attempts in the form of edicts aimed at outlawing the undesirable practice. The modern-day passion for gambling, whether in the Western-imported form of horse-racing or the home-grown and extremely popular game of *mah jeuk* or *mah jong*, is eloquent testimony to their miserable failure. The imperial edict against the evils of gambling in the South China region begins sententiously: "From earliest days loafers and idlers have been anathema to those who rule. But gamblers are worse than mere idlers…" Their warnings live on, even in today's Hong Kong, in the official government warnings of the negative effects of the gambling habit as well as in the tightly regulated framework for gambling in the Territory. The Manchus were nevertheless soon preoccupied with the implications of another vice,

potentially even more destructive of the social fabric than gambling, namely the smoking of opium. They could have had little intimation of the outcome of their campaign against the importation of this popular but debilitating recreational drug.

The Manchus regarded themselves by now as *bona fide* Chinese. The undoubted tendency of the Han Chinese to assimilate conquering outsiders into their own culture is to a considerable extent true in the cases of both the Mongols and the Manchus. Despite this, the Celestial Empire remained vulnerable to its enemies, both interior and exterior. The Manchus' assumptions of absolute superiority simply compounded the problem. Warning signs of British intentions to win special trading concessions on an equal footing with the Portuguese were evident with the visit of the British government envoy Lord Macartney to Peking in 1793. Between 1793 and the mid-1830s Britain, now the pre-eminent sea power in the world, determined to wrest trading concessions from the Chinese government, although Macartney himself dismissed as a wild suggestion the notion that British negotiators should push for the concession of a Macao-like enclave or insular station.

The huge corporate monopoly that was the British East India Company controlled the lucrative tea trade between China, India and Europe. China was not at all interested in balancing trade by importing products from Britain. The currency used to buy Chinese tea, silk and porcelain was silver, and until the early nineteenth century it had been in plentiful supply. Yet Western trade practices were disrupted by the Napoleonic Wars and their aftermath, which resulted in a serious shortage of silver: hence the introduction of opium smuggling, which was to shape the future of the nondescript fishing community on the South China coast.

The emerging breed of Western capitalist adventurers, even less scrupulous about trade agreements and cultural differences than the East India Company, exhorted the British government to "open up" the Chinese market by force of arms. What they had to sell was opium from British-administered Bengal. The opium trade was illegal in China, having been banned by the Manchus. Officially, smoking opium was illegal, but in practice the habit was widely adopted, with officials turning a blind eye. In Europe there was no such prohibition on the smoking of opium, but the populations of European countries were never targeted in the aggressive way that the Chinese market was.

A further problem, more worrying from the point of view of the stability of the Chinese economy, was that the silver originally earned from the trade in tea was now flowing back to the coffers of the Western barbarians in payment for the supply of opium. We may reflect that today's contentious World Trade Organization and balance-of-trade negotiations, as well as the debate about the legalization of certain recreational drugs, remarkably parallel the nineteenth-century state of affairs. It was only in China, where opium was banned, that the drug ravaged the population. The new self-styled *taipans* (the Cantonese word simply means "big boss"), who spearheaded this illicit trade and established factories in Canton at the head of the Pearl River, were able to flout the imperial edict with virtual impunity, partly, it has to be said, thanks to the collusion of the Canton customs authorities. The endemic corruption, which was to speed the demise of the Manchu empire at the beginning of the twentieth century, certainly facilitated the smuggling, which proved much more profitable than the legal trade being conducted via Canton and the Pearl River. In a 1992 mainland Chinese film, entitled simply *The Opium War*, and timed perhaps to remind restless Hong Kongers of their antecedents in the run-up to 1997, the lavish colour epic portrayed the events of the 1830s and 1840s in black and white terms, in short, Chinese heroes and British villains. The 1964 Hollywood tub-thumper, *Fifty-five Days in Peking*, was, of course, an equally one-sided and jingoistic take on the events of the Boxer Rising in Peking in 1900, seen from a diametrically opposed perspective. A degree of cautionary scepticism is therefore advisable in assessing any representations of these events.

What is clear, however, is that British sea-power gave the nation an unprecedented ascendancy in asserting coercive trade relations. After a number of unsuccessful overtures in attempting to widen the limited trade from Canton, Britain's third Superintendent of Trade in the region, Captain Charles Elliot, was sent with a brief from the Foreign Secretary, the wily and long-serving Lord Palmerston, to gain further concessions and open up other trading ports. To what extent British attitudes were influenced by the heads of opium smuggling companies, later to become household names in international trade, William Jardine (the "iron-headed old rat", as he was dubbed by Chinese negotiators) and fellow Scotsmen James Matheson and James Innes, is arguable. Elliot himself, a skilled naval officer and later a diplomat, as a principled Christian gentleman, considered the smuggling and smugglers of opium repugnant. References to Elliot in the Canton traders' news bulletins of the early 1840s make it clear that the loathing was reciprocated. Ironically, Elliot's Chinese counterpart in negotiations, Commissioner Lin Zexu, as an incorruptible Confucian, shared Elliot's convictions. Unlike Elliot, however, he was empowered to do something to stop the abuse of trade agreements. Lin seized and burned stocks of opium at Canton, precipitating the uneven war, which was to end in the cession of Hong Kong.

One of the problems about negotiations, which, in an uncanny pattern of historical repetition, was to be echoed by the joint talks leading up to the Handover in 1997, stemmed from the deep-seated culture clash between the participants. The Chinese considered the foreign interlopers in the Middle Kingdom (the centre of the world) as intrinsically inferior, and their emphasis on the pre-eminence of trade—the lowest level of occupation in the Chinese hierarchy, placed below intellectuals and poets, soldiers and even peasants in social consequence—both risible and contemptible. As representative of the Qing emperor and as a learned Confucian and statesman, it was unimaginable for Lin to accept the suggestion that Queen Victoria and her representatives should be accorded honour and status equal to his emperor.

In the light of this cultural divide, compounded by problems of wording and interpretation, which have continued in China's negotiations with Western powers to the present day, the clash of armies and navies was inevitable. It was assumed by the opium smugglers, who clearly had Palmerston's ear, that Elliot's mission would bring them the prize of Canton, or another favourably located island or port in its place, such as Chusan or Formosa—modern-day Taiwan. Yet after besieging the city of Canton from the sea and having the city at his mercy, Elliot decided to refrain from further bloodshed. Impressed by the natural deep-water harbour at Lei Yue Mun at the tip of the Kowloon peninsula, Elliot moderated his demands by claiming possession of Hong Kong and trading concessions in a few other ports.

The possession of Hong Kong on 26 January 1841 by a small contingent of British sailors and marines from HMS *Sulphur*, under the command of Captain Sir Edward Belcher, is commemorated now only in the name of a small street in Hong Kong Island's Sheung Wan

Possession Street, the place of "possession"—165 years later.

district, which is still, nine years after the Handover, called Possession Street, in spite of the inevitable colonial associations of the word. There is no monument to Elliot, nor any street named after him, but Belcher's slightly unfortunate name lives on, not only in the form of a street named after him in nearby Kennedy Town, but also in the fashionably located residential complex, the Belchers, in Pokfulam Road near Hong Kong University.

Imagining Possession
Timothy Mo's scrupulously researched and widely acclaimed 1986 historical novel, *An Insular Possession*, imagines the event through the eyes of the novel's historical protagonists recording the occasion for the readers of their bulletin. Hong Kong-born and British educated, Mo's fine inter-cultural sensibility (he is ethnically Eurasian) and appreciation of the delicious ironies of history puts the reader inside the heads of his cast of "players" in the story of Hong Kong's annexation by the British:

Formal occupation of Hong Kong. This event took place on Tuesday the 26th inst. A small detachment was landed from the Sulphur surveying vessel, Edmund [sic] Belcher captain, and arriving on the narrow rocky beach of the north-west of the island, proceeded to a small knoll overlooking the harbour, where, amid three loud huzzas and under a discharge of musketry, the Union Jack was raised. The British merchantmen and men-of-war lying in the harbour responded with a feu de joie of their cannon, which echoed and re-echoed off the massive granite peak, which commands the anchorage. The kites and seagulls soared and screamed in alarm, no less than the lousy Chinese soldier on the spit of land opposite the island [Tsim Sha Tsui on the tip of Kowloon].

This is a fine day for all foreigners and not merely the British merchants alone. Free and unrestricted entry and departure from the port, where no imposts [duties] shall be levied, such is the order of the day and desire of Captain Elliot. He should declare Hong Kong a neutral as well as a free port... At last we shall have a sanctuary and, still more important a point d'appui from which all China may in the fullness of time be opened.

Shortly after this report in Mo's epic novel the reader is treated to an account of soldiers and sailors, including the historically important Major William Caine and Lieutenant William Pedder, after whom Caine Road and Pedder Street and the Pedder Building in Central District are named, playing cricket on the beach at Tsim Sha Tsui (the sandy spit with a Cantonese name that evokes the image of a bird's beak). This lively episode includes a conversation between the puzzled American onlookers, Gideon Chase, a real-life participant in the events and later a Chinese scholar, translator and academic, and the fictional Walter Eastman, in which they conclude that the slow game of cricket "could be adapted into a game more suited to the spirit of the New World" by getting rid of the wickets, having just one batsman and creating "more drama in running a circle or triangle." This sly reference to the modern American sport of baseball mischievously implies that Mo's characters were responsible for its invention on the beach at Kowloon, a fanciful notion perhaps, but not without a degree of credibility given the circumstances.

Mo's protagonists accompany the roguish, larger-than-life painter

Harry O'Rourke, on a painting expedition to the Peak on Hong Kong Island, from which they have an even more majestic panorama than do today's tourists. O'Rourke was a real-life Macao-based artist, less famous than his Irish compatriot George Chinnery whose many paintings and sketches of Macao, Hong Kong and the Pearl River have survived (unlike those of O'Rourke). Gideon's reaction anticipates that of many a traveller in the years that followed: "Heavens! What a prospect!" Gideon is amazed, delighted. There is neither haze nor cloud, perfect weather after last month's savage rains. The air is so transparent one might see for ever. The harbour is like a glass of green liqueur, its masts as big as match-sticks, the chequered hulls of the men-of-war the size of dominoes." Even Jardine's *godowns* (pidgin English for warehouses, and still a recognised term in Hong Kong), presumably packed with opium, are clearly visible a mile and a half to the east.

Twenty years prior to Mo's historically authentic tale of possession, the "foundation myth" of Hong Kong had been presented in more strictly fictional form in the 1966 novel, *Tai-Pan*, by British writer and former naval officer James Clavell. Dirk Struan, the novel's protagonist, is a thinly disguised fictional incarnation of the king of *taipans*, William Jardine, whose name, even today, is strongly associated with corporate Hong Kong. Like Jardine, Struan founds a dynastic merchant house based on opium trading that comes to dominate Hong Kong. The sequel novel, *Noble House*, brings the story of this company forward into the twentieth century.

One might argue that using fictional *alter egos* for the principal players was unnecessary, e.g. William Longstaff for Charles Elliot, Captain Glessing for the real-life Captain Edward Belcher and even one, Horatio Sinclair, as Gideon Chase. Other novelists of early Hong Kong such as Dean Barrett (*Hangman's Point*, 1998) happily fuse fictional protagonists with factual participants of the action. Clavell's version, in spite of excellent explanations of the development of the opium trade and the taking of Hong Kong, jars the more one knows about the real-life players. Both the novel and Daryl Duke's film adaptation, starring Bryan Brown as Struan and the lissome Joan Chen as his Chinese mistress May-may, offer authentic and atmospheric depictions of the "Possession ceremony" on the beach at Sheung Wan. Struan's rival, Tyler Brock, (possibly either Thomas Dent from the great rival trading house of Dent's or the irascible and chauvinistic James

Innes) describes the island as a "poxy rock". As they wait bareheaded in the wind for the ceremony to begin, "Struan looked up at the foothills to an outcrop where the kirk [St. John's Cathedral presumably] would be. He could see the kirk in his mind's eye and the town and the quays and warehouses and homes and gardens. The Great House where the Tai-pan would hold court over the generations."

The events of January 1841 are presented very differently in a 1992 short story entitled *Chronicle of a City* by Hong Kong-born writer Yu Feng—a pen-name for his full Cantonese name Yu Hon-king. The narrator, or perhaps the writer himself, links the "bitter events" experienced by his father, grandfather and great-grandfather in Hong Kong. In this wonderfully evocative tale, presented as oral history handed down from father to son, the unnamed great-grandfather, as a boy of ten, witnesses the British party landing at a stony beach on the island to which he has been taken to work by relatives. Although he hides among the rocks, the boy is discovered by the "red-haired devils"—soldiers and sailors in Commodore Bremer's advance party. Some of them beat him and had it not been for the cannon volleys from the big ships in the harbour, the sound of bugles and the fusillade of musket fire from the other soldiers, which fortunately distracts the boy's tormentors, the narrator reflects that his ancestor would not have survived. He wryly observes that

> the fact that I, his great-grandson, was able to be born over a hundred years later because of the ceremony by which Britain took possession of Hong Kong must be one of the absurdities of history... For a while the ground trembled and the mountains shook. Maybe the founding of a city was no more than that. Just that.

As the boy makes his painful way back home along the stony beach after the soldiers have gone, he spots their red, white and blue flag, which he wraps around himself in place of his torn clothing, after hurling the empty flagpole defiantly toward the seemingly western-moving mountain. His great-grandson, the narrator, recounts that he has tried to trace his forebear's footsteps on that eventful day in what is now the reclaimed land on which the busy streets of Western District and Sheung Wan are built, trying to hear the rumble of the cannons of history in his head above the roar of the traffic. He concludes: "in that city, which had been old Hong Kong, everything had but a fleeting presence and the people were good at forgetting; they were too busy looking to the future; that stony beach had lain long buried under the city, forgotten."

The alienated viewpoint of Yu Feng's narrative gives us an insight into the bemused reaction by Hong Kong's small population to the annexation of Hong Kong. As was the case 156 years later in the corresponding retrocession ceremony, a greatly increased population could only watch a momentous ceremony in which they were mere pawns in the play of greater powers. Ironically, though Elliot remains uncommemorated and generally unappreciated in the scheme of things, his actions receive a kind of backhanded appreciation in Yu Feng's piquant short story. In Mo's novel Elliot is presented sympathetically, especially in the scene in which, shortly before his recall, Elliot's cool-headed leadership during a severe typhoon saves the occupants of the small ship *Louisa*, in which Gideon Chase is also travelling as interpreter and translator.

"An Insular Station"

At the same time, the disappointment of the future *taipans*, Innes and Jardine, that Elliot had settled for terms in the treaty that involved no further cessions of islands on the east coast of China was transmitted swiftly to London and to Palmerston himself. In a letter to Queen Victoria in April 1841, Palmerston blamed Elliot for disregarding his instructions and not pressing home his advantage over the ill-equipped Chinese navy: "Even the cession of Hong Kong has been coupled with a condition about the payment of duties, which would render that island not a possession of the British Crown, but like Macao, a settlement held by sufferance in the territory of the Crown of China." The Queen, while piqued by what she calls Elliot's "strange conduct", consoled herself with the thought that she could call herself Princess of Hong Kong, in addition to Princess Royal. Elliot's sound naval and military reasoning for electing Hong Kong and abandoning the island of Chusan cut little ice with the irate Palmerston, who, under the influence of the traders' lobby, declared his dissatisfaction with "the barren island with hardly a house on it." He dismissed Hong Kong as "a desert island, only good for the Canton traders to retire to", and recalled Elliot, but did not rescind his annexation of Hong Kong.

Palmerston's lack of prescience about Hong Kong's potential for future development was, of course, shared by his Chinese counterparts. While despising the troublesome barbarians and treating them with the disdain they merited, it was clearly politic to make a minor concession to them. Plagued with internal disturbances and insurrections in this period, which culminated in the great upheavals of the Taiping Rebellion, the Manchus could afford to lose a minor territorial outpost that most of them probably never knew existed until Elliot made his demands. For their part, they were mystified that the foreign devils could be satisfied with such an insignificant prize. Perhaps this perception and the initial treaty lulled them into a false sense of security, for which they later paid when more aggressive and unprincipled successors to Elliot, Hong Kong's first and third governors, Pottinger and Bowring, in attempts to please both the influential opium *taipans* and their Whitehall masters, undertook a series of further gunboat sorties up the Pearl River. These culminated in the Treaty of Nanking in which the cession of Hong Kong was ratified. The real prizes were to be five treaty ports with consular representation, including Shanghai.

Although it was never the British government's intention to keep Hong Kong when more desirable enclaves could be obtained, Elliot's vision and nautical experience were to prove—with the advantage of hindsight—a great blessing to his country. By the time Palmerston and subsequently his Tory counterparts in the new government had established that Hong Kong was not a long-term option and could be traded back to the Chinese in return for a more valuable "insular station", Hong Kong had already begun to be settled by opportunist adventurers, both Chinese and European. In the early days, as contemporary historical accounts reveal, it had all the features of a gold-rush town, particularly on the north side of Hong Kong Island. As trade developed, its sheltered harbour and protective garrison and navy presence discouraged piracy and attracted fortune-seekers. Within a few months the population more than tripled to approximately 15,000. Once more permanent buildings including the *godowns* of the opium traders were constructed, it was always going to be difficult for the first governor, Henry Pottinger, to surrender the new insular possession. Pottinger's ambivalent legacy (he was certainly instrumental in obtaining the territory, though he and the opium *taipans* openly expressed their mutual antipathy for each other) is celebrated in what Mo describes as "the rather mean alley of Pottinger Street", in fact a bustling market street.

Hong Kong was actually first administered by Elliot's and subsequently Pottinger's deputy, Alexander Johnston, who showed great initiative in making the permanent settlement of the island as much of a *fait accompli* as he could. At the time of the British taking possession, according to Johnston's notes on Hong Kong, there were few public buildings with the exception of temples at Chekchu (Stanley), Sokonpo (near Causeway Bay) and Shekpaiwan (Aberdeen). The English nomenclatures commemorate the names of English political gods such as Tory foreign secretary Lord Aberdeen, whom Johnston and other pioneers realized needed to be placated, if their brief was to be exceeded. Johnston noted that there were a few red deer on the island and a profusion of indigenous fruits, including lychee, mango, longan and pear, as well as fresh water and abundant vegetables. He subsequently engaged in energetic development, including a census of the population, which was estimated as 4,350 in May 1841, not taking into account the itinerant boat-people. Johnston recorded his first impressions and measurements of the island as follows:

> On landing and examining the island of Hongkong, the N. and N.E. side is found to be separated from the S. and S.W. by one continued range of hills, in no place less than 500 feet, in most parts upward of 1,000, and on more than one pinnacle 1,741 feet above the level of the sea by barometrical observation. When to this is added that the utmost breadth of the island does not exceed four or five miles, it may easily be imagined that the descent to the sea on either side is very abrupt.

By the following January, exactly a year after possession, the new enclave was developing rapidly and the facilities included a growing range of shops, the Victoria Hotel and the obligatory brothel and gambling house, the latter boasting ornate Venetian-style architecture, to complement the military barracks and naval headquarters. Most of these buildings sprang up on the new thoroughfare, Queen's Road, which skirted the northern waterfront of the island.

Johnston seemed to share Elliot's enthusiasm for the choice of

Hong Kong, and like Elliot and unlike the more bellicose Pottinger, proved a capable and decisive figure in promoting Hong Kong's development. Both men not only made the necessary leap of faith and imagination, but were prepared to take liberties in the pursuit of their duties according to their own lights. Had they acted more obediently and less decisively, had they heeded their faraway masters' literal instructions that the island was to be no more than a temporary military post and a possible negotiating gambit, Hong Kong would have had a very different destiny. Elliot's enlightened decision that Chinese residents should be subject to Chinese law and British residents to British was another important factor in encouraging the human resources of the new colony not only to stay but also to increase in numbers. Elliot's concern for the native population for all its paternalist overtones was nonetheless sincere:

> If the preservation of Hong Kong is of such first-rate importance for our own trade and interests, it is to the full as much so, as an act of justice and protection to the Native population upon which we have been so long dependent for assistance and supply. Indescribably dreadful instances of the hostility between these people and the government are within our certain knowledge, and they cannot be abandoned without the most fatal consequences.

Elliot's differences of perspective from his powerful compatriot politicians, for whom Hong Kong was of much less consequence than trade relations with the Chinese, can be seen to anticipate the dilemma of Britain's final governor, Chris Patten. Indeed, the historical resemblances and correspondences are nothing short of uncanny, and seem to suggest the circular nature of a narrative rather than the conventional linear view of historical progress. It is important to recognize, as Elliot seemed to do, that this narrative will be a shared one. As poet P. K. Leung (Leung Ping-kwan) has pointed out, many Hong Kong writers have avoided the responsibility of telling the city's tale, preferring to tell their personal stories, like Yu Feng, from the margins. He adds that none of these voices should be suppressed. In his own poem entitled *Fragments of a Northern Song Dynasty Fish-shaped Pot*, Leung writes these telling lines comparing Hong Kong to a fragment of greater China:

Those empowered to write history with a stroke of the pen
incorporated the southern kilns into those of the north,
producing a complete history

The fragments say: Please carefully study our grain.
Don't read us into
Your history

Perhaps it is when these many voices sing in chorus that the texture and complexity of the story of Hong Kong can be felt. Timothy Mo allows Elliot's and Gideon Chase's strange mix of pragmatism and idealism to be felt and heard once again. Chase observes in his unfinished and unpublished autobiography that the mere facts of history cannot do justice to the turbulent events:

And in these watersheds of change, that which is new and that
which is old, the revolutionary and the ancient, invention in its
infancy and that which is to become extinct, all come together in a
medley of the shocking and the incongruous… Treaties, Congresses,
Convention mean nothing, except to the participants—the stuff of
history is less tangible, but lies in a popular mood whose ebbs and
flows are not measurable by the month or year.

chapter two

CENTRES OF POWER AND IMAGINATION: CENTRAL AND ADMIRALTY

A "Floating" City

In her novella *Marvels of a Floating City*, Hong Kong author Xi Xi (pronounced Sai-sai in Cantonese and Shee-shee in Mandarin) imagines the city as a miraculous land mass floating in the air above the sea and out of reach of pirates:

> *The only witnesses were the grandparents of our grandparents... The descendants of these grandparents gradually settled down in the floating city and gradually adapted themselves to its conditions... Most people believed that the floating city would continue hanging steadily in the air, neither rising nor sinking for ever.*

As a vivid image-laden allegory of the founding of a great city this whimsically conceived fable has something in common with the creation myths that emanate from various world cultures. Based originally on an exhibition of René Magritte's paintings at City Hall in Edinburgh Place in Central, the story unfolds as a series of vignettes based on the surreal images depicted in the paintings. The image of the floating city itself is inspired by Magritte's *Castle in the Pyrenees*, while other well-known Magritte works such as *Time Transfixed* and *The Mind's Gaze* are juxtaposed with short but surprisingly apposite meditations on Hong Kong's past, present and future.

Xi Xi's own literary creation myth encompasses also the uncertainty and ambivalent feelings during the Sino-British joint negotiations in the mid-1980s about Hong Kong's future after its inevitable return to China in 1997. Throughout the 1980s and 1990s the city's mood-swings, as charted by fluctuations in the local stock market's Hang Seng Index, ran the gamut from bullish, boom-induced confidence to the deep pessimism that followed in the wake of the 4 June 1989 massacre of pro-democracy protestors in Tiananmen Square,

Legislative Council Building (LEGCO), Central (foreground).

Beijing. The ending of Xi Xi's significantly cross-cultural and mixed-medium creative work leaves the reader reflecting on the ambivalence of Mona Lisa's smile on the poster advertising the next exhibition at City Hall. The teacher and her students, to whom she has been explaining the pictures in the exhibition, are observed by people outside. "Suddenly the observers at the window come face-to-face with the students and their teacher. From the solemn looks on the observers' faces one can detect how things are going. If it is a tragedy, their faces will be sorrowful; if it is a comedy, they will of course smile." The author, and perhaps the teacher too, are interpreting the significance of some familiar paintings to Western eyes, through the prism of Hong Kong's cultural and political experience. The famously ambiguous nature of the meaning of the Mona Lisa smile parallels the ambivalent, sphinx-like face of the city's future. Xi Xi's idiosyncratically naïve style may not be every Hong Kong reader's cup of tea. Yet in this short but exquisite work she expresses Hong Kong's unique East-West fusion, its fragile almost miraculous existence and its uncertain future at the time of writing.

Culturally Hong Kong is a curious hybrid, as Xi Xi's imaginative tale suggests. Central District, where City Hall is located, was formerly known as Victoria, and has been the hub of cultural development and diversity since its modest beginnings in the years following British possession. One of the government's loudly proclaimed objectives in the aftermath of Hong Kong's reunification with China has been to transform a sophisticated and cosmopolitan financial centre into "Asia's World City". Indeed, if this claim on the pennants and banners of the Hong Kong Tourist Authority is to be believed, it already is one. Chief Executive Donald Tsang's government has no monopoly on hyperbole and self-delusion among contemporary world governments, but some would say it is a premature claim. Nevertheless, the ambition to be regarded as a world city typifies the attitude that Hong Kong is distinct from other Chinese cities. Nowhere is this spirit of diversity more marked than in its former centre, Victoria (in fact, for a long time its one and only significant conurbation).

The modern Central is without argument a thriving, truly international commercial district, comparable with London and New York in respect of its modern skyscraper skyline, and ranked third in the world behind the above-mentioned cities in terms of its financial turnover. Its special blend of ultra-modern glass and chrome edifices—especially banks, hotels and shopping centres—towering above angular 1950s and 1960s modernist-looking buildings, which in turn rub shoulders with the small residue of elegant colonial structures in the city centre, is a monument to both progress and forgetfulness. Indeed, photographs of the Central waterfront from the 1950s have more in common with those taken in the mid-nineteenth century than they do with contemporary images of the city's dramatically imposing skyline.

As Hong Kong cultural critic Ackbar Abbas has eloquently argued, the rapid transformations that Hong Kong has undergone, particularly in the last forty years, have conferred something of a cultural amnesia on the city. Words like conservation and heritage were, until very recently, unfamiliar to many in Hong Kong, signifying foreign notions strangely hostile to progress. Land has always been at such a premium in this crowded city that since the expansion of the late Sixties and Seventies most buildings were considered to have a limited shelf-life, if not built-in obsolescence. Present time seemed the only relevant time-frame as buildings were erected with dazzling speed. Many Hong Kong residents have experienced the feeling of only becoming aware of a new building's presence weeks or months after its completion. Almost immediately it becomes taken for granted, as if it has always been there.

Only now in the new millennium is Hong Kong developing a hitherto undetected consciousness of its past and making the exciting discovery that it actually has a heritage. The relocation of one of its oldest colonial buildings, Murray House, from Central to the quieter environs of Stanley on the south side of Hong Kong Island, involving the painstaking reconstruction of the carefully dismantled stonework of the building, is evidence of a growing awareness on the part of the broader community. Younger generations of Hong Kongers, born and bred here, perceive the territory not as a temporary place for making money, as their forefathers had done, but as their home. They have instinctively grasped that a distinctive sense of communal identity depends on tempering the previously accepted utilitarian approach to living space and creating a feeling of post-modern urban chic from the eclectic constructions and spaces bequeathed to them in what has frankly always been a somewhat arbitrary and profit-driven approach to urban development.

A Walk through Central District: around Statue Square

It is impossible to discern today the original contours of what became Victoria in the 1840s, when communications linking army posts on the north side of Hong Kong Island metamorphosed into a main road and a straggling settlement of tents and mat-sheds. For one thing, an enormous amount of land reclamation over a period of a hundred and sixty years has entirely transformed the appearance of the waterfront. The fact that it continues to be known as Victoria Harbour, even in the aftermath of the handover of sovereignty to China, tells us much about the quirky and pragmatic nature of the city and its inhabitants, as well, of course, about the virtual deification of Queen Victoria at the high point of British imperialism in the mid to late nineteenth century. Victoria Port, as it was known, was the hub of seagoing operations until reclamation work and the acquisition of Kowloon began to push the docks first east and subsequently north.

In Dean Barrett's novel of a wild frontier Hong Kong in the year 1857, *Hangman's Point*, there is an imaginative sketch of the Central area seen through the eyes of his rough-and-ready protagonist, innkeeper Andrew Adams:

> *Below Wellington Street was Stanley Street and below that was Queen's Road, the town's main thoroughfare stretching from east to west along the harbour. Below a mass of grey clouds obscuring the faintest of blue skies, he could glimpse wharves, Chinese markets known as' bazaars', residences, offices, stores, go-downs [warehouses] of the Europeans, and the Oriental Bank Building. Men in top hats and morning coats entered offices of some of the leading merchants and traders.*

Jules Verne's popular classic *Around the World in Eighty Days* (1873) likewise conjures up an imaginative description of the waterfront about twenty years later based on Verne's prodigious reading. His hero, phlegmatic British gentleman, Phileas Fogg, who is traversing the globe in order to win a bet, lands briefly at Victoria Port in the company of his valet, Passepartout and the delectable Princess Aouda. Verne gives an amusing description through the eyes of his fictional Frenchman Passepartout, who, unlike Verne himself, did actually visit the place, if only in Verne's imagination:

Hong Kong has vanquished Macao in the struggle for Chinese trade, and now the greater part of the transportation of Chinese goods finds its depot at the former place. Docks, hospitals, wharves, a Gothic cathedral, a government house, macadamized streets give to Hong Kong the appearance of a town in Kent or Surrey, transferred by some strange magic to the antipodes. Passepartout wandered with his hands in his pockets towards the Victoria Port, gazing as he went at the curious palanquins and other modes of conveyance, and the groups of Chinese, Japanese and Europeans who passed to and fro in the streets. Hong Kong seemed to him not unlike Bombay, Calcutta and Singapore, since, like them, it betrayed everywhere the evidence of English supremacy.

So many of the colonial associations that have survived in the names of streets and buildings in Central bear testimony not only to its past, but also perhaps to its future. The *laissez-faire* policy that is supposed to have been the cornerstone of the city's development under the free-market system that turned the city from a colonial backwater into an affluent first-world metropolis can also be observed operating in a rather different cultural context since the Handover. There has been relatively little attempt to change names in an attempt to eradicate the past, as has been common in other post-colonial environments. This can be seen as one simple and immediately visible instance of the Chinese government's good faith in implementing the late patriarch Deng Xiaoping's imaginative one country-two systems concept for Hong Kong's future.

To return to our stroll through the varied and colourful streets of Central, we start, like Passepartout, in the harbour, or to be more precise where the waters of the harbour once flowed. The present-day City Hall was constructed belatedly in 1962 to replace the Victorian original, demolished to make way for the Hong Kong Bank in the 1930s. The second incarnations of both City Hall and the Star Ferry Buildings, like other buildings in their immediate vicinity, are built on reclaimed land. Now a multi-purpose public venue and performance hall, very much in the spirit of the original colonial style building, the major difference is the cultural eclecticism of City Hall's presentations, from Western musical recitals and concerts to Asian dance and musical forms as well as indigenous Chinese theatre and music, both traditional and modern. Even the original staple of performance, the musical or light opera, as performed by local amateurs, has remained, but at the same time changed almost out of recognition. The Hong Kong Singers, formed by European expatriates in 1931, but now multi-national and multi-ethnic in composition, in contrast to the virtual apartheid of former colonial entertainments, perform a broad repertoire of musicals here on a regular basis, produced with a degree of professionalism and polish unthinkable in earlier, more parochial days. The low squat performance venue of City Hall is partnered by its High Block with recital rooms and administrative facilities, as well as a marriage registry. As recently as the late 1970s this block dominated the skyline but now it is dwarfed by the forest of skyscrapers behind it.

As we stroll from the Star Ferry terminal area towards the heart of Central we need to imagine we are still walking on water, since it is not until we reach Queen's Road Central that we stand on *terra firma*, at least historically speaking. To the right as we leave the Star Ferry is Jardine House, a name redolent of Hong Kong's opium-fuelled prosperity. Dr. William Jardine is probably the most famous name among the self-styled *taipans* who exercised more control over the affairs of the territory than any governor. Although the man himself returned to Britain to enter politics and died in the early 1840s, the Jardine-Matheson partnership and its subsequent dynasty remained one of the most prosperous and influential of the *hongs* (trading companies) in the Crown Colony.

The Jardine Building was originally known in the 1970s as the Connaught Building and set the scene for a brilliant short story of that period by Song Mu, entitled *The Man Who Jumped off the Connaught Centre*. In this tale, a mainland man commits suicide and the reader is party to the callous responses of various Hong Kong Chinese witnesses of the event, one of whom uses the graphic detail as raw material for a film script he is writing. The story sardonically captures the Hong Konger's lack of sympathy for and sense of superiority over his country bumpkin mainland cousins. To a large extent, the 1989 Tiananmen massacre of unarmed demonstrating students was to change that perception.

Crossing by underpass the busy Connaught Road (named after Queen Victoria's younger son, the Duke of Connaught, who visited Hong Kong and officially inaugurated the huge waterfront reclamation and Central extension programme of the late 1880s), we arrive at the

Thomas Jackson. Statue Square, Central.

Prince's Building, adjacent to what may be considered Central's central plaza, Statue Square. The Prince's Building (named after a Prince of Wales and not the eponymous American recording artist, who performed at Hong Kong's 2003 Harbour Fest!), is one of the Centres, or fashionable shopping centres, of Central, bristling with the brand names so beloved of tourists, Hong Kong people and now China mainland visitors alike. This may be a shopping paradise to those with a bottomless wallet or hyperactive plastic, but the astronomical rents ensure that bargain-hunters are conspicuous by their absence.

Statue Square, which plays host to Christmas and Chinese Lunar New Year celebrations, seems at first sight to be a misnomer. After careful inspection, one statue can be located facing the Legislative Council Building on the east side of the square. This solitary figure is the likeness of Sir Thomas Jackson, one of the key players in the founding of the Hong Kong and Shanghai Bank, or to use its more globally familiar acronym, HSBC, the headquarters of which look down from the south of the square across Des Voeux Road approvingly on their favourite son. Many of Hong Kong Island's roads and streets are named after governors and other British colonial administrators, and this one is no exception. William Des Voeux was governor for four years spanning the ambitious reclamation and road building programme of the late nineteenth century. To return to Jackson, it seems rather appropriate that when the occupying Japanese army removed the other statues from the square including Edward VII, George V, Queen Mary and even the Empress of India herself, they managed to leave Jackson as the sole occupant of Statue Square, a fitting monument to Hong Kong's greater predilection for mammon than majesty. Queen Victoria's intact effigy was rescued from a shipyard in Yokohama and restored to Hong Kong after the Second World War, only not in her former pride of place. Much to her lack of amusement, she was relocated in her own park in Causeway Bay.

One of the main instigators of Hong Kong's rapid expansion in the last decade of the nineteenth century was Sir Catchick Paul Chater, after whom Chater Road and Chater Garden, located opposite Statue Square, are named. This Armenian, Calcutta-born bank clerk worked his way up to become one of Hong Kong's earliest non-British tycoons and most generous benefactors. Statue Square was also the result of his philanthropy and endeavour, and he played a central role in the vigorous reclamation initiative of the 1880s and 1990s which radically transformed today's Central District. An enthusiastic cricketer, Chater's name adorned the Hong Kong Cricket Club at Chater Garden in Central right up until 1977. For much of that time cricket was played on prime real estate right next to the waterfront. Chater Garden is now a public park where some of Hong Kong's many *tai chi* practitioners can be observed—if one is an early riser. *Tai Chi*, the basis of martial arts but practised at a much more leisurely pace than the Bruce Lee and Jackie Chan variety, is connected with the idea of using the flow of the body's *chi* (force or strength).

Speaking of the ubiquitous Jackie Chan, one of the most internationally recognizable faces of Hong Kong, a dramatic opening scene from his film *New Police Story*, a 2004 sequel to his popular Eighties *Police Story* movies, is set in Chater Road in Central. Jackie, now Inspector Chan, arrives on the scene after a number of his colleagues are gunned down by a bloodthirsty gang of young, game-obsessed cyber-gangsters. In typical Hong Kong film location style, the setting of the heist switches abruptly and inexplicably from the Tsim Sha Tsui waterfront across on Kowloon-side to Central. Using this most prestigious area of Central as backdrop to the gang's outrageously spectacular slaughter of cops works as a strong signifier of their audacity. To make matters worse, their bloody deeds are committed only a stone's throw from the Legislative Council Building, where Hong Kong's lawmakers meet. This rather elegant, almost neoclassical building, designed and built in 1912 as the Supreme Court, has long been a place of symbolic importance. Its architects, Webb and Bell, also designed the facades of Buckingham Palace and the Victoria and Albert Museum, so the sharp-eyed may spot some subtle similarities. On the domed roof above the pedestal of the building stands the blindfolded figure of the Greek goddess of justice, Themis, holding the conventional scales of justice.

The Legislative Council (LEGCO) started life in the Crown Colony as a rubber stamping mechanism for the decisions of the governor's executive council caucus. When Hong Kong's last governor Chris Patten introduced last-minute attempts at broadening the extremely limited base of representative democracy in the Territory, expectations of democratic procedure being introduced in Hong Kong's fifty-year grace period of non-convergence with the mainland political system were suddenly raised. Indeed, the Basic Law, which covers all such matters, and resulted from the joint Sino-British negotiations, actually envisages the possibility of greater democratic representation in the future. What form this kind of political development will take and, for example, how soon Hong Kong's Chief Executive can be directly elected remains a subject of hot dispute, however. One Beijing politician colourfully repudiated Patten's attempt to ensure a more widely elected Legislative Council as "the deathbed repentance of a whore who wishes to preserve her chastity."

Even after the 1997 transfer of sovereignty to Beijing and the relative lack of at least direct and obvious interference from the Chinese government, the LEGCO building has witnessed more controversy and strife than was customary in the generally sleepier colonial era. There appears to have been a general apathy toward politics in earlier times, though not perhaps from all quarters of the community, as the serious riots of 1967 demonstrated. Here on the balustrade of the LEGCO building on the eve of the 1997 Handover, barrister Martin Lee, then leader of Hong Kong's fledgling Democrat party, barricaded himself and a group of supporters in as a highly visible protest about the political arrangements of the Handover, particularly the disbanding of Patten's elected Legislative Council in favour of a Beijing-approved provisional legislature. Lee and other feisty pro-democracy fighters, such as Civic Exchange leader Christine Loh and Frontier party leader Emily Lau, have continued to press vociferously for a greater degree of transparency and democratic representation in Hong Kong's future political structure.

Probably the most high-profile thorn in the side of first Chief Executive Tung Chee-hwa's administration, however, was the veteran street protestor-turned-lawmaker, "Longhair" Leung Kwok-hung. Leung's inspiration in the struggle against what he and an increasing number of others in Hong Kong have seen as government cronyism in public affairs is the iconic Argentinian activist, Che Guevara. When Longhair was sworn in as one of the newly elected lawmakers in 2004, he insisted on being allowed to wear his trademark Che Guevara T-shirt. In spite of attempts to apply a rigorous dress code to LEGCO meetings, Longhair, elected by a significantly large majority in his Kowloon constituency, continues to embody a growing trend towards popular activism and civil disobedience.

An ideological divide that had been masked by the 156 years of colonialism has started to emerge. One analogy for the conservative-progressive antagonism that is slowly shifting political boundaries in Hong Kong would be the deep mutual antipathy between present-day Republicans and Democrats in the United States. Ironically, though, social progressives, normally seen as being on the political left in Western countries, are ranked against the pro-Beijing alliance of working-class conservatives and big business interests, many of whom forged close links with the Communist Party leadership in the years leading up to the Handover. Stability and prosperity have long been Hong Kong's mantra, but with an estimated US$121 billion reserve fund, to shore it up against unforeseen events such as the Asian economic crisis (1998-2002), Hong Kong people are becoming a little less worried about rocking the boat and a little more sceptical about the supposed trickle-down effect of its prosperity. An unlikely ally of the progressive faction in Hong Kong is popular Roman Catholic primate of the Special Administrative Region, Bishop Joseph Zen (recently elevated to Cardinal by Pope Benedict), who has spoken out against the government's public relations humbug on the thorny issue of universal suffrage.

Two other noteworthy buildings in the vicinity of Statue Square are the Mandarin Oriental Hotel and the Ritz-Carlton, two of Central's most luxurious hotels. The original colonnaded Hong Kong Hotel, which graced the waterfront and housed many illustrious visitors including Shaw and Kipling, has long disappeared, but these two five-star hotels have their own more recent literary associations. The Ritz-Carlton is built on the site of the former Sutherland House, where the Foreign Correspondents' Club used to be located. It was from here that John Le Carré plotted the story of *The Honourable Schoolboy*, the second novel in his Smiley trilogy of the 1970s, and critically acclaimed as the outstanding English novel of that decade. Richard Hughes, the Australian journalist and doyen of the FCC, on whom Le Carré's memorable correspondent/agent Old Craw was reputedly based, coined the famous aphorism about Hong Kong—"borrowed place, borrowed time."

Of that more in later chapters, but let us head back along Chater Road in the direction of the Mandarin Oriental Hotel. We pass the Hong Kong Club, which is also not devoid of historical and literary pedigree, and the Cenotaph, where the November remembrance ceremony continues to take place to honour the dead of both world wars. One war veteran and long-time Hong Kong resident, the late Jack Edwards, whose book about his internment under the Japanese occupation, *Banzai, You Bastards* (1991), is as uncompromising as it sounds, was ever-present at the ceremony alongside a gradually diminishing number of former comrades. Others, such as Arthur Gomes and Osler Thomas, have also written compellingly of their war-time experiences. One of the photographic highlights of the Handover year occurred on a windy day at the Cenotaph when a Scots guardsman's kilt blew up, revealing the stark truth about the prevailing wisdom on how the kilt is in fact worn. The scoop photo is now on display in the present-day Foreign Correspondents' Club and has passed into the annals of Hong Kong legend.

Approaching the Mandarin Oriental one is ill-prepared for its sumptuous interior, as its exterior appears somewhat less grand than the famous Peninsula Hotel across the harbour in TST (the local shorthand for Tsim Sha Tsui). In the penthouse bar of the Mandarin Tony Parsons' first-person narrator Alfie Budd in *One For My Baby* (a superior novel to that author's best-selling *Man and Boy* in the view of this writer) meets his destined other half, Rose, and nearly gets into a brawl with her accompanying beau, the beefy, blond, corporate, all-British Josh. "Who are you this week, pal? Stamford Raffles? Cecil Rhodes? Scott of the Antarctic?... We're guests in this place [i.e. Hong Kong]. Britain no longer rules the waves. We should remember our manners." Alfie's lecture on how to make oneself slightly more acceptably British in post-Handover Hong Kong is not of purely literary relevance. However, it should be borne in mind that the chinless (or as Parsons amusingly puts it "lipless") wonders who used to parade through Central's business area on Friday nights on their way to the amusements of nearby Lan Kwai Fong, Central's entertainment hotspot, are now more likely to be firm-jawed Americans and Australians, given the rapid recent turnover in Hong Kong's expatriate population.

Leslie Cheung, one of Hong Kong's greatest singers and movie stars of the last twenty-five years, fell to his death in a presumed suicide jump from an upper floor of the hotel during Hong Kong's *annus horribilis* of 2003, the year of the SARS (severe acute respiratory syndrome) outbreak. An outstanding artist, one of Cheung's greatest screen roles was as a cross-dressing Chinese opera singer in the 1993 Chen Kaige film *Farewell My Concubine*. His extensive filmography (including modern Hong Kong classics such as *Rouge, Days of Being Wild* and *A Better Tomorrow*) and discography had made him a dearly loved figure on the creative scene, and his heartbroken fans, dismayed by his death at the relatively young age of 46, stood vigil for many days outside the hotel. The culturally sensitive Mandarin Oriental management made every allowance for their right to mourn Cheung's premature passing, in spite of worries about potential disruption to the routine of the hotel itself. Known simply to his legion of fans by his English name, Leslie, his memory will continue to be cherished. His name will remain a legend, roughly equivalent to that of an Elvis or a Lennon in local Hong Kong terms.

Before we leave Chater Road and head in the direction of the new Hong Kong Bank, the former Government House and the lower Mid-

Levels, we should take a look at the Hong Kong Club, formerly one of the most elegant colonial edifices in the Territory. The new club was offered by developers in the early 1980s as bait for surrendering the extremely valuable and, with the fast-approaching Handover, symbolically anachronistic, four-storey building. Still an elegant building in its own modern curvilinear style, its office space above the new club headquarters, eloquently proclaims where power really resides in today's world. For a long time Chinese were barred from membership or admittance, unless they were carrying out work or serving the members.

Christopher New's fictional Hong Kong university lecturer, Dmitri Johnson, the protagonist of his *China Coast Trilogy*, meets his former Cambridge classmate, Peter Frankam, now a high-ranking civil servant in the Hong Kong government in the hallowed but gloomy environs of the club in a memorable scene from the second novel, *The Chinese Box*. New was himself an academic in the Philosophy Department of Hong Kong University and he knew his subject intimately. His is one of the very best of fictional-documentary depictions of Hong Kong in the 1960s and 1970s. Dmitri, having embarked on an affair with Chinese ballet teacher, Mila, is about to be given the hint by the well-connected Peter that his affair is becoming common knowledge among a disapproving expatriate community. Dmitri and Mila had been together when they witnessed a clear case of police brutality against an injured protestor involved in the 1967 riots. After the man is reported to have died in custody, they register a complaint, and prepare to give their testimony at the court hearing. Frankam's attempt to intimidate his "friend" in the opulent colonial environs of the Hong Kong Club does not work, however. After various topics of conversation including terrorism—a reference to the civil disturbances taking place outside—and the state of the stock market, Frankam steers discussion round to his own impending promotion to Director General, and to Dmitri's "extramural activities"—a clever pun on non-approved and therefore clandestine outside teaching. Finally Dmitri makes his escape from the (to him) oppressive surroundings of the Hong Kong Club. As he makes his way towards Statue Square, pondering on the likelihood of an official conspiracy to cover up the incident, he sees a beggar in the shade of the Court of Justice (later the Legislative Council Building) holding out his plastic mug hopefully in spite of the lack of human response.

Dmitri decides he will be like this beggar when the court case comes around: "I'll hold up my evidence like he holds up his mug."

Crossing Statue Square with a disenchanted Dmitri, we arrive at the tramline along Des Voeux Road. The Hong Kong tram system stretches from Kennedy Town in Western District to Shau Kei Wan on the north-east of the island. The section between Central and Causeway Bay is the busiest, and the two-Hong Kong dollar fare places the ride on a par with the Star Ferry as one of the cheapest tourist experiences in the developed world. Old photographs of Hong Kong trams in the 1920s indicate that the design of the trams has not altered radically, except that they are now all double-deckers. Dmitri has the public transport options of taking a slow tram or an equally slow bus, but not today's preferred option, the Mass Transit Railway, which was begun in Central in the late 1970s. Now one of the most convenient, comfortable and regular metropolitan train services anywhere in the world, the mainly subterranean MTR serves Hong Kong Island and Kowloon, while the overground Kowloon-Canton Railway (KCR) connects Kowloon, the New Territories and the Hong Kong-Chinese border. Rejecting the opportunity to turn back into the cavernous mouth of the MTR entrance, we cross Des Voeux Road and look instead at the equally cavernous mouth of one of the two bronze lions that guard the imposing HSBC headquarters spanning Des Voeux Road and Queen's Road parallel to it.

Before considering Norman Foster's now world-famous and award-winning architectural design, these Western, realistic-looking bronze lions, as distinct from their more stylized Chinese counterparts, certainly merit a mention in their own right. They were cast by W. W. Wagstaff, a British fine arts professor at the National Academy of Arts in Hangzhou in the 1930s and named Stitt and Stephen after two senior bank executives. Stitt and Stephen were brought to Hong Kong to stand guard at the original Hong Kong Bank and fulfil the customary function of lion guardians of all shapes and sizes in Chinese lore, that of warding off evil spirits. They still stand defiantly, pock-marked by bullets from Japanese soldiers during the doomed defence of Hong Kong, but unbowed and oblivious to the remarkable transformation in the appearance of their ward. Hong Kong writer and academic Lo Wai-luen, or Xiao Si (little thoughts) as her Mandarin pen-name playfully styles her, writes about these bronze lions in one of her Hong Kong short stories. She complains about the lack of a door or lobby to the new bank building and remains unimpressed by the longest free-standing escalator in the world, which rises up from the open space to the banking hall above. To her the new building is "like an unfinished factory, its body cold and stiff and exposed". But what the writer-narrator has really come to see are the bronze lions. A tourist passer-by stares at the sight of what seems to be a local person engrossed in the fine detail of the lions: "The more imposing of the pair, the lion with the open mouth had sustained many injuries... For fifty years, he had opened his mouth, but said nothing. Well, someone born and bred in Hong Kong is looking for the first time at the lions, who have been here for more than five decades. Would you understand that, Sir?"

No, we probably wouldn't, she clearly thinks, so we leave Xiao Si stroking the lions' paws to have some of their fabled luck conferred on her. We can now observe the HK$5.2 billion HSBC headquarters more closely. It stands next to the old Bank of China Building with its tiered, neoclassical facade, intended when it was built in 1950 to impose itself grandly on the Central skyline. Now dwarfed by its neighbours, it modestly plays host to entrepreneur David Tang's retro chic China Club. This building looks down on both the Legislative Council Building and the Cenotaph below. Seen from the shore level, the three older structures rise symmetrically one behind the other, reaffirming perhaps the maxim that size isn't everything, and asserting the twin harmonies of perspective and geometric fusion. The greatest asset of Foster's design for the HSBC building from a Chinese cultural perspective is supposed to be its *fung shui* (literally water-wind. This refers to the Chinese science of natural balance, connected to the concept of *yin-yang* dualism). In other words, the building is ideally situated to catch the *chi* (force) coming down from the Peak, and at the same time receive the energy that emanates from the waters of the harbour. It also stands in a favourable position to ward off any potentially negative *chi* (force) from its close rival, the Bank of China.

Admiring Foster's bold design as we walk beneath it, we try to imagine the scene on any given Sunday, when this open space, like so many of the other open spaces of Central, becomes the temporary property of thousands of Filipina domestic helpers enjoying their rest day. Songs, often of a religious variety, as well as incessant and enthusiastic chat, are the order of the day. On Sundays Central quite

HSBC Headquarters and the Bank of China flanking the Cheung Kong Building.

literally belongs to the Filipinas, who are so preoccupied with their own affairs that they have hardly a glance to bestow on curious or not-so-curious passers-by. In the streets of Central, specially pedestrianized for these huge Sunday crowds, there is group singing, group dancing, group sport and sometimes group theatre. In fact, every Sunday is a street carnival of sorts. It is not that the participants resent the presence of others; simply that they are so intent on asserting their own cultural expression that they are entirely un-selfconscious. They work extremely hard for six days a week, and on the seventh, after attending mass at the Catholic Church, enjoy themselves come rain or shine. Visiting Caribbean poet Lasana M. Sekou describes them thus in his poem, "hong kong sunday", written for a writing workshop visit to Hong Kong Baptist University:

> *a morning. a mass. to a day of seatings in Central. ground like crop*
> *circles*

a chapel silent chatter. Filipinas in sacrament. the familiar
communion, the other feng shui.

Another memorable depiction of the Sunday scene in the heart of Central can be found in 2002 Nobel laureate Gao Xingjian's novel, *One Man's Bible*. Gao, a dissident in self-elected exile in France came to Hong Kong for a visit in 1995, and his semi-autobiographical novel records his impressions of a city living on borrowed time. This passage also provides a vivid mental picture of Central's stark contrasts and seeming contradictions:

> *The Bank of China Building, glass from top to bottom, reflects, like a mirror, the strands of white clouds in a blue sky. The sharp corner of the triangular building is knife-thin, and Hong Kong people say that it is like a meat cleaver cutting through the heart of the city and destroying the excellent feng shui of the island. The building of some finance group alongside has been fitted with some odd metal contraptions, futilely, to resist the baleful influences of the Bank of China Building. This is how Hong Kong people deal with the problem.*

Towards the Mid-Levels
A little further along Queen's Road, on the opposite side from the HSBC building, are three of Central's oldest streets, Ice House Street, Duddell Street and Wyndham Street. They have been utterly transformed by development, but one interesting vestige of the past are the steep and broad steps connecting Duddell Street with the winding Ice House Street. Flanking the steps are handsome Victorian-period gas-lamps, which are listed as declared public monuments. Walking back down Ice House Street, after a brief pause for breath, we reach Queen's Road once more. At the intersection we can take a pleasant, tree-lined footpath, climbing gently above Queen's Road. This is named Battery Path, and in the early days of the colony it led up to the Murray Gun Battery above. As we walk, we pass the elegant former French Mission House, now the Court of Final Appeal and see the Hong Kong Government Offices to the right and St. John's Cathedral directly in front. Poet and academic Agnes Lam's poem "Bamboo and Bauhinia" evokes the experience of standing on this leafy path near the cathedral,

an oasis of relative calm from the busy streets below. The convergence of the bamboo (Hong Kong scaffolding is constructed of bamboo; its main virtue is its flexibility in high winds) and the bauhinia (the flower of which is the emblem of post-Handover Hong Kong) is in the poet's imagination metaphorical and pertinent to Hong Kong's dualistic past and future:

Bamboo and bauhinia
leaves move
lightly
on the slope
of Battery Lane…
Grazing against each other,
folding, unfolding
A rustling tune in the Central breeze

It is difficult to imagine the panoramic view of Victoria and the harbour that St. John's Cathedral commanded when it was completed in 1849, but the spire of the Gothic-style church is now rather unremarkable, and the building hemmed in by Central's modern giants. Money was raised to pay for the construction by renting out pews to Hong Kong's great and good, with the governor's family naturally expected to occupy the front pew. In a notoriously quarrelsome social context, families competed to get the best pews as a marker of their social status in the expatriate community. The best artistic representation of the cathedral in the early years was done by visiting *Illustrated London News* artist-journalist Charles Wirgman in 1857 and reproduced in Arthur Hacker's delightful compendium, *The Hong Kong Visitor's Book—A Historical Who's Who*. Wirgman depicted an imposing ecclesiastical building, roughly the size of a large village church in Britain, set against dark hills to the rear. In the foreground commercial and social intercourse is being conducted in an open flat area by members of both the Chinese and the expatriate community.

Nowadays the cathedral is still well attended, and is also used for musical choral performances and occasional performances such as the Youth Arts Festival's *Godspell* (1999) and the Stage Renegades' Aids Concern fund-raising production of T. S. Eliot's verse play, *Murder in the Cathedral* (1993). The picturesque front porch of the cathedral is used as the setting for the scene, in which Tom Stewart, John Lanchester's protagonist in his Hong Kong novel *Fragrant Harbour*, meets sinologist and poet, Wilfred Austen. The meeting is a fateful one for Stewart, and one cannot help feeling that Lanchester's portrayal of the kindly but acerbic Austen owes more than a little to short-term Hong Kong resident and British pacifist, W. H. Auden.

On the other side of Garden Road, opposite St. John's Cathedral and slightly further up the hill, can be seen a very elegant colonial-era building, behind which lies the entrance to the Peak Tram. This building is known as the Helena May Institute, after its founder, the indefatigable wife of 1912-19 governor Francis May, and was designed as a home for single ladies. Still used as a ladies' club, the Helena May, with its graceful high-ceilinged ballroom-cum-dining room, peaceful garden and spacious dance school in its basement, is reminiscent of a more sedate chapter in Hong Kong's history. The Helena May and the cathedral are twin havens of serenity in an otherwise hyperactive location.

Government House
Walking up from these two buildings to Government House in Upper Albert Road, it is clear that much of Hong Kong's colonial development was controlled by the centre of power in Central from the combination of church and government, with the elegant colonnaded army headquarters at Flagstaff House (see below) and the army barracks and headquarters below next to Tamar naval basin, slightly east of Edinburgh Place and City Hall. The Tamar site was named after the floating naval headquarters provided by HMS Tamar, which was moored off Central until the 1950s. After the 1997 Handover the Tamar site was used variously as a funfair site and the venue for a Rock Music festival event known as Harbour Fest. It is now somewhat controversially scheduled to be the site of expensive new government offices in 2010. In the previous decade it played host to part of the extensive Handover ceremony on 30 June 1997, when last governor Chris Patten's tearful farewell transmitted the dominant mood to the rain gods. The unremitting rain throughout the celebrations was taken by some, on the other hand, as a portent of purification and renewal. Patten and family took their last farewell of Government House in a simple and dignified ceremony.

In contrast to the HSBC's excellent *fung shui*, Government House, which like the cathedral commanded a clear view over the harbour, lost both its outlook and its own favourable *fung shui* when the seventy-storey new Bank of China Building, with its angular geometric design and jutting tubular antennae, was built. According to Andrew Yeoh in *Hong Kong: A Guide to Recent Architecture*, the "structural metaphor" of the strong but graceful edifice is based on "the sturdy flexible tube" of the bamboo cane. But the new Bank of China represented something else, something more threatening to the established centres of power in the territory. In one symbolic stroke it seemed that the potency of the Chinese mainland's growing financial power and influence had planted a dagger deep into the heart of the seat of British power in Government House. At least that was how the new configuration and power relationship were interpreted by the Chinese in Hong Kong, even if the rulers themselves were unaware of the implications of the changes. Under the last four governors, Lord Murray MacLehose, Sir Edward Youde, Sir David Wilson and Lord Christopher Patten, it has to be said that a real effort was made to leave Hong Kong in as viable and vibrant a state as was humanly possible given the inevitability of the cession of power. Little wonder with the energetic programme of urban renewal and development and the civil service localization policy begun under MacLehose and sustained right up to the end of Patten's tenure of office that little attention was paid to such intangibles as *fung shui*. Yet the writing was as much on the reflective walls of the Bank of China as it was on the paper of the Basic Law.

Government House was completed in 1855 under the supervision of Sir Charles Cleverley, the first colonial Surveyor General of Hong Kong, after initial work on it began in 1851. Seen from the exterior in Upper Albert Road, its odd architectural amalgamation of Eastern and Western cultures is nothing if not distinctive. The building was home to every governor from the unpopular Sir John Bowring (1854-9) – unpopular with the expatriate community, that is - to the more generally liked Patten (1992-7), who, nevertheless, encountered his own share of opprobrium from his modern-day detractors.

In 1942 the building was rebuilt and the roof modified with the addition of Shinto-style towers to suit the tastes of the occupying Japanese Commander. After the British regained control there were too many other urgent affairs to be dealt with to bother about the offending structural modifications. So there it remains, looking rather incongruously like a miniature Buddhist temple. Some architects are of the opinion that it lends a certain style and character to the building that had been absent from the original design, and I must agree that they have a point. Tung Chee-hwa's post-Handover government only used it for wining and dining visiting dignitaries. Tung himself studiously avoided being associated with the building, believing it would bring him bad *fung shui*, which in retrospect is rather amusing considering his misfortunes in office. 2nd Chief Executive, Donald Tsang, by contrast, spent a cool $14 million of taxpayers' money on renovations for himself and his fish so that they would be comfortable when they moved into Government House in January 2006.

In Hong Kong-born novelist Louis Dung Kai-cheung's wonderfully ironic 1997 work, *The Atlas: Archeology of an Imaginary City*, the recorded comments of Governor William Des Voeux in his real-life 1903 memoirs are skilfully and humorously juxtaposed with the imagined comments of Chris Patten on the subject of The View from Government House. Using maps of the city, old and new, as reference points but retaining an imaginative sweep in his creative documentary, Dung writes that after the gradual encroachment of the Bank of China and other tall buildings on its sightlines "Government House has become an inland building." Des Voeux's original diary, as quoted in Dung's piece, reads, "Beneath, the air was quite clear and consequently, though the vessels in the harbour were invisible in the darkness, their innumerable lights seemed like another hemisphere of stars even more numerous than the others..." Dung's pastiche, purportedly based on comments his semi-fictional Patten is alleged to have made to his gardener, reads: "Beneath the air was quite clear and consequently, though the buildings in the city were invisible in the darkness, their innumerable lights seemed like another hemisphere of stars even more numerous than the others..." Thus Dung amusingly and topically superimposes modern historical fiction on documented historical fact.

Patten, with his more down-to-earth and informal style, was generally appreciated by Hong Kongers, except for influential tycoons, who deemed his efforts at broadening the base of public representation unnecessary and injurious to their own representations to the Communist Party leadership in Beijing. History generally repeats itself, so it is unsurprising to know that war-time governor Sir Mark Young also tried to introduce a modicum of democratic representation after the Japanese occupation, but was thwarted by the local entrepreneurial elite, just as Patten's attempted democratic reforms seem to have been undermined by an alliance of magnates and mandarins.

Poet Louise Ho evokes the era of internal confrontation and strife during the anti-colonial demonstrations of the 1960s in the poem "Hong Kong Riots 1967" from her 2001 collection *New Ends, Old Beginnings*. She depicts a single guard in a sentry box outside Government House at the time of the riots. Her opening words of encouragement can be read as an exhortation to Hong Kong people to stand their ground, too, in the coming years of turbulence:

Stand your ground
even if for only two foot square.
Rain or shine
surrounded by crowds
the sentry stood
khaki shorts
rifle in hand
still as a statue
and held his ground
of two foot square.
This too is pomp and circumstance
without fanfare.

Opposite Government House on the south side of Upper Albert Road and eastward across Garden Road and Cotton Tree Drive are Central District's green spaces. The Botanical Gardens and Hong Kong Park, respectively, resemble two vital lungs close to the heart of Hong Kong's often breathless capital. Comparisons with the effective blend of parks, buildings and waterways that one finds in London are not unreasonable. The park, completed in 1991, represented an ambitious attempt to complement the nineteenth-century Botanical Gardens and provide an ecologically friendly leisure environment above Central and Admiralty. It includes an ingeniously elegant and airy hi-tech aviary for a wonderful variety of bird species, as well as a number of artful miniature gardens, pools, rockeries and some vivid pink flamingos. Set harmoniously and somehow fittingly within the 25-acre space is the dazzling white and strikingly graceful 1846 colonial building Flagstaff House, now home to over five hundred pieces of earth-ware and porcelain tea-ware. Other colonial buildings have been adapted for modern purposes, in particular the Hong Kong Visual Arts Centre and the Marriage Registry. There is also a replica of a Roman amphitheatre adjacent to both the Edwardian-era registry office and the Asian-style landscape gardens, underlining Hong Kong's spirit of cultural eclecticism. Hong Kong Park, with its magnificent aviary, its harmonious landscaping and artificial lake, was an impressive achievement that has given Hong Kongers, crowded as they are into small apartments, a place to indulge their tastes for taking Sunday strolls and elaborately staged photographs.

By contrast, the Botanical Gardens can be seen as less dependent on stylish artifice. In spite of the more natural-looking character of these gardens, acknowledged for their success in preserving several endangered species of bird, they are no more part of the original landscape than the more obviously artificial Hong Kong Park. Eminent Victorian botanist Charles Ford, the Botanical Gardens' first superintendent from 1871 to 1903, succeeded spectacularly in his ambitious scheme of tree planting and plant propagation, to such an extent that the once barren-looking terrain of Hong Kong Island itself was dramatically transformed by the end of the century. Ford's ingenuity and imaginative approach to the landscaping and greening of the city of Victoria, has left modern-day residents much to be thankful for.

The Sorrows of Central Prison and the Joys of the Fringe Club

Walking downhill again from the former Government House, we reach the distinctive, red-brick Dairy Farm building, which dates from 1913. Built as a distribution outlet for the sale of fresh milk for Dr. Patrick Manson's Dairy Farm company, which he set up to improve hygiene and counter the effects of unhealthy diet in late Victorian and Edwardian Hong Kong, the building now houses the Hong Kong Fringe Club and the latest incarnation of the Foreign Correspondents' Club. The FCC is a magnet for international journalists as well as a good place to wine and dine and attend topical lunch-time talks by writers and commentators.

The Hong Kong Fringte Club, Central.

The Fringe Club, in addition to regular cross-cultural programme of arts events, hosts an annual City Festival with artists coming from many countries, particularly other Asian cultural contexts. There is a surprisingly varied programme of dance, drama and music in the two small theatres and the bar, as well as a permanent exhibition venue for photographers and visual artists to display their work. A regular event nowadays, the Man Literary Festival, welcomes Asian and Western writers every March to the Fringe Club. Recent guest speakers have included writers of international reputation alongside emerging younger writers from China, Hong Kong and elsewhere in Asia. Long-time Fringe director Benny Chia has his finger on the cultural pulse of the city, and the venue is popular with culture vultures, both young and old, Asian and Caucasian. A few Hong Kong movies have used the lively and hospitable Fringe Club as a location for scenes. One such is director Peter Chan's transgender comedy *He's the Woman, She's the Man*, starring Leslie Cheung and Anita Yuen. On the opposite side of the road, at the corner of Lower Albert Road and best viewed from the roof terrace of the Fringe Club, stands the Anglican Bishop's House, the oldest still inhabited Western-style building with its octagonal tower, on which are inscribed the Bishop's eight crosses.

From the Fringe Club it is a short walk across to the entertainment district of Lan Kwai Fong, with its numerous bars and restaurants. Lan Kwai Fong (literally "Orchid and Osmanthus Square" with reference to its tradition for exotic flower sellers) was transformed by a group of entrepreneurs two decades ago from a run-down network of poky streets into a crowded all-night magnet for Hong Kong's serious partying types. Nowadays, the vibrant community of Lan Kwai Fong organizes the district's own small Rio-style street carnival every October. The lively little cul-de-sac off Lan Kwai Fong, in addition to being a great place to eat *al fresco* was home to a well-known and fashionable pub, frequented by the arty, hip and politically anarchic, and named Club 64 (or June 4th Bar) in memory of the massacred Tiananmen students. The bar has moved to a site above Lan Kwai Fong in Peel Street off Hollywood Road. It now goes under the name July 1st Bar in reference to the ground-breaking mass protests against Tung Chee-hwa's over-cautious administration that took place in Hong Kong on 1 July 2003.

On New Year's Eve 1992 when Lan Kwai Fong was packed with people celebrating the New Year, there was a panic stampede as a result of overcrowding and pushing which resulted in the deaths of twenty revellers. The Lan Kwai Fong Tragedy shocked many of its habitual patrons, and although it has recovered its expatriate and non-Chinese clientele, there remains an air of melancholy about the place for many Chinese. This feeling is expressed by one of Hong Kong's best-known contemporary writers Leung Ping-kwan in his short piece, *The Sorrows of Lan Kwai Fong*. "Lan Kwai Fong always makes me think of Hong Kong. The space we have is a mixed, hybrid space, a crowded and dangerous space, carnival-like even in times of crisis, heavenly and not far from disasters, easily accessible and also easily appropriated—by political, economic and other forces." A tribute to those who died was recorded by two of Hong Kong's DJs under the artistic pseudonym of "Softhard". Entitled *Today is the Last Day*, the song movingly evokes the confusion and terror of those involved: "This is the day, the last day, a hydrogen balloon floats up to heaven..." Nevertheless, Lan Kwai Fong has retained its appeal as a nightspot and also a sanctuary for avant-garde arts groups, such as the popular Edward Lam Dance Company, as well as a growing number of small art galleries.

Another arts hub is planned at what is now the Central Police Station and Magistracy complex, which includes Victoria Prison. Many of the original colonial buildings in this complex are still in use. The interior white and blue-trimmed low police building was used briefly as a putative Police Training School in the first of Alan Mak's and Andrew Lau's dark but highly acclaimed *Infernal Affairs* film trilogy. Central Police Station, conversely, was depicted as one of the ultra-modern glass and chrome skyscrapers of the Cyberport, which is located on the south-west coast of the island. In a case of life following art (not an uncommon phenomenon in Hong Kong these days), a brand new glass and chrome police headquarters has been built in Wan Chai.

Victoria Prison incidentally housed a number of famous inmates, some of a literary disposition. Chinese leftists Ai Wu and Dai Wangshu, writing about their sojourns in Victoria Prison in the 1930s, left their mark in the power of their imagery. Ai Wu, writing of his long-held dream to visit Hong Kong, spent his brief stay as "a guest of her majesty": "I often compared China to a loving mother and Hong Kong to her young daughter. At the mere thought of this I could hardly resist the temptation to see this gorgeous young lady." After his expulsion he states, "The deepest impression I am left with of Hong Kong is the cruelty of imperialism and the unbearable stink of the night-bucket! This I will never forget." Dai Wangshu, by contrast, focuses in his poem "An Old and Worn-out Hand" on his imaginative reconstruction of the wretched life of a fellow prisoner, whose hand-marks on the cell wall he fancies he can discern. In fact, this poem is generally considered by Chinese literary critics to be a landmark in the twentieth-century rupture with traditional Chinese literary aesthetics in favour of a distinctively modernist voice.

Close to the prison and the old Central Police Station is Pottinger Street, named after first governor Sir Henry. This steeply climbing pedestrian path is fringed by stalls selling party fancy dress, coloured wigs and humorous appendages as well as electrical goods and various other inexpensive kinds of merchandise. It offers commanding views in both upward and downward directions, and gives a wonderful impression of the character of old Central District. In the 1960s Hong Kong artist Dong Kong-man produced a series of vibrantly coloured poster images of the city for the Hong Kong Tourist Association. The series was called "Hong Kong—British Crown Colony", and one of the best in the series was a poster of Pottinger Street bathed in bright light and seen from a cubist-cum-impressionist perspective, full of people buying and selling on the steps or strolling with birds in cages. On Wellington Street, which bisects the steps of Pottinger Street, bicycles and rickshaws enhance the effect of the scenic representation. Something of this old-fashioned atmosphere persists in the look of Pottinger Street even today. It is not so surprising given the fact that, like Ladder Street in Western District, it was one of the earliest streets in the colony and was always unsuitable for traffic other than of the biped variety.

On the streets below Pottinger Street, Wellington Street (named after the Iron Duke of Waterloo fame) and Stanley Street, we find two of Central's oldest and most reputed eating establishments. Yung Kee Restaurant on Wellington Street is famed far and wide for its duck and goose specialities, while Luk Yu Teahouse's credentials are clearly discernible in its venerable wooden shop-front and authentically old-fashioned interior. In either restaurant the diner is tempted to dally and let the world go frenetically by outside. The slow pace is in stark contrast to the fast food shops (*tsa tsaan teng*) on the opposite side of both streets. Inside the delightful Luk Yu time seems to stand still, peace and quiet reign, and Chinese tea is king. Peace and quiet were rudely shattered a few years ago when a Triad (Hong Kong Mafia) breakfast-time assassination took place there, but fortunately the contract killing appears to have been an isolated incident.

Filming On the Mid-Levels Escalator

Rising from the Central Market area and neatly crossing over Hollywood Road on its way up to the Mid-Levels is the 2,600-foot Hillside Escalator, the longest of its kind in the world. Open at the sides and with a curved glass roof to keep off the rain, the escalator is another genuinely enjoyable (and free) tourist ride, although if one wishes to ride up one must wait for the morning rush-hour transporting commuters from the Mid-Levels of Caine Road (named after Hong Kong's first colonial magistrate and founder of its prison) and Robinson Road to finish at 10.00 a.m. and for the direction of the escalator to be reversed. The Central escalator, to be precise a combination of travellators and escalators, moves approximately 36,000 people per day. With older tenement-style buildings only a few feet away from the escalator in places, it is tempting to peep at residents' domestic surroundings. This peculiarly Hong Kong juxtaposition of public and private spaces is evoked by Hong Kong's most famous international film director of recent times, Wong Kar-wai. In his 1993 masterpiece *Chungking Express*, the wacky but lovable Faye Wong spies on the melancholy policeman (played by *In the Mood for Love*'s Tony Leung) she fancies, and plucks up the courage to steal into his flat, which is located right beside the escalator. In a number of skilful shots Wong Kar-wai's cinematographer Christopher Doyle captures the voyeuristic but exciting nature of the escalator ride and the near-impossibility of privacy in this crowded environment.

Another film that uses the Central section of the escalator as backdrop for an intimate tale of a dysfunctional love is Hong Kong-born director Wayne Wang's allegory of the 1997 Handover, *The Chinese Box* (no relation to Christopher New's novel). According to some commentators, the protagonists are intended to symbolize China, Hong Kong and Britain respectively. Jeremy Irons plays a journalist living in a small apartment adjacent to the escalator (possibly the same one inhabited by Tony Leung!) and wandering wistfully around Central locations looking for love and a scoop for his UK-based newspaper. The women involved, bar owner Gong Li and arty eccentric Maggie Cheung—the female lead of Wong Kar-wai's international hit *In the Mood for* Love—make the film visually appealing (in spite of the facial disfigurement of the charismatic Cheung's character), as do the stunning shots of Central and the atmospheric escalator scenes. Sadly, however, when poor Irons dies of an untreatable form of leukaemia (fortunately not on the escalator), one feels strangely relieved.

SoHo, Egg Tarts and the IFC

If we elect instead to keep travelling up the escalator, having shaken off the persistent Faye Wong, we reach the so-called SoHo area of Central, consisting of bars and restaurants in streets radiating from the escalator spine of Shelley Street. If one is inclined to literary things, and approves of the radicalism of the young romantic poet Percy Bysshe, husband of Mary Shelley and friend of Byron, then one might reasonably assume the street is named after him. On the other hand, it might derive its name from his wife, creator of Frankenstein. True to Hong Kong form, however, the street is most probably named after Sir John Davis' Attorney General, A. E. Shelley, who left the colony under the cloud of suspicion of committing fraud—not a serious impediment to getting a street named after one, it would seem.

SoHo provides a wider range of international cuisines than can be found anywhere else in Central, and a whole escalator culture seems to have emerged since the previously unremarkable Staunton Street, Elgin Street (named after the son of the British earl who purloined the Elgin marbles for the British Museum) and Shelley Street metamorphosed into a gourmet's paradise. Lorette Roberts' *Sketches of SoHo*, a beautiful and imaginative book of sketches, water colours, personal observations and factual information, constitutes the perfect guidebook and cultural introduction to the area. Her artwork, featuring shop-fronts, door knockers, elegant old windows, general oddities and local inhabitants of various ethnic types, does ample justice to the diverse activities in this fascinating network of streets. The area is also home to many of Hong Kong's arts galleries. Roberts' artistic eye reveals the riot of colour to be found in the streets too, from the profusion of reds in the lantern shop to the fanciful idea that typical Hong Kong road works signage is "like a piece of installation art". As Roberts points out in her introduction: "Like an onion it [SoHo] has its layer upon layer to peel away, revealing a village—a hybrid cosmos… What a cornucopia of culture, and how I have enjoyed painting it and its people!" It is just as well she has documented SoHo since, if the Hong Kong Government's euphemistically named Urban Renewal Authority gets its way, much of one of Central's most appealing and historically rich areas may disappear by 2010.

Further up on the Mid-Levels steps and parallel to the escalator is a memorial plaque to honour the memory of Dr. José Rizal, Filipino revolutionary, who lived in Hong Kong at the turn of the nineteenth century in the exotic-sounding street, Rednaxela Terrace. The name was originally written down by a sign-writer illiterate in English, if not Chinese. That can be the only explanation for writing the name Alexander the wrong way round—unless the sign-writer had imbibed one over the eight, or unless there really was a mysterious Mr. or Ms. Rednaxela. We shall never know, but if there was, his name has survived and stands proudly to this day.

Nearer the top of the escalator at Robinson Road are two beautiful old buildings, which date back to an earlier era and fittingly project a more contemplative aura than that of the scene below. The Jamia Mosque, with its wrought-iron gates and banyan trees, was designed as a place of worship for the Punjabi Muslim policemen stationed at Central Police Station in the early years of colonial rule. It retains an air of reclusion and serenity to this day. Several minutes walk from the escalator on Robinson Road is the finely carved, Hispanic-style Ohel Leah Synagogue. The synagogue was founded by entrepreneur Sir Jacob Sassoon, in memory of his mother. The Sassoon family, to whom British First World War poet Siegfried Sassoon was related, were made wealthy by the success of David Sassoon, who settled in Hong Kong in the 1840s. Sassoon family fortunes originated in the 19th century opium trade that flourished between Bombay and Shanghai, for which they cornered the market.

If we now wait for the downward escalator run for the morning commuters it will mean spending an entire night carousing in one of the many bars or restaurants and sleeping on the steps adjacent to the escalator itself. However, we can make the most of the opportunity to revisit the lower part of Central by walking down to Hollywood Road, crossing into the former red-light district of Lyndhurst Terrace (*Baaifat Gaai* or Flower Stall Street in its more evocative Cantonese moniker). This is also where China's first president Sun Yat-sen lived when he was in Hong Kong at the end of the nineteenth and beginning of the twentieth century. A former Victoria College, Central, schoolboy, Dr. Sun, as he became after studying medicine in Hong Kong, together with like-minded members of his secret organization, plotted the overthrow of the decaying Manchu Qing Dynasty from Hong Kong's Central District. It is ironic to think that Hong Kong's infamous Triad Societies were originally formed for the same purpose by Ming Dynasty survivors, that of overthrowing the hated Qing Dynasty. Unfortunately, or fortunately for many Hong Kong film directors and movie stars, the scope of their activities became increasingly less laudable as time passed. Wall plaques in Wellington Street, Hollywood Road and Lyndhurst Terrace commemorate Dr. Sun's achievements.

Having been exiled to Macau and arrested in London by Qing Dynasty spies and British upholders of the Chinese imperial system, Dr. Sun overcame all obstacles and became President of China's first republic shortly after the 1911 revolution in China. He returned to Hong Kong in 1923 to give a speech at Hong Kong University, of which more in a later chapter.

A more recent political figure, namely the last governor, or Lord Patten, as he is now known, gained a reputation as a regular patron of the immensely popular bakery in Lyndhurst Terrace, Tai Cheong, which opened its doors for business on the same spot for over fifty years. "Fei Pang" (fat Patten), as he was affectionately dubbed, was always partial to their *daan taats*, or egg pastries. Tai Cheong, which used to have long queues outside every Saturday and Sunday morning, closed in June 2005, not because the most reputed Chinese patisserie in Hong Kong was losing business, far from it. In a typical example of Hong Kong's sometimes cynical and opportunistic *laissez-faire* approach, greedy landlords have speculated outrageously with non-negotiable increases of over a hundred, and in some cases two hundred, per cent on already high rents.

In the case of Tai Cheong, Patten, still a regular visitor to Hong Kong, and incidentally to Beijing too, raised the issue in an email to the *South China Morning Post* in May 2005. "Everyone knows that in my judgment they made the best egg tarts in the world," he averred. Immediately Legislative Councillors started to take an interest, sensing a celebrity, and thus newsworthy, case, with the potential of political capital to be gained. Perhaps the government of the present Chief Executive, Donald Tsang, will prove itself more assertive than the previous one in legislating against the "greed is good" brigade, before this part of Central loses its charm and idiosyncratic, small-business ethos. The happy postscript is that Tai Cheong re-opened in new premises on the opposite side of Lyndhurst Terrace three months later and continues to do good business.

Land speculation is of course nothing new, and can be traced back to the earliest colonial days and the very first land sales on Hong Kong Island. Talking of imagination, as we are in this book, some acknowledgment is due to the brazen audacity of creative profit-making on the part of rapacious landlords and property speculators in this city, but history tells us it has always been thus in any metropolis. The opening chapters of Han Suyin's 1951 autobiographical novel, *A Many-Splendoured Thing*, recount the rampant property and rental speculation in Hong Kong, and especially in Central, in 1949, when landlords profited shamelessly from the misery and dire need of the hundreds of thousands of mainland Chinese, who fled to the Territory to escape Mao Tse-tung's victorious communist troops.

As we reach Queen's Road Central once more we can walk down the fashionable and busy Pedder Street (named after Lieutenant William Pedder, who accompanied Elliot and stayed on like Caine and Johnston to make his home in Hong Kong). Pedder became harbour master, and from his Central Building headquarters supervised the busy harbour trade. Of course, the watermark at this stage of Hong Kong's development was very close to Queen's Road. It is hard to imagine the South China Sea lapping at one's ankles as one approaches the smart Landmark shopping centre, but the plaque on the wall of the Landmark, informing us of this fact, reinforces the logic of the name. We can only imagine that we are swimming briskly as we cross the busy Des Voeux and Connaught roads once more. We arrive first at the busy and prestigious office environment of Exchange Square, on the podium of which stands an imposing 1968 Henry Moore sculpture, *Oval With Points*, set atop a fountain and another bronze piece with a watery setting, Elisabeth Frink's *Water Buffalo Standing*. Both are vigorous and assertive works that resonate with the confidence appropriate to a building that houses Hong Kong's stock exchange. A third sculpture specially purchased for display here is Taiwanese artist Ju Ming's *Tai Chi—Single Whip*, which has a specifically Chinese cultural connotation. However, if we examine the abstract Moore sculpture, on closer inspection it turns out to represent the figure 8, which fittingly signifies wealth and prosperity in Chinese culture.

A stone's throw from Exchange Square is Hong Kong's newest wonder, the towering, rocket-shaped International Finance Centre, or as it is commonly known, the IFC. The lower structure, One IFC, houses Central's Airport Express terminus. The prominent 1,400-foot spire of Two IFC, home to the Hong Kong Monetary Authority, is, for the present at least, the tallest building in Hong Kong and the fifth tallest in the world. It was designed by internationally acclaimed architect Cesar Pelli (making a change from Norman Foster.) There is, unusually perhaps, some truth in the developers' hyperbole about IFC being "a city within a city". While its shopping facilities and supremely comfortable multiplex cinemas can be readily appreciated by the consumer, and its office space by company employees, the most impressive view of the IFC is from the opposite Kowloon-side. From there it appears to be some kind of extra-terrestrial space capsule (with a curious battery-shaver-like head) that has landed directly in front of Hong Kong's Peak, in a post-modern version of H. G. Wells' *War of the Worlds*. Hong Kong disaster movies have simulated attacks on Central's Bank of China and Wan Chai's Convention and Exhibition Centre, and it seems unlikely that the IFC's potential as a site of the fictional imagination will remain untapped for long.

At this point we can consider a restful visit to one of the Outlying Islands from the Ferry Piers facing the IFC or return to the MTR to seek Suzie Wong in old Wan Chai. Suzie's charms win out and we head back in the direction of the MTR to travel past Admiralty and another hotel hub at Pacific Place to Wan Chai. On second thoughts, let's take a tram and imagine what the view must have been like for Richard Mason, the documenter, if not the creator, of the *World of Suzie Wong* when he arrived in Hong Kong in the early 1950s.

chapter three

"SUZIE'S WORLD": FROM WAN CHAI TO HAPPY VALLEY

Literary and Linguistic Antecedents

I crossed Hennessey Road, with its clattering trams and two huge modernesque cinemas showing American films, and came out on the waterfront by the Mission to Seamen. Next to the Mission was a big hotel called the Luk Kwok, famous for Chinese wedding receptions and obviously too expensive for me even to try... Sampans tied up amongst the junks tossed sickeningly in the wash of passing boats. Across the road from the quay were narrow, open-fronted shops, between which dark staircases led up to crowded tenement rooms; and along the pavement children played hopscotch whilst shovelling rice into their mouths from bowls, for all Chinese children seemed to eat on the move... I leant on the sun-warmed stone. A rickshaw went by, the coolie's broad grimy feet making a slapping sound on the road. Then my eyes fell on an illuminated sign amongst the shops. The blue neon tubes were twisted into the complicated, decorative shapes of Chinese characters. I recognized the last two. They meant hotel.

Richard Mason, *The World of Suzie Wong,* 1957

When Richard Mason arrived in Hong Kong in 1956, he stepped off the Star Ferry in Wan Chai (like his fictional hero Robert Lomax) and checked into the then harbour-front Luk Kwok Hotel (whereas his hero checked into its fictional neighbour, the Nam Kok), looking for inspiration for his next novel. Already moderately successful, this former student of W. H. Auden had decided on Hong Kong as a suitably exotic locale for his yet-to-be-started work. Auden had marked his and co-writer Christopher Isherwood's brief passage through Hong Kong on their way to China's war with the Japanese invaders with a sonnet entitled simply "Hong Kong". (Their resulting 1939 prose and poetry collection was entitled *Journey to a War*):

Waterfront, Wanchai, with Hong Kong (Bauhinia) and PRC flags. IFC building in background (right).

The leading characters are wise and witty
Substantial men of birth and education
With wide experience of administration
They know the manners of a modern city.

Only the servants enter unexpected;
Their silence has a fresh dramatic use:
Here in the East the bankers have erected
A worthy temple to the Comic Muse

It would be nice to think that Hong Kong's comic muse could be the great twentieth-century humorist, P. G. Wodehouse, but Pelham Grenville, named after Hong Kong friends of his Hong Kong Police Force father, only lived in Hong Kong for a few months as a two-year-old. He did, of course, work for the Hong Kong Shanghai Bank in London, but high finance's loss became comic literature's gain when he resigned to devote himself to such delightfully comic creations as Jeeves and Wooster. Some commentators have observed that the sharp, often sly observation about class difference below the smooth surface of his writing somehow reflect a consciousness shaped by the Hong Kong social situation. Wodehouse certainly knew about Hong Kong, but even for a precocious two-year-old, such powers of observation would be quite miraculous.

In modern-day Hong Kong the comic muse could be hugely popular actor-director Stephen Chow, whose clever, special-effects movie spoofs on aspects of Chinese and Hong Kong culture, including *Shaolin Soccer* and *Kung Fu Hustle*, have now reached the sort of international markets formerly reserved for Bruce Lee and Jackie Chan. Perhaps, though, if we interpret the word comic in a different way, we can consider as modern muses those commercial comic book writers from Hong Kong and Japan, whose output is greedily devoured by the younger Hong Kong reading public on buses and the Mass Transit Railway.

To return to Auden, the final lines of his sonnet refer to the ugly situation of the late 1930s as world war loomed: "We cannot postulate a General Will; For what we are, we have ourselves to blame." Mason's experience of that war and his post-war younger-generation sensibility enabled him to depict with devastating accuracy, unclouded by patriotic or nationalistic sentiment, the manners of both masters and servants. His basic humanistic and egalitarian instincts as a writer inform the semi-autobiographical novel, *The World of Suzie Wong*, which was born from his Hong Kong experience. They also prompted him to explore the less privileged and affluent sectors of the community, and place the literary, and subsequently social and cultural focus on a new class of servants—the so-called bar-girls or yum-yum girls. Yum, or yam as it is written in the Yale transcription system for Cantonese Romanization, means drink, and the term signified the practice of buying girls, who frequented the bar, a drink at an extremely inflated price, as a prelude to sex, either "short-time" or "all-night", depending on the price paid.

Mason's novel took the lid off the post-Victorian gentility of the colony and challenged the complacency and sexual hypocrisy of "the wise and witty". In addition, *The World of Suzie Wong* chronicled a transformation in Hong Kong's way of life and provided a candid, though admittedly somewhat romanticized, portrait of its emergent "service economy". Hong Kong's economic success story was beginning to be written at this time by former Shanghai entrepreneurs, who had moved their manufacturing resources to Hong Kong in anticipation of the 1949 communist victory in the civil war in China. Factories and sweat shops were beginning to proliferate, but the sex industry, which had been amply represented by the brothels of Shek Tong Tsui, Tai Ping Shan and Lyndhurst Terrace in earlier eras, also began to flourish once again in Wan Chai. The increasing number of US naval ships docking for R and R (rest and recreation) in the friendly port of Hong Kong, supplementing the existing squads of thirsty British sailors, resulted in a business boom for Wan Chai bars, hotels and of course those who lived in parasitical or symbiotic relationship with them.

Mason captures this period in Hong Kong's development beautifully, from the sleepy colonial city to the more vibrant modern metropolis. The novel and the film adaptation, with which it is invariably confused as though they were somehow ideologically and culturally inseparable, did not convince a good number of sceptics, especially in Hong Kong itself, who saw evidence of patriarchy, paternalism and gross oversimplification in what was represented by the story. Nevertheless, Suzie's name has become, for better or worse, irrevocably associated with Wan Chai, as the existing bars that carry this fictional heroine's name attest. There is, of course, much more to Wan

Chai than its firmly cemented association with Suzie, though. It is an area that is worth exploring for its perhaps surprisingly rich historical and cultural roots. The name means literally "little bay" (the second word in Chinese being a diminutive), and like many place-names in Hong Kong it contains the word for bay—"waan", to render the sound in accurate transliteration.

Old Wan Chai: Schemes and Fantasies

We have every reason to assume that there was not much happening in Wan Chai before the advent of Western sailors in the 1840s and then again in the 1950s and 1960s. The indigenous fishing activity, on which the livelihood of many generations of pre-colonization Hong Kong depended, was based primarily on the south side of the island. After the British colony was established, the area between the new town of Victoria and the East Point warehouses of the *hongs* (trading companies), which was off-handedly described as Little Bay, increased in strategic importance. The location of Wan Chai, close to Victoria, yet cut off from it by the navy and army barracks and docks, and its close proximity to these bases ultimately determined its development as a recreation focus and shopping emporium for servicemen. When the Victoria district was declared out of bounds to off-duty military and navy personnel around the turn of the twentieth century, Wan Chai's taverns and whorehouses started to flourish. Wan Chai's western demarcation point became the garrison at Arsenal Street. Beyond that lay the navy base, referred to as Admiralty, which included the area still known today as Tamar. In the east it was bordered by a hill that came to be called Morrison Hill, after the missionary and gifted linguist, Robert Morrison, whose missionary zeal led him to translate the bible into Chinese, and whose Christian proselytizing fervour was undoubtedly one of the motivating forces behind the early evangelization of Hong Kong.

East of Morrison Hill and the rice paddies of Belcher Valley (named after himself by a rather conceited Captain Edward Belcher) were the *godowns* of the Jardine-Matheson company, situated roughly where the modern Excelsior Hotel in Causeway Bay now stands. According to one local legend, a young naval officer's proposal of marriage was rejected at the appropriately named Repulse Bay, but subsequently accepted in Belcher's Valley, prompting the change of name to Happy Valley. Happy Valley has become a focal point for sport, particularly horse-racing, which is both extremely popular across all sections of the community, and a source of huge income for educational and charitable enterprises through the donations of the Hong Kong Jockey Club. Nestling against the hill to the west with an excellent view of the racecourse is Happy Valley Cemetery, the bucolic last resting place of many expatriates and prominent Eurasians and Chinese citizens, who were buried here in the nineteenth and twentieth centuries.

Another landmark in the area close to Happy Valley and above the bustling streets of Wan Chai is an original natural feature of the landscape, a rock formation jutting from the hill at an improbable 45 degree angle. Known as Lovers' Rock or Yan Yuen Sek (Marriage Fate Rock) in Cantonese, this has long been a place of pilgrimage for unmarried women desirous of felicitous marriage omens, and couples, or even parents and grandparents, seeking happy portents of a son and heir. Indeed, every August at the so-called Maidens' Festival a handful of hopeful maidens can be observed climbing the 30-foot high rock and lighting joss sticks. Their fellow maidens are nowadays to be found below in Causeway Bay's bustling bargain boutiques, engaged equally single-mindedly in a different kind of quest. The starkly phallic form and imposing situation of Lovers' Rock remind us that, when it comes to fertility rites and superstitions, human imagination is truly universal, in spite of the cultural variations brought by many centuries of civilization. There seems little doubt that long before Little Bay was transformed into the centre of amorous activity in Hong Kong's otherwise abstemious cultural psyche, the primitive priapic deity above Wan Chai was playing its part in promoting the continuation of the species.

On Morrison Hill and behind the Ruttonjee Hospital—a former naval hospital, founded thanks to the endowment of the Parsee merchant family of that name—there are stone steps and a gateway leading to what is now Wan Chai Road, but was formerly known as Spring Gardens. This was an up-market,   residential district with a short promenade built right on the Wan Chai waterfront, as it was in the 1840s. In later decades it was transformed, almost inevitably, into a brothel district. Today, Spring Garden Lane, off Wan Chai Road, with its fast-food shops and modest high-rise accommodation, bears little resemblance to Murdoch Bruce's lithograph of 1846, which depicts the fashionable and elegantly colonnaded new colonial houses, one of which was home to the new governor George Bonham, and the broad promenade skirting a small harbour for sampans and navy gigs. Another longer distance view of Spring Gardens by a more renowned artist of the East, George Chinnery, depicts a serene settlement of apparently weathered colonial buildings, with barques and sampans moored off the quay. In the background the hills above Wan Chai merge with a cloudy sky, contrasting with and offsetting the tranquil water below. Not perhaps one of Chinnery's best-known works, the pen and ink and watercolour representation, completed in the same year as Bruce's, shows the same uncanny affinity with his subject that is evident in Chinnery's consummately skilful and numerous depictions of the Tanka boat people.

In those days Wan Chai was a little less than a mile long and the bay was unsuitable for large vessels. Gradually land was reclaimed under a succession of governors and schemes. The grandest of such schemes never quite took off, although it can be seen as a forerunner of all subsequent land reclamation plans. Had it done so, modern Wan Chai would be called Bowrington after its proponent, Governor Sir John Bowring, a Chinese language scholar, former Liberal MP and generally controversial figure in the early colonial era. For thumbnail sketches of Bowring, the acquisitive government attorney, William Bridges and well-meaning police superintendent, Charles May, one should read Dean Barrett's *Hangman's Point*, set in Hong Kong in the year 1857:

> *Adams made way for eight neatly dressed Chinese bearers carrying a large chair at the centre of their two poles… As the chair passed the man inside peered out and Adams found himself face to face with Sir John Bowring. With his high forehead and pince-nez practically down to the tip of his nose, the fourth governor of Hong Kong seemed to scrutinize everything he passed with a tinge of scepticism. Bowring regarded Adams closely, registering neither approval nor disapproval, and then passed from sight.*

Having embarked on a number of ill-advised escapades, including the disastrous 1856 *Arrow* incident involving a gunboat sortie to Canton, Bowring's reputation for grandiose schemes and self-promotion had fast become legendary in the colony. His vaunted Praya reclamation plan linking Causeway Bay or East Point with Victoria and continuing as far as Western District or Navy Bay (Sai Ying Pun) was nothing if not ambitious. In fact, Bowring's concept of reclamation and a *praya* or promenade running along the shoreline and linking east and west is what subsequently happened. The single thoroughfare of Queen's Road was for too long the only transport link between the various commercial and military establishments on the island. One pivotal point of the development was to be the waterfront of Wan Chai. Bowring bullied the community into accepting his plans and even pledging money, but after work was begun on a new canal, dubbed the Bowrington Canal and the first street of the new town area, which was named Bowrington Street, Bowring's visionary plans were amazingly voted down. This rejection, occasioned more by spite and animosity toward Bowring among Legislative Council members than fiscal prudence, spelled the end of Wan Chai's brief early promise of spectacular development.

Bowrington Street remains to this day a small but lively open market thoroughfare, but Bowrington Canal was filled in and the present-day Canal Road East and West are distinguishable only by the deafeningly noisy flyover that soars above them, under which street sleepers and others take up temporary abode and various street activities continue to flourish. Today's city planners, in partnership with ever-hopeful development companies, eye the waterfront between Central and Wan Chai greedily, as the government's controversial plan for supposedly beautifying the harbour and easing traffic congestion on this, one of the busiest stretches of the island, are argued both in and out of court. Something tells me that Bowring's scheme, despite the man's undeniable self-importance and vanity, was more ecologically friendly than today's scheme. For all his faults, Bowring was not working in excessively close collusion with land developers.

The Affair of the Poisoned Bread

Another famously dramatic event in Bowring's incident-packed governorship also featured Wan Chai. After Bowring's unwarranted aggression against the Chinese forces in Canton, following a minor squabble that spiralled out of control, the authorities in Canton initiated covert operations to strike against the Western interlopers in the heart of Hong Kong in January of 1857. One method had been to put a price on the foreign devils' heads, but a more cost-effective strategy presented itself when the Yee Sing Bakery, situated between Queen's Road and the present-day Southorn Playground in Wan Chai, gained contracts to supply most of the expatriate community with their bread and biscuits. The proprietor, one Cheong Ah-Lum, was doing excellent business, and although he was prosecuted for what became known as the great poisoning incident, he was, as transpired, clearly not the culprit. By seven 'o clock one morning the first tell-tale signs of arsenic poisoning were manifesting themselves, though not so much among the Western expatriate community, the presumed intended targets, as the Indian and Parsee community. The poisoners had perhaps rather foolishly forgotten that they also liked to eat bread. Word of the poison outbreak spread rapidly and the majority of the non-Chinese community avoided eating the arsenic-laced bread. For some strange reason, however, the message never reached the hated Sir John Bowring, and both he and his wife suffered terrible pain and nausea. The iron constitution of Bowring, which complemented his armour-plated skin, enabled him to survive. His wife was not so lucky and her death later that year in England is likely to have been hastened by the poisoning she experienced, though it may not have been the direct cause.

The fact that nobody died as an immediate result of poisoning was almost certainly thanks to the excessive zeal of Cheong's two foremen, who were the real culprits. They put far too much arsenic in the mix, which, instead of guaranteeing the desired deadly effect, caused victims to vomit up the poison before it could be absorbed into the bloodstream. The noxious reactions were still preferable to death, and enabled emetics to be judiciously applied by Hong Kong's doctors, who were to be called upon in large numbers again in later emergencies, such as the bubonic plague epidemics of the late nineteenth century and the SARS scare of the early twenty-first.

The unfortunate owner of the bakery had caught a ferry boat to Macau, the Portuguese enclave across the Pearl River delta. He had chosen this day of all days to take his sons for a trip, perhaps to enjoy a baker's holiday checking out the delightful Portuguese-style egg tarts, for which Macau pastry makers were renowned. Not surprisingly, his apparent flight was taken as tacit admission of guilt. When the wretched Ah-Lum was apprehended, one mitigating circumstance, however, was noted. Both his sons were suffering from acute food poisoning, brought on by eating the contaminated bread and exacerbated by the motion of the boat. This fact helped to save the baker's life. At his subsequent trial the ranting public prosecutor (Bowring's nemesis and would-be governor, Attorney-General Thomas Chisholm Anstey) opined to the jury that, even if there were grave doubts as to Ah-Lum's culpability, he should still be hanged. Bowring had made a strong and principled stand against those who wanted to administer the summary retribution of lynching Ah-Lum outside his now non-operational Queen's Road establishment. He insisted on proper judiciary proceedings. When Anstey pleaded that it "was better to hang the wrong man than confess that British sagacity and activity have failed to discover the real criminals," the jury disagreed by a majority of five to one.

In spite of misgivings about British justice and its flaws, perversions and miscarriages, it is only fair to say that the rule of law, British-style, has continued to be seen as a bastion of defence of Hong Kong's rights, following the Handover. At the time of writing this book, when the rule of law in China remains a goal rather than any sort of reality, we must reflect thankfully that Anstey's cynical idea of justice that the accused can be assumed guilty unless proven innocent, never really caught on in the territory. The unpredictable and erratic Bowring subsequently detained poor Ah-Lum with a view to deportation under an ordinance he had hastily introduced as a sop to the "hang 'em and flog 'em enthusiasts, of which there were many among the expatriates in that era, as Timothy Mo's *An Insular Possession* indicates. The reactionary news organ *Friend of China,* which appears alongside other documentary devices in Mo's epic historically accurate novel, was successful in suing Ah-Lum for damages following his acquittal. His defence attorney, the corrupt Dr. William Bridges, after whom Bridges Street in Central is thoughtfully named, managed to sneak him out of jail and smuggle him out of the territory and over the border.

The same thing happened half a century later with Vietnamese revolutionary, Ho Chi Minh, much to the chagrin of the French police in Indo-China, when they were seeking his extradition from Hong Kong. Ho Chi Minh, of course, went on to inspire greater things than

Ah-Lum was to do, although the latter did ply his baker's trade in Vietnam after his expulsion. On balance, then, the famous Ah-Lum affair was less a victory for the British judicial system than it ought to have been—more like a draw, in fact. For a sympathetic portrayal of Ah-Lum and a compelling account of the poisoned bread affair, see Barrett's *Hangman's Point*, which offers a colourful, but balanced, blend of fact and fiction.

Anstey subsequently fought an embittered but successful legal campaign against Bowring, Bridges and their Cantonese-speaking ally, Daniel Caldwell, who was the Civil Service's interpreter and pirate catcher. Caldwell was a gifted but highly ambivalent figure. Like Bridges, he took advantage of his office for his own pecuniary ends, but his peculiar role as official "Protector of Chinese" and his choice of a Chinese spouse in an era when the ideological concept of miscegenation was becoming widely accepted in the West, makes him something of a maverick in early Hong Kong society, despite his official position in the Civil Service.

Eventually the accident-prone Bowring, who had unwittingly engineered the collapse of Palmerston's Liberal government with his high-profile and trumped up sortie against China, was replaced as governor, and Bridges, Anstey and Caldwell were all rejected for reinstatement as part of the new governor Hercules Robinson's clean sweep. Ah-Lum had the last laugh, as he was permitted to return to Hong Kong. Bowring returned to England, remarried and continued to harry and be harried by the press. The only other acknowledgement of his colourful presence in Hong Kong, apart from the vestiges of Bowrington in East Wan Chai, is the rather nondescript Bowring Street in Jordan on Kowloon-side. If the proposed Central-Wan Chai link becomes a reality, it is unlikely to be named after him in honour of his grand scheme.

From Ship Street to Sugar Street: Temples, Trams and a Post Office

Wan Chai is full of nautical references in the names of streets—e.g. Ship Street, Sampan Street, Schooner Street, which is hardly surprising given its waterfront setting, albeit a different setting in the early days of the colony than that of today. Even now its personality is decidedly split between the cultural district of Wan Chai North, the area north of the busy Gloucester Road leading to and from the busy cross-harbour tunnel, and Wan Chai South, which has a different kind of cultural tradition. Beyond the "girlie bars" of the Lockhart Road district and a short walk away are the bustling local shops and markets in the network of streets connecting the main thoroughfares of Hennessey Road, Johnston Road and Queen's Road. The northern section, which includes the busy Convention and Exhibition Centre, with its 1997 extension built specially for the Handover and boasting a magnificent seagull-design wavy roof, as well as the Academy for Performing Arts, the Arts Centre, Government Offices and Central Plaza, the tallest building in Wan Chai, stands on reclaimed land. It was reclaimed in three swathes starting in the 1880s. Development continued in the 1920s, when Morrison Hill was substantially flattened to provide earth for the project. Then, in the late 1960s and 1970s what is now known as Wan Chai North was developed as a waterfront and an access road for the new cross-harbour tunnel.

Ship Street, a steeply ascending street leading up from Queen's Road, being close to the original waterfront, was home to ships' chandler's establishments and a shipyard. Just around the corner on Queen's Road East is the oldest proper religious building still extant in Hong Kong, begun in 1847 not long after the British annexation of the island, when it stood right on the then waterfront. The Hung Shing Temple developed from a small shrine built in the shelter of a big rock dedicated to the Dragon, Kong, legendary ruler of the South China Sea in Chinese lore and protector of seafarers against typhoons. The small fishing community originally living on the site had instituted worship centuries before at the place where the temple was completed in the 1860s. Other deities to be found here include Lung Mo (literally, the dragon mother), the Sun and Moon gods (whose presence is also reflected in the names of Sun and Moon Streets, both in relatively close proximity), Lady Kam Fa (Golden Flower), the protector of pregnant women, Kwun Yam, the goddess of mercy, the City God, Shing Wong ("City King") and in a peaceful upper room the Lord Buddha. The picturesque old banyan tree that spreads it beneficent branches over the roof of the temple and elegantly typical Shekwan pottery roof border complete a wonderfully harmonious scene, all the more valuable for its aura of peaceful contemplation in the noisy environs of the present-day Queen's Road, the thoroughfare for traffic heading in the direction of Happy Valley and Causeway Bay.

The Blue House, Wan Chai

Not far from the Hung Shing Temple on Ship Street and a little further east is Stone Nullah Lane, where Wan Chai's famous 1920s Blue House is located. This eye-catching former tenement building is being transformed into a local museum. There is another historically interesting temple here, and like the Hung Shing Temple, it dates from the 1860s. This one, the Pak Tai Temple, is more attractively set in the quiet, leafy surroundings of Wan Chai Gap. It contains a bronze statue of the god Pak Tai (literally King of the North), a Taoist deity connected both with water and wealth, the two words being metaphorically connected and thus synonymous in vernacular Cantonese. Hence the temple remains popular with Hong Kong adherents of the Taoist teaching, as well as those pragmatic residents who will happily invoke any auspicious omens from a variety of creeds. The statue dates back to the Ming Dynasty and the early seventeenth century, although it is unclear how it ended up in the temple. The legend of Pak Tai is illustrative of Hong Kong thinking concerning water and wealth. Those developers, who wish to turn water into land, leading inexorably to wealth, are doubtless inspired by Pak Tai's fate. His dirty bath water was magically transformed into gold, as a result of which he acquired the status of a god. Whether future generations of Hong Kong citizens will revere these rapacious latter-day Pak Tais when Hong Kong's harbour has dwindled to the size of a large boating pond is open to question.

A highly interesting feature of all temples, and indeed of the various festivals in honour of departed ancestors, involves the burning of fake paper money and other paper objects designed to enhance the quality of life of these ancestors in the netherworld. The present-day Pak Tai Temple is particularly fascinating, as model icons of the trappings of material wealth, such as luxury cars, houses and even servants are daily recreated in paper and bamboo miniature by a team of craftsmen. The Western proverb to the effect that when it comes to wealth "you can't take it with you when you go" is clearly alien to Chinese concepts of the possibilities of the after-life. Not only the more old-fashioned rich, but also relatively poor and marginalized citizens like Suzie Wong, as Mason's book recounts, indulge in this practice. Following the death of her baby in a house collapse during torrential rainstorms, Suzie burns paper replicas of objects he will need in the next life, including a house, books, clothes, million dollar notes and a bridge to facilitate his passage to a better life. Having burnt them on the narrator's (Robert Lomax) balcony at the Nam Kok Hotel, she confides in him that she does not really believe in the culturally ingrained superstition. For her the half-belief is a way to mitigate the aching gap left by her child's death. "Believing—and not believing. She had always been good at that," reflects the narrator, aptly describing the typical Hong Kong approach to merging the practical with the transcendental.

Another superstition involving paper that can be witnessed in the older parts of Wan Chai is the custom of "beating the devil". This includes the battering and cursing of paper effigies of one's enemies. For fifty dollars a time local people pay Wan Chai's street ritual performers to beat those they hate at certain auspicious times, especially the White Tiger Festival in March and the Hungry Ghost Festival in August. Patrons of the street rituals, many of them from the younger generation, appear to place great faith in the efficacy of this peculiar practice.

Before heading east towards Happy Valley and Causeway Bay, we should note two other buildings redolent of an entirely different cultural perspective actually standing on Queen's Road in close proximity to the Chinese temples. The Old Wan Chai Post Office, now the Wan Chai Environmental Resource Centre, was built in 1915 on the site of Wan Chai's main public latrine. The unusually shaped, long and low whitewashed building forms an unlikely alliance with the Hung Shing Temple in providing a strong contrast to the predominantly tall office buildings in the vicinity. The most prominent of these is the imposing, tubular-shaped "Babel" formed by abrasive tycoon Gordon Wu's Hopewell Centre (named after the spring and well on the original site), which has one entrance in the heart of Wan Chai and the other in the Kennedy Road Mid-Levels area above Wan Chai.

Sugar Street: Sugar and Silver and All Things Nice...

The next stage on the tour is what was originally considered the eastern point of the old Wan Chai, now known as Causeway Bay. To get there we can jump on a tram (or as local people dubbed them "ding-dings" after the sound of the original bell) heading east along Johnston Road. This road, crossing old Wan Chai and parallel to Queen's Road, is named after Sir Reginald Johnston, tutor to the last Qing emperor, Pu Yi. (Johnston was portrayed by Peter O'Toole in the Bertolucci film *The Last Emperor*.) Some time after the fall of the Manchu Dynasty, Johnston served as commissioner to Weihaiwei, a small British enclave in China, which, like Hong Kong, became an historical anomaly. He presided over its return to Chinese sovereignty in 1930.

The tram will take us through East Wan Chai and through Causeway Bay along the busy Hennessey Road, named after John Pope Hennessey, an Irishman and, like Bowring, an unpopular governor in expatriate circles. In most cases, the unpopular governors tended to be unpopular with the expatriate population on account of their often justifiable interference with Hong Kong's legendary *laissez-faire* administrative system. For most of the colonial era such actions usually made them correspondingly more popular with the local community. This is especially true of the unpredictable Hennessey, whose main failing (amid, to be fair, a number of important and progressive reforms) lay in his deep-rooted objections to the introduction of flush toilets and a proper public water supply in Hong Kong. If we alight at the tram stop after the Japanese department store, Sogo, we arrive at Sugar Street, which is one of Hong Kong's historical landmarks for a number of reasons.

Louis Dung features Sugar Street in his wonderfully evocative blend of fact and fiction about Hong Kong of the past and future entitled *The Atlas: Archeology of an Imaginary City*. Hong Kong, as he conceives it, no longer exists, and the central idea of the book is that the history of its districts and streets is being reconstructed by future historians, who unearth its fantastical as well as its factual aspects. One fascinating point about Dung's book is its implication that recounting the history of any place is a highly arbitrary, selective and interpretative process, and that intersecting cultures will inevitably represent the "truth" of history according to their own different lights.

In the passage about Sugar Street we are told that Tong Gaai (the Cantonese for sugar is *tong*) was originally home to the Hong Kong government coin mint, built in 1866. Investment in the new Hong Kong mint proved ill-judged when daily production failed miserably to meet expectations. The site was sold to Jardine's in 1868 and the mint machinery sold to Japan, with a net loss of 300 per cent on the original investment. Dung recounts the local legend that the mint failed because, in spite of melted silver being poured into the machinery, "sparkling white sugar grains emerged." According to the myth, Queen Victoria herself became addicted to the Sugar Street Mint's special

brand of sparkling sugar. Legend has it that, after the acquisition of the Sugar Street factory by Jardine's, raw sugar was fed into the new machinery, which was turned inexplicably and wondrously into glinting, sweet-tasting silver coins. As a matter of fact, the factory was destroyed by the savage 1874 typhoon and its entire stock swept into the South China Sea. Fishermen in Victoria Harbour testified that their catch, after the typhoon had abated, tasted bizarrely sweet.

Another of Hong Kong's enduring legends is connected with the Seven Sisters Rocks (Tsat Tsz Mui Shek), formerly situated off the northern coastline but now buried under reclaimed land in Tsat Tsz Mui (Seven Sisters) Road in North Point, just east of Causeway Bay. According to folklore the sisters in question were condemned to be married off against their wishes (something like the Chinese equivalent of *Seven Brides for Seven Brothers!*) and committed suicide by throwing themselves hand-in-hand into the sea very close to today's busy King's Road thoroughfare. They metamorphosed into a chain of rocks representing the seven sisters from tallest to smallest, according to the folk tale. When archeological excavations were conducted in the Tsat Tsz Mui Road area in the Fifties, anecdotal reports circulated that seven combs containing seven locks of hair were unearthed on the site.

Victoria Park: Painting the Town Red...

A stone's throw from the now rather nondescript Sugar Street lies Victoria Park, so called because of the statue of Queen Victoria (created by the sculptor Raggi for her Diamond Jubilee in 1897) that sits at its southern entrance contemplating the walkers, joggers, sports players, lovers and—at Chinese New Year—huge crowds and eager merchandisers with supreme detachment. This statue with orb and sceptre and regal countenance is, of course, the same one that sat in its pomp in Statue Square in the heart of Central prior to the advent of the Japanese troops in December 1941. Her miraculous recovery from a Japanese breaker's yard after the war may have conferred on her the unlikely status of Hong Kong's talisman. When Victoria Park was built in the early 1950s on reclaimed land—like so many other familiar features of modern-day Hong Kong—it covered the typhoon shelter and part of the round causeway from which the area took its English name. The remains of the old causeway connecting the Causeway Bay dam built in the bay in the early 1900s are covered by the present-day

Protest placards, Victoria Park, Causeway Bay.

Tung Lo Wan Road behind the park. In fact, the Chinese name, Tung Lo Wan, or Bronze Gong Bay, has absolutely nothing in common with the English counterpart, which is often the case with Hong Kong place names. Other local names it enjoyed were Hung Heung Lo (Red Incense Burner) and Lin Fa Kung (Lotus Palace), the latter name presumably connected with that of Causeway Bay's Lin Fa Kung temple.

It is hard to imagine what the area was like previously, as one strolls today through the spacious and leafy Victoria Park, or mingles with the crowds at Chinese New Year in the flower market, where kumquat trees are sold in great numbers as symbols of prosperity for the year ahead. Looking at old photographs of the district before the reclamation that started in the 1930s, one can see trams skirting the waterfront, and pedestrians strolling in leisurely fashion close to where the park is situated today. Yet, like many places we take for granted in present-day Hong Kong, much of the land was either permanently under water, or flooded during the extensive rainy season.

In the modern era Victoria Park has also become emblematic of public space and grassroots meetings for the expression of popular sentiment. Following the Tiananmen Square massacre on June 4 1989, there was a huge outpouring of public grief in the form of a mass march. The focal point for this collective exhibition of sorrow and apprehension about the mainland government's brutal suppression of dissent was almost inevitably Victoria Park. Hong Kong's own democracy activists helped to co-ordinate the escape of many high-profile dissidents, who fled the subsequent swift crackdown on the mainland. As they gathered in thousands in Victoria Park that fateful year, they lit candles that would be relit each succeeding year without fail to ensure that the memory of the students who died on or near the square would not be extinguished. Louise Ho's moving tribute to the fallen, entitled "New Year's Eve, 1989" echoes the terrible beauty of Yeats' poem "Easter 1916":

> The shadows of June the fourth
> Are the shadows of a gesture
> They say, but how shall you and I
> Name them, one by one?
> There were so many,
> Crushed, shot, taken, all overwhelmed,
> Cut down without a finished thought or cry
>
> ...Then this compact commercial enclave
> First time ever, rose up as one.
> Before we went our separate ways again
> We thought as one
> We spoke as one,
> We too have changed, if not 'utterly'
> And something beautiful was born

Following the SARS crisis, five years of economic stagnation and the Hong Kong government's determination to please Beijing by imposing a sweeping anti-subversion ordinance under the Basic Law, Hong Kong people again took to the streets in the 1 July 2003 demonstration. Again the focal point for the three-quarters of a million-strong march was Victoria Park and its ultimate destination the

Government Offices in Lower Albert Road in Central. The spectacular success of the march, when the Tung administration backed down over the imposition of the ordinance (the so-called Article 23), proved that Hong Kong people were not as apathetic as had been thought. It also proved that Victoria Park is now firmly established as an unofficial site of popular protest.

David Clarke in his authoritative study, *Hong Kong Art—Culture and Decolonization*, muses wryly that by association with photographs and sketches of rallies held in Victoria Park, Queen Victoria's statue is in truly post-modern fashion effectively losing its "colonial connotations": "Victoria somehow becomes a participant in the demonstration." He goes on to speculate: "Rather than seeing this as a nostalgic fondness of Hong Kong people for colonial rule one should interpret it as an attempt to assert a sense of identity in the face of post-Handover uncertainty."

In 1995, with the Handover two years away, Mainland artist Pun Sing-lui saw Queen Victoria's likeness rather differently and photographed himself with a Chinese communist flag standing in front of the statue. This was a prelude to his attention-grabbing art happening at Victoria Park, when he painted the former Empress red and chipped away at her nose with a hammer. Whether the red was intended to signify blood or the red flag was a moot point—briefly, anyway, for the art protest seemed to elicit little patriotic sympathy or sustained interest from a sceptical Hong Kong public.

Clarke also makes the perceptive point that, during the annual 4 June remembrance gathering, effigies representing the Beijing students' sculpture, *The Goddess of Democracy*, and the earlier *Monument to the People's Heroes*, are recreated as emblems intended to transform Victoria Park temporarily into a kind of Tiananmen Square, enabling "a specific kind of imagined community to come into being." A more recent artefact, *The Goddess of Democracy Stone Wall*, in fact made out of wood, looks particularly effective in the atmospheric, candlelit memorial gathering: "a ghostly luminescent goddess, standing among the crowds of demonstrators," to quote Clarke.

Still today, June 4 continues to be commemorated with artistic events, happenings and performance artists. The park has also become a venue for a live music festival. Now an annual event in Hong Kong's pleasantest month of November, the original 2003 Rockit Festival in

Victoria Park was conceived as an alternative and inexpensive music jamboree, set up to compete with the high-profile international rock festival that was promoted by the government and designed to rekindle confidence in post-SARS Hong Kong. While the Harbour Fest was mired in organizational difficulties and has not been repeated, the Rockit Festival of garage, hip-hop, techno and rap has gone from strength to strength with each passing year. Local Hong Kong bands share the bill with non-celebrity international acts and their lyrics are often politically charged.

Mad Dogs and Englishmen: Noel Coward and the Noonday Gun

In Hong Kong
They strike a gong
And fire off a noonday gun
To reprimand each inmate
Who's in late.

In these lines from his song *Mad Dogs and Englishmen* British playwright Noel Coward immortalized Causeway Bay's noonday gun, which was originally located outside the Jardine East Point *godown* and which boomed out every day at noon. Its rather prosaic purpose was not, in fact, to warn soldiers to return to barracks, but simply to inform Hong Kong residents, many of whom carried no timepiece, that it was midday. It continues, quixotically some might say, to serve this purpose, despite the fact that Hong Kong's population has no shortage of time-checking devices, many of them very expensive. There is a story (somewhat apocryphal it should be noted) that the original reason for the naval salute was to punish a breach of colonial etiquette, when the Jardine-Matheson *taipan* was greeted over-zealously by his subordinates with a 21-gun salute, normally reserved only for high-ranking dignitaries of governor rank. In consequence, the Jardine *hong* was ordered to fire off a gun each day in perpetuity on the stroke of noon. However, the existence of noonday guns in other former colonial cities such as Cape Town, indicate that the practice was not peculiar to Hong Kong. The Hong Kong gun was made in Portsmouth in 1901, as the highly polished brass plaque informs us.

Having confused the issue in his famous song lyric—while at the same time making an intriguing reference to the bronze gong after which Tung Lo Wan is named—Coward was fashionably late for his own appointment to fire the noonday gun, when he stayed in Hong Kong in March 1968. Hong Kongers, who set their watches by the noonday gun, would have found them running three minutes slow on that day. Coward's depiction of mad dogs and Englishmen venturing recklessly out into the blazing midday sun is probably more apposite of Anglo-Indian colonial types, but it is nonetheless true in general that expatriates manage to be either over-dressed or under-dressed for Hong Kong weather on any particular day.

Crossing the busy Gloucester Road to the World Trade Centre (*sic!*), which is close to the noonday gun, we come to the Excelsior Hotel, where Coward stayed. It commands an impressive panoramic view across the harbour to Kowloon. The literary reference in its Dickens Bar belies the nature of the place. Wood-panelled and bristling with sporting memorabilia, it is less a nod in the direction of London's many Dickens pubs than a strong reminder of the sporting venues in the vicinity that have in their own way come to characterize the former East Point.

The Hong Kong Stadium: at Sixes and Sevens

Not far from here in So Kon Po is the new Hong Kong Stadium, completed in 1994, where the annual International Rugby Sevens tournament in March brings in visitors from all over the world. March 2005 saw Hong Kong host the Rugby World Cup Sevens for the second time, but it is not widely known that Rugby Sevens was actually invented in Hong Kong in 1975 by members of the HK Rugby Football Union. At first permission to introduce this innovative form of rugby was refused by stuffy administrators in Twickenham. Fortunately, the Hong Kong rugby devotees persisted until they overcame official resistance. Thanks to their imaginative endeavour a new type of rugby at international level was introduced on 28 March 1976. Not a year has gone by since without the stadium reverberating to the sounds of vociferous and competitive, but good-natured, support. The idea of a Rugby World Cup in the normal fifteen-a-side code was not introduced until two decades after the Sevens competition was born, and since then the fluid and exciting Sevens form of the game has also caught on at international level. Hong Kong can claim much credit for pioneering internationalism in the game in the face of reactionary opposition at a time when there was insufficient standardization of codes. Great names to have graced the Sevens include New Zealand's Eric Rush and Jonah Lomu, Australia's David Campese and former England captain Lawrence Dallaglio, but the undisputed wizard of this imaginative, creative, fast-thinking and instinctive game is the incomparable Waisale Serevi, whose Fiji side has won more times than any other. Serevi recently announced his retirement after winning the trophy for the eleventh time and the World Cup Sevens in Hong Kong on two occasions. It has been pointed out by Hong Kong wits that if anyone wanted to obliterate the entire expatriate population of Hong Kong in one fell swoop, dropping a bomb on the stadium during Rugby Sevens weekend would be a good way to do it. A slight exaggeration perhaps, but the point is well made.

An idiosyncratic offshoot of another great English sport of international stature was, like the Sevens, made in Hong Kong. The International Cricket Sixes Competition was initially held in Kowloon Cricket Club. It migrated to the then brand new stadium, located just above So Kon Po in Caroline Hill Road. International names like Steve Waugh, Wasim Akram, Brian Lara and Andrew "Freddie" Flintoff have graced the event, but cricket proved less attractive, not for sponsors Swire (Cathay Pacific), but for international visitors and local people. The return to the serene and lush environs of Kowloon Cricket Club in Jordan ensured the ongoing viability of the event, which has started to spark interest in the Sixes game among local schools and increasingly overseas. Not So Loud Theatre Company's 1998 play *At Sixes and Sevens* at Hong Kong Fringe Club was a witty thespian tribute to both events, casting light on ingrained expatriate habits in Hong Kong that are tribal perhaps, but less aggressively so nowadays than at the height of Empire.

Happy Valley: the Turf and the Sod

Gamyat ng-keui gwai gu toh, tajiu gwantai ya seung tung
Today my body returns to earth, tomorrow will be your turn.

A little less stark and certainly less chilling than the inscription that stood above the entrance to Nazi concentration camps, this gentle reminder of our mortality that can be seen above the gate of Happy Valley cemetery gives pause for thought—but only to Chinese readers, since it is written in classical Chinese. Happy Valley (Pau Ma Tei in Cantonese), cool and shaded and the closest thing to an English glade on an otherwise "barren rock", was originally planned as the site of the main settlement in the early 1840s.

Yet the city of Victoria was established not here, but a couple of miles west in what is now Central District. There were two reasons for this change of plan. One was the unfavourable *fung shui* according to the lore of Chinese geomancy, and the other, probably not unconnected with the first, was the high incidence of fatalities in the neighbourhood owing to the prevalence of mosquitoes. Not surprisingly, therefore, the expatriate cemetery on Hong Kong Island was moved here from its original Wan Chai site in 1845, presumably because it was very handy for the cemetery to be near the source of business. Malaria, carried by mosquitoes in the advantageous breeding conditions of Happy Valley, was one of the main killers. One of the main causes of malarial mosquitoes infesting the area had been rice cultivation, which was banned shortly afterwards. The area was drained and covered and became dominated by sports fields and the racecourse, nicely harmonizing with the graveyards to the west, which nestle snugly against the hills leading to Wong Nai Chung Gap.

There are a number of distinct sections of the Happy Valley Cemetery: the Parsee Cemetery (Parsees were Indian merchants of Persian ancestry), the Roman Catholic Cemetery, the Islamic Cemetery, the Hindu Cemetery and the largest, the Colonial Cemetery known simply as the Hong Kong Cemetery, with the majority of its inmates assumed to be generally of Church of England or similar denomination. It is clear from a visit to Happy Valley that the composition of Hong Kong's population from the mid-nineteenth century onwards was far more ethnically and culturally mixed than is usually acknowledged. Many of the graves bear witness to the styles of the period as well as to cultural differences, and Gothic, Celtic, Russian and Armenian crosses and carvings are to be seen. To the eye of the twenty-first-century visitor, perhaps one of the most powerful indictments of the entrenched European class system and cavalier attitude to loss of life among the lower orders can be seen in the monument to unnamed soldiers, who died of fever and other causes in 1840s Hong Kong. One is struck by the callousness of the simple legend "Died of Fever, 1848: 9 sergeants, 8 corporals, 4 drummers, 67 privates, 4 women, 4 children." More than half a century later in the Great War they were still seen as expendable, their deaths hardly registering, except as a statistic. Soldiers were not even buried at state expense until the late nineteenth century, their funeral expenses being defrayed by auction of their underclothes.

Noted residents of the Happy Valley Cemetery, in addition to the expected senior colonial and military figures, include Sir Robert Ho Tung, the first Eurasian to be knighted and to live on the exclusive Peak, Sir Kai Ho-kai, London-trained barrister and later Hong Kong legislator, who became the first Chinese person to be knighted, and Armenian Sir Catchick Paul Chater, after whom Chater Road in Central is named. All of these people worked extremely hard to overcome institutionalized racial prejudices, and all of them contributed significantly to Hong Kong's development with their philanthropy. Missionary Karl Gutzlaff also lies here in a plain grave befitting a Lutheran. His ambitious aspiration to proselytize the whole of China failed and he died at the age of 48, apparently worn out by his efforts. Arthur Waley, sinologist and English translator of the early Chinese poetry collection, *The Book of Songs*, described him in his documentary study *The Opium War through Chinese Eyes* as "a cross between parson, pirate, charlatan and genius, philanthropist and crook". In sum, an eminently representative colonial figure, some might say.

Another former real-life denizen of Hong Kong now at rest in Happy Valley is Mary Ah-Yow Caldwell, Chinese wife of the slippery and resourceful "pirate-catcher" Daniel Caldwell, referred to above in connection with Bowring and the Ah-Lum trial. Christopher New's *A Change of Flag*, the final part of his *China Coast Trilogy* of novels, pictures his fictional protagonists, Hong Kong University lecturer Dimitri Johnson and Eurasian businessman and amateur historian Michael Denton, visiting the grave of this remarkable woman. Denton identifies Mary Caldwell with his own (fictional) mother, since both were rescued from brothels in Shanghai, where their job had been entertaining the clients with Chinese opera songs and more.

Michael stood for a moment looking at the grave. It was so quiet they could hear the leaves rustling and the flutter of birds' wings. It

couldn't have been much quieter when Mary Ah Yow Caldwell was
buried here, the Chinese wife of an enigmatic Englishman, whose
obscure descendants apparently still left flowers on her grave—as he
still left flowers on his mother's grave, the Chinese wife of another
enigmatic Englishman.

Somerset Maugham paints a memorable picture of Happy Valley in the opening chapters of his (in its day) controversial novel, *The Painted Veil.* Taking his cue from a story in Dante, he imagines the life of bored wife Kitty Fane, wife of stolid government bacteriologist, Walter, in colonial Hong Kong. She has a torrid affair with a dashing senior government officer, Charles Townsend, and as the novel opens she is caught with her lover in their Happy Valley house "after tiffin": "Their house stood in the Happy Valley on the side of the hill, for they could not afford to live on the more eligible but expensive Peak." Fane forces his wife to accompany him on a dangerous mission to Guangdong province across the border in China, an area gripped by a serious cholera epidemic, to punish her for her infidelity, which changes her shallow outlook on life utterly. She survives, but her husband does not. Greta Garbo played Kitty in the 1934 film version, highlighting the central role of the female protagonist in Maugham's story.

Maugham was sued for libel because his first version used the name Lane, of whom there were not a few in Hong Kong. After changing it to Fane, he was once again sued for libel by an Assistant Colonial Secretary of that name. "It seemed to me strange that the temporary occupant of so insignificant a post should think himself aimed at, but in order to save trouble I changed Hong Kong to an imaginary colony of Tching-Yen," he noted caustically in his preface. Although the original Hong Kong-set novel was recalled, some sixty copies survived. In modern reprints the name of the "imaginary territory" has fortunately reverted to Hong Kong.

Happy Valley is also, of course, home to one of the most famous racetracks in the world, which dates back to 1884, although horse-racing had been a leisure activity among the officer class and wealthy entrepreneurs from the very beginning of the colonial era. The swampy area of Happy Valley was drained to create a rough track and makeshift stands were erected, gradually replaced by grander structures. The Hong Kong Jockey Club, formed in 1884 when work on the racecourse was begun, grew into the most significant source of charitable and philanthropic funding in Hong Kong after the switch from amateur racing to professional in the post-Second World War period.

The racecourse was the site of one of Hong Kong's most catastrophic fires in March 1918 when temporary bamboo and rattan "mat-shed" stands collapsed under the weight of excessive numbers onto the charcoal braziers below, where food was being prepared. Eyes were averted in the other stands from the start of a race to the unfolding disaster at the side of the track. Over a thousand people were killed or injured, but the death toll could have been even higher had soldiers not been on hand to prevent a total stampede.

Hong Kong's noted passion for gambling and horse-racing in particular has proved a great social leveller, bringing together governors, *taipans*, expatriates and local Chinese, tourists and civil servants, rich and poor alike. The Jockey Club today spends an estimated HK$1 billion a year on worthy causes, a staggering sum that gives an indication of the kind of revenue generated at the track and at Jockey Club betting shops. One of Hong Kong's most popular horses of recent times, its Red Rum, one might say, was Silent Witness (an unintentionally suitable name, considering the cemetery in close proximity), a strong if unorthodox racer ridden by champion jockey Felix Coetzee. Unbeaten for seventeen races, Silent Witness was unable to extend his record, being pipped at the post in May 2005 at the Sha Tin racecourse.

Times Square and the Lee Theatre: Larger Than Life...

Only in Hong Kong (to use the title of satirical Hong Kong writer Nury Vittachi's amusing book of the same name) is it possible to have a replica Times Square. This one does not by any stretch of the imagination bear any real resemblance to its better known New York namesake. You could be forgiven for supposing that you had suddenly left the busy, commercially vibrant and rather down-to-earth environment of Causeway Bay and been mysteriously transported to hi-tech Tokyo when you arrive in this decidedly twenty-first-century locale, a mere stone's throw from the eternally rumbling trams of Hennessey Road and the flyover traversing what was once Bowrington, now prosaically known as Canal Road. Ann Hui's film *Ordinary Heroes* opens with her factual-fictional radical priest, A-Kam, tending to the street sleepers for whom Bowring's imaginary Eden is now a more humble dwelling, one with constant traffic overhead. Times Square is a different kind of paradise than the one Bowring had envisaged, a shopping paradise, and one with prohibitive prices. Despite its proximity, it might as well be the Mandarin Oriental as far as the less fortunate are concerned.

The first thing that strikes you about Times Square is probably not its derivative name, but the inescapable screen that dominates the busy thoroughfare and entrance to the shopping plaza as well as the surrounding area. Like the ubiquitous giant screens and skyscrapers of real-life Tokyo and the sinister and intrusive screens of the futuristic film (of which Ridley Scott's *Bladerunner*, with its futurist Los Angeles setting modelled on both Hong Kong and Tokyo, is an outstanding example), it exercises an magnetic attraction on the throngs heading towards or away from the blocks of offices and the spacious shopping mall behind it. The continuous diet of soft news, celebrity plugs and advertising does not seem to have left the consumers with a jaded palate, and doubtless some of Hong Kong's sharp young executives have determined in their MBA dissertations that there is a relationship between the giant screen and consumers' shopping habits. Fixed in the glare of the screen, they may be sufficiently distracted or even hypnotized to embark on an injudicious shopping spree on eventually arriving in the huge atrium of the mall.

A two-minute walk from Times Square on Leighton Road in the direction of Leighton Hill and the sports stadium is the Golden Lee Plaza, a tall modern building with a pastiche dome intended to evoke memories of the original Lee Theatre, which stood on this site and was for many years one of the main cultural hubs of the Wan Chai district. This beautifully designed building, boasting one of Hong Kong's most elegant cinemas, was erected by the Lee Hysan family in 1925 and coincided with the advent of cinema to Hong Kong as a culturally established entertainment form. It was at this time that Hong Kong's film pioneer Lai Man-wai was pursuing his many film projects, the results of which could be seen at the Lee Theatre, with its outstanding baroque interior design. The Lee Theatre was also for many years home to Hong Kong's most popular traditional form of entertainment, namely Cantonese Opera, and many of its stars performed here or were viewed on the silver screen, as Lai Man-wai and other directors increasingly turned to the stage for inspiration for their films. Both stage and screen forms of entertainment were on offer at the Lee Theatre until the early 1990s, when one of the Wan Chai district's greatest landmarks made way for the present Golden Lee building. Not entirely a monument to shopping and business, the modern Golden Lee Cinema, with its stylish art deco design and nostalgic mural, may go some way to placating the ghosts of earlier times.

Also in the vicinity and connected with cinema were two restaurants that have survived Hong Kong's high turnover rate for small businesses and made a name for themselves in the process. Queens Café, which boasted the best cakes and bread east of Central—perhaps this claim remains true to this day—was used for a brief scene in Wong Kar-wai's early masterpiece *Days of Being Wild* (1991), starring Leslie Cheung, in which it features as his indulgent auntie's favourite haunt for playing mahjong. The Queens Café restaurant migrated to the more up-market environs of Kowloon Tong's Festival Walk in the mid 1990s, but before it did, it served as the meeting place and provided the name for the Queens Café Company, an amateur theatre group. Wong Kar-wai's most internationally recognized film *In the Mood for Love* (2001), based on a novella by Hong Kong writer Liu Yichang, also made affectionate use of the Wan Chai and Causeway Bay streets and eating places, particularly the Goldfinch Restaurant, a traditional 1960s establishment that has remained with the same family proprietors for the past forty years—which is unusual in the Hong Kong context. Of course, the restaurant owners feel entitled to trade on the popularity of the film and include a special In the Mood for Love menu for two, echoing the scene in which Chow (Tony Leung) and Su (Maggie Cheung) dip strips of meat in mustard, a very Asian approach to the Goldfinch's primarily Western cuisine of pepper steak, lobster and cheese and borscht soup.

In the sequel to *In the Mood for Love*, the quirky but engaging *2046*, the narrative shuttles back and forth between the 1960s and 2046. This year is significant because it is the expiry date of the no-change arrangement for Hong Kong's governance and the point at which Hong Kong's administrative system and political culture are expected to have "converged" with that of China. Wong Kar-wai imagined his protagonist Chow, a writer of newspaper instalments in

Hong Kong's popular fantasy novel genre, living in the Oriental Hotel in Wan Chai. Although the hotel is as fictitious as Robert and Suzie's Nam Kok, Wan Chai's streets and buildings took on a larger-than-life quality in the movie that made the neon-lit hotel and surrounding streets both authentically real and yet surreal.

The Battle of Wan Chai

Wan Chai is also significant for its role in the fall of Hong Kong in World War II and subsequently in VJ (Victory in Japan) Day, as historians have noted. The Japanese had begun their invasion on 8 December 1941, advancing inexorably across the border and backed up by vastly superior aerial power. Hong Kong's military positions and coastal defences were simply overrun. One of the last and bitterest confrontations took place in Wan Chai. In this doomed conflict soldiers of the Middlesex Regiment, aptly nicknamed the Diehards, distinguished themselves with their extraordinary courage. In fierce close combat—house to house as their redrawn lines in O'Brien Road were breached—they held up the Japanese troops and sold their lives dearly. On Christmas Day General Maltby, commander of British forces, and Governor Sir Mark Young were driven through the tattered remnants of the British lines to proffer their surrender.

John Lanchester's novel *Fragrant Harbour* (2002) conveys a sense of the heroism and self-sacrifice during this bitter chapter in the Hong Kong story. His hero, hotelier Tom Stewart, recruited as a resistance leader by the army, experiences the aftermath of the battle as he is brought back to Wan Chai, a prisoner of the Japanese, and housed in a former Wan Chai brothel along with other civilians who are being used by the Japanese to maintain normal services in the newly conquered Territory. Shocked by the carnage and the cruelty of the invaders, he determines to make contact with other resistance factions and eventually links up with his former employee, now a member of the Triads, on the roof of the tenement in which he is housed. Stewart survives both the occupation and the brutal experiences of internment in the Stanley Camp, but subsequent events make him realize that the Triad organizations were acting opportunistically in smuggling radio equipment to the resistance. In fact, as the novel shows, the Japanese occupation gave a foothold to Triads in the expansion of their operations that they never subsequently relinquished.

In strict contrast to the self-serving Triads, the prostitutes of Wan Chai, who came to be known as the "Angels of Wan Chai" by the internees at Sham Shui Po prisoner of war camp, smuggled in food, soap and other items out of the goodness of their hearts and often at great personal risk. There were fewer girlie bars before the 1950s in Wan Chai, and the Angels were street walkers who frequented the China Fleet Club in Wan Chai and other locations where soldiers were to be found. Arthur Hacker, long-time resident of Hong Kong and artist and historian of Wan Chai, quotes one British veteran, who recalled that the Angels of Wan Chai were in their own way as heroic as the Diehards: "During the fighting they carried ammunition and supplies to the Hong Kong defenders. After the surrender they daily risked their life from trigger-happy Jap guards to bring food they could hardly spare to the inmates of Shamshuipo [the Kowloon-side internment camp]. We always toast these gallant beautiful ladies at our reunions."

The celebrations for Victory over Japan took place at Southorn Playground, still to this day very much in the heart of Wan Chai, on 9 October 1945 and were also intended as a nod in the direction of Chiang Kai-shek's s brittle and moribund nationalist regime north of the border. At the time of writing, plans are underway to transform the concrete public space of Southorn Playground into a futuristic hi-tech sports hub combined with an urban regeneration leisure site. But we run ahead of ourselves. By the time that Richard Mason arrived in the area, ten years after the VJ ceremony, the fast-increasing number of bars in the area gave the ex-Angels a more comfortable environment in which to conduct their business.

If You Knew Suzie…

The World of Suzie Wong was Richard Mason's lasting bequest to Hong Kong. Despite the fact that he only spent three months at the characterful old Luk Kwok Hotel (on the site of the present modernized high-rise Luk Kwok, but with a commanding view over the harbour in those days) chatting to the bar-girls and researching the material he needed for the novel, Mason almost accidentally created a myth on which Wan Chai's reputation was built. Richard Quine's 1960 film version, despite offering some of the best location shooting ever for a foreign film made in Hong Kong, and despite a feisty performance by Hong Kong-born Nancy Kwan as Suzie, is at heart a Hollywood travesty. Transforming Mason's alter ego Robert Lomax, a quintessentially egalitarian British post-war type, into an American played unconvincingly by a miscast William Holden, ranks alongside the cinematic appropriation by Americans of the escape from Colditz. Nonetheless, reaching a wider audience inevitably than Mason's book, the film version also played an important part in promoting Wan Chai to the world. The book was out of print for many years but its reappearance in the early 1990s coincided with Wan Chai's recovery like a phoenix from the ashes after the somewhat leaner years of the 1970s and 1980s. The Americans, having retreated from Vietnam, no longer patronized Hong Kong's R&R facilities as they had in the preceding decades.

Wan Chai's temporary decline is charted in Angie Chen's 1986 Hong Kong film *My Name Aint Suzie*, with is memorable performances from leading female actors Patricia Ha Man-jik and singer Deanie Yip, who won a best supporting actress award for her portrayal of a ruthless, lesbian businesswoman. She supports the indomitable former teenage bar girl and street prostitute, Mei-li, who decides to strike out on her own after her strong-mindedness gets her into trouble with the brothel madam. A fiercely feminist film in its underlying implications, *My Name Aint Suzie* was seen as a local backlash to the westernized sentimental stereotyping of bar-girls represented by *The World of Suzie Wong*. One of the famous Shaw Brothers films, the often trivial and escapist style of this "Hollywood of the East" film company belies the seriousness of the subject matter in Chen's hard-hitting riposte to Suzie in *My Name Aint Suzie* with its "noirish", downbeat ending.

Unlike Mason's Suzie, who is rescued from the vicissitudes of her precarious life as a bar-girl and from the round of "short times" or "all-nighters" with her sailor clientele, Mei-li (her name closely resembles Suzie's Chinese name Mee-ling), having been raped by a gang of boys which puts an end to her life on the Aberdeen fishing boats, becomes a teenage prostitute and after many struggles a bar owner and madam in her own right. The potential male rescuer in the form of the ubiquitous Eurasian actor and star of *Infernal Affairs*, Anthony Wong (Anthony Perry in this earlier incarnation), turns out to be a love-rat and leaves Mei-li in the lurch. She survives thanks to her own ingenuity in a world in which protection rackets and cut-throat competition are the norm. Her departure from Wan Chai for the more lucrative pastures of Tsim

Sha Tsui coincides with the fading of Wan Chai's glory days, and the images of the now run-down district in the latter part of the film, especially in the shots of empty dilapidated streets and sparse customers, symbolize the transition of Hong Kong toward an altogether less romanticized and more hard-nosed era.

Thai and Filipina prostitutes started to replace the local Suzies as bar-girls. Many of these bar-girls, as Mason points out with genuine sympathy, have nowhere else to go but the streets, where they have no future and no security in their old age. Perhaps more of an attack on the screen version of Suzie Wong than Mason's novel, Angie Chen's film evokes a troubled Wan Chai and a world in which gentlemen like Lomax, and even to some extent the sailors he depicts, have been replaced by cold-hearted gangsters in the guise of businessmen. All males in the world Chen depicts are predatory and unscrupulous, and a woman's only comfort in this harsh world is to confide in her own sex.

Mason's Lomax, a painter in the novel rather than a writer like his creator, paints a picture of a more leisurely Hong Kong, recovering from the hardship of the Second World War. What the book does admirably is to confront stereotypes about Hong Kong people and especially, its *demi-monde*. In his three-month stay Mason obviously developed a genuine appreciation of Hong Kong and its non-Western residents. Whether or not Mason himself while staying at the Luk Kwok Hotel was quite as abstemious as Lomax is at the Nam Kok is questionable, but irrelevant, since his record of events is fictionalized. Mason claimed that Suzie was not derived from a single model, but was rather a compound of several that he knew. For all that, she is one of the more recognizable fictional creations of the twentieth century.

Mason's book was instrumental in promoting more enlightened attitudes toward sex, prostitution, the ambivalent predicament of the Eurasian community and mixed marriage as well as challenging the hypocrisy of what he portrays as outdated ideas about morality, miscegenation and racial superiority, still unfortunately prevalent in the West. Quine's film, needless to say, strips away Mason's progressive agenda entirely, and reduces the story to romantic melodrama, though one not entirely without respect for Chinese culture and with a strong emphasis on authentic Hong Kong locale.

One reason that Suzie and her fellow denizens of the Nam Kok—skinny, good-hearted Gwenny Lee, Minnie Ho, Wednesday Lulu,

Typhoo, Little Alice *et al*—come to life in Mason's novel is not just the precise description of the writer's narrative, but especially the brilliant rendering of their conversation and badinage in authentic "Chinglish" dialogue, which reproduces Cantonese English of the period more credibly than Timothy Mo's over-systematic and contrived substitution of past tense for present tense, for example, in *The Monkey King*. Here, Typhoo, one of the yum-yum girls is explaining to the newly arrived Robert about the sailors' over-estimation of their sexual capabilities before they "make lovey":

> *"Sure, every sailor same-same," Typhoo grinned. "He think, 'Minute my ship reach Hong Kong I catch girl, make lovey nine, ten, twelve times.' What happen? He make love once, twice— finish!"... Little Alice's giggles boiled up again. "You all crazy! If my boyfriend go to sleep, I hit him. I say, 'Hey, come on. Me sex- starve!'" "You got plenty cheek taking sailors' money," Typhoo said. "You enjoy making lovey so much why don't you pay sailors!"*

The scrupulous Robert virtuously decides he would not take a girl, "because, although I thought many of them very attractive, I did not see how it would work out if I was living among them." Then he encounters the mercurial Suzie who pretends she does not know him, although they have already met on the Wan Chai ferry, and their hesitant courtship, defying the impossibility of their situation, slowly develops. Lomax, at this point an impoverished artist, cannot afford to keep Suzie and Suzie is too proud to expect him to. What is impressive about the novel is that Mason never flinches from showing the reader both the seedy and harsh side of Hong Kong life as well as its magic, and the former is never described salaciously or gratuitously. When Suzie develops tuberculosis we are given an insight into the heavy toll this killer disease was exacting on the Territory in the post-war years, and the graphic details of the way people died. More of a documentary fiction that evokes a period than a romantic novel, *The World of Suzie Wong*, seems to have come in for unjustified criticism—often by those who may only be familiar with the film as opposed to the novel. It is undoubtedly a work by a writer with his heart in the right place.

It is said that Mason was well liked and greatly appreciated by the bar-girls for bringing them to the attention of the outside world. As

Arthur Hacker has pointed out: "In its own way the book is as much a social history of Wan Chai at the time, as Christopher Isherwood's *Goodbye to Berlin* is of Germany in the 1930s... Without Suzie, Wan Chai would be just another urban district of Hong Kong. Suzie gave the place a certain touch of glamour, if perhaps a little tarnished, an identity, an individuality." Other fictional bar-girls, such as Chaplin's Russian Countess played by Sophia Loren in the great silent comedian's frothy romantic comedy *A Countess from Hong Kong* (1967), are no match for Suzie in the popularity stakes. The actress Tsai Chin who played Suzie in the play version of the novel recalls that the slinky Chinese *cheong sam*, as worn by Suzie and her colleagues, became a fashion item in the West, despite not being designed with the Western female figure in mind. Unsurprisingly the trend did not last, though *cheong sams* are still very much in evidence as elegant wear for special occasions among the generally slimmer and more petite women in Hong Kong.

North Wan Chai: the Imagination Soars

Today one cannot envisage Wan Chai without its new cultural and commercial appendage to the north of Gloucester Road on the newest piece of reclaimed land and, in particular, Wong's and Ouyang's elegant and assured extension to the Hong Kong Convention and Exhibition Centre, jutting jauntily out into the harbour. It was here on the dangerously sloping roof that the thrilling finale to Jackie Chan's *New Police Story* was shot. This extension to the Convention and Exhibition Centre, completed weeks before the Handover ceremony in June 1997, was designed to host the historic occasion, which it did with aplomb. It now seems as if its soaring bird's wing roof has been a permanent feature of Wan Chai's varied skyline, backed by the impressive dimensions of the oddly misnamed Central Plaza (it is in Wan Chai rather than Central, either an oversight on the part of the architect or a bold statement about where Hong Kong Island's centre really ought to be), which was the eighth tallest building in the world when it was erected in the late 1990s. One of Hong Kong's early examples of post-modern architecture, with its dazzling array of colours at night from its pyramid top and its gold neon floodlighting, the Central Plaza stands at an angle which permits many of its offices to have excellent harbour-front views.

Central Plaza and the Hong Kong Convention and Exhibition Centre.

The same cannot be said for the Academy for Performing Arts, which commands superb harbour views, but, presumably to aid the concentration of staff and students alike, has windows facing only the inshore side, which strikes the casual visitor as bizarre in the extreme. The Academy, which was built thanks to Hong Kong Jockey Club subvention (thereby underlining the connection between the sport of kings and the arts) not only produces talented young dancers, musicians and actors, but also plays host to many performances in the Hong Kong Arts Festival in its well-appointed theatre spaces. One Academy graduate, Colleen Lee Ka-ling, won a runner-up place in the prestigious international Chopin competition in Warsaw in 2005, a feather in the cap not only of the pianist herself, but also of the sometimes under-appreciated arts academy.

In June 2004 the Academy played host to Hong Kong's very own stellar jazz guitarist, Eugene Pao, a widely respected figure among fellow jazz musicians on the world circuit. Pao, a modern jazz fusion artiste, and a highly inventive one to boot, paid the city of his birth a compliment with a breezily optimistic and exciting piece entitled "Voice of the City". The listener is left in no doubt which city he had in mind when he composed it. In turns hectic, neurotic, confident and exuberant, "Voice of the City" epitomizes the spirit of Hong Kong in a way that few film scores or songs have been able to. The live album, entitled simply 'The Eugene Pao Project' (available on EZMOOD Records), gives the listener a flavour of Pao's Hong Kong-style eclecticism, and oscillates between the Jazz Club (in Central, but now sadly defunct) intimacy and Queen Elizabeth Stadium (also in Wan Chai) vitality of Pao's wide-ranging, improvisatory live performances.

Finally one cannot do justice to a tour of North Wan Chai without due mention of the Hong Kong Arts Centre, opened in 1977 by Governor Sir Murray MacLehose and expertly managed on a shoestring since then. This oddly designed beanpole of a building is a dynamic venue, playing host to art exhibitions and installations, film festivals and premieres of local independent work, as well as dance, drama and even pantomime. In addition it has galleries, a café and language teaching facilities, and is home to the Goethe Institute, as well as the Hong Kong Arts Festival offices.

What is impressive about the Arts Centre is its workaday atmosphere and creative buzz. Schoolchildren, tourists, locals and arts buffs mingle freely and comfortably in its surprisingly open and spacious interior. In the 200-seater Shouson Theatre, donated in commemoration of philanthropist Shouson Chow by his widow, it has one of the best and most intimate performance spaces in Asia. Built on a small patch of reclaimed land donated by a government keen to be seen as non-philistine and supportive of arts development, the Arts Centre has thrived in spite of its difficulties in making ends meet without further subsidy. To quote architecture critic Juanita Cheung: "Like a breath of fresh air, it stands out against the sad, granite aesthetic of its corporate neighbours. Unlike most buildings in this city, the centre is not trying to look expensive, and this lack of pretension strikes you as somehow being honest, and has you rooting for its success. In a subtle way, it is as close as you get to an alternative space in Hong Kong."

The Arts Centre's special feature for the 2005 Festival was an imaginative recreation of the Seventies spirit of Xi Xi's celebrated novel *My City*, ingeniously renamed *i-city* for the digitally conscious generations that have grown up since that defining era for the Territory. One of the other interesting productions arising out of this imaginary concept of *i-city* was the collection of animated shorts, *i-city [animation]*. Among the delightfully creative nine animated pieces is Stella So Man-yee's *Lonely Moon*, a nostalgic tram trip through the Hong Kong of the 1950s and 1960s heading surrealistically towards the moon rather than the terrestrial terminals of the island. On the way the animal passengers pile up the city's treasures, including old-style restaurants, for preservation on the double-decker tram's superstructure. Another popular production at the Shouson Theatre was local, avant-garde group Zuni Icosahedron's satirical spoof *East-Wing, West-Wing, the Chief Executive is Missing*, in which former Chief Executive, Tung Chee-hwa, was represented as a cardboard cut-out.

At present the controversial Wan Chai reclamation plan envisages even greater depredations on Wan Chai's share of Hong Kong Harbour. Perhaps the graceful and striking new wing of the Hong Kong Convention and Exhibition Centre could be seen in years to come as the tip of a development iceberg, which will permit the harbour's dimensions to be further reduced for the greater glory of mammon. As raconteur Clive James in an entertaining one-man show at the Academy for Performing Art's Lyric Theatre in 2003 wryly remarked, "It won't be long before the Star Ferry is stationary and passengers simply walk on one end in Kowloon and off at the other in Central or Wan Chai." If you can have roll-on, roll-off ferries, then why not walk-on, walk-off ones? Perhaps it is not as far-fetched and whimsical as one may imagine.

chapter four
"THE GREAT LEARNING":
POKFULAM, HONG KONG
UNIVERSITY AND WESTERN
DISTRICT

Western: an Introduction

The area west of Central, beyond the trendy SoHo district and neighbouring Sheung Wan extending to the western shoreline, has come to be known loosely as Western District or just "Western". The name *Sai Wan* (west area) in Cantonese refers more specifically to the residential areas on the north-west coast known as Sai Ying Pun and Kennedy Town. Difficult to categorize, the entire stretch west of Central is more heterogeneous than homogeneous in its modern-day form. It extends along Caine Road and Hollywood Road, Queen's Road West, Des Voeux Road and Connaught Road, all running virtually in parallel away from Central towards Sai Ying Pun, the western part of the old city of Victoria. Beyond this district is the bustling community of Kennedy Town—named after late Victorian governor Sir Arthur Kennedy—from which one can take the pleasantly winding and leafy Victoria Road to the north-western tip of the island at Sandy Bay, famed for its spectacular sunset, and the ultra-modern seaside Cyberport complex. The mix of high-density residential and commercial buildings along the northern shoreline and Mid-Levels gives way to more sparsely populated and undulating streets and roads west of Kennedy Town and round this western headland towards the scenic south side of the island.

The reader should bear in mind at this point that "western" is used purely in the geographical sense, and that as in many other areas of Hong Kong, Chinese and Westernized features of culture and lifestyle rub shoulders with one another in that typically unpredictable, apparently arbitrary but constantly stimulating fashion that has come to characterize Hong Kong.

The north-western part of the island includes some of Hong Kong's most culturally, educationally and medically significant and yet diverse buildings, from Man-Mo Temple to Hong Kong University. Moreover, in its Sai Ying Pun heartland it has retained a strong sense of enduring Chineseness that has obstinately resisted the concessions to modernity of many adjacent streets and areas. Yet a stone's throw from here evolved the westernized education of the Central School (later Queen's College), King's College and the University of Hong Kong, acknowledged in retrospect by Dr. Sun as the cradle of his own revolutionary ideals for transforming China. As we shall see, Western District, no less than Wan Chai and Causeway Bay, is rich in historical, cultural and ideological heritage, which makes it an integral part of the body of the metropolis. If Central is the head and Wan Chai and Causeway Bay, respectively, the heart, then Western District has a powerful claim to being gastronomically, the stomach, and educationally, the very soul of the city.

Along Hollywood Road

One account has it that Hollywood Road acquired its glitzy name not from Hong Kong's ongoing love affair with the frequently formulaic products of the Los Angeles film industry, but from a place in England. Hollywood was the name of the country seat in Westbury-on-Trym near Bristol of Sir John Davis, Hong Kong's second governor. Davis, who succeeded Pottinger in 1844, was almost universally reviled by the expatriate community on account of his even-handedness towards both locals and expatriates and his efforts to introduce a system of taxation that only marginally reduced the substantial profit margins of the traders. Davis' period of governorship ended in 1848, but his memory lives on, not only in the road that bears his name, Mount Davis Road in the Pokfulam district, which lies further west, but also perhaps in this most culturally significant of thoroughfares, Hollywood Road. A more prosaic and conflicting theory is that the old Hollywood Road area was dotted with holly shrubs. However, the holly plant is not indigenous to Hong Kong, so these would have had to be imported. As in other matters of name derivation in Hong Kong, conjecture is often all one has to go on, and certainty is often clouded in local legend and cross-cultural misunderstanding or approximation.

Sheung Wan streets, west of Central.

Hollywood Road, which runs from the old Central Police Station at its Central end to Possession Street and Possession Point, represents a quintessentially Hong Kong cultural blend. Not an artificially designed and cliché-ridden East-West mix, but a genuine and non-contrived co-existence of Chinese culture and commerce with aspects of Britishness, especially in its antique shops and second-hand shops. The majority of establishments are, however, distinctly Chinese. In the exodus from the communist takeover of the mainland, and especially in the harsh years of the Cultural Revolution, many genuine antiques found their way here. China's antiquities and historical treasures were considered part of a reactionary and contemptible feudal tradition, and in consequence little valued. Hollywood Road became the focal point for a trade in statues, figurines, ceramics and other artefacts from China, many of which were snapped up by avid Western collectors.

When demand started to outstrip supply, the shopkeepers resorted to obtaining high quality fakes, many of which were, themselves, hundreds of years old. Nowadays it can be difficult to discern the genuine antique even when buying from professional and reputable dealers. The same is also true of antique Chinese furniture, which can easily be stained to give the appearance of centuries-old rosewood or mahogany. What matters perhaps more for tourists and collectors in this busy yet leisurely street is the thrill of searching and believing that they have acquired a piece of great value. After all, value might well be said to reside principally in the belief systems of the imagination.

Creative imagination, rather than value, is uppermost in the minds of the idiosyncratic artists who exhibit at the interestingly maverick studio known as Para/Site in Po Yan Street just off Hollywood Road. One of the best places to enjoy installation art, the studio is a testament to the never-say-die attitude among its co-operative founders. Their preference to exhibit in Western and Sheung Wan, "an area in which the traces of Hong Kong history have not yet been erased," to quote David Clarke, has meant hopping from location to location at the whim of fortune and fluctuations in the property rental market. Now in Po Yan Street, the gallery has a longer-term home and exhibitions, such as the 2004 Mapping Identities by curator and whimsical artist Oscar Ho, have given the visitor, whether local or overseas, an insight into Hong Kong's resilient, distinctive, quirky and tongue-in-cheek culture.

Part of the Mapping Identities exhibition was Ho's series of art works Stories around Town, consisting of tall tales and spoofs based on current rumours during the nervous Nineties. Ho's most glorious send-up of official identity narratives was his widely believed hoax piece based on a fish called Lo Ting. This half-fish half-man was purported to be the ancestor of the Tanka tribes from whom indigenous Hong Kongers were descended. Playing on the word *yue* in Cantonese (meaning fish), he propagated the myth that the Yue people, who preceded the Tanka, were in fact fish-men. Subsequently Ho decided to continue producing absurd art works on the basis that Hong Kong reality provided plenty of raw material for creative exploitation.

Talking of fish, there are a number of places of cultural, historical and gastronomical interest along the Hollywood Road antiques route. On the corner of Aberdeen Street is the old-fashioned Lin Heung Restaurant, still functioning as a *yum cha* establishment in the style of old Hong Kong. *Yum cha* (tea-drinking) together with eating *dim sum* (little heart, i.e. snacks and delicacies) is an integral part of Chinese culture everywhere, and nowhere more so than in food-conscious Hong Kong. *Dim sum* food comprises various types of dumpling containing pork, shrimp and vegetable, as well as spring rolls, rice and meat wrapped in lotus leaves, and, not perhaps for the more squeamish, chicken toes. Most *dim sum* restaurants have been modernized, so it is particularly gratifying to see a traditional teahouse of this kind continuing to thrive. Everything about the place from the décor and fittings to the food and even the till is un-selfconsciously redolent of an earlier era. Needless to say, the food is both authentic and excellent. It offers an attractive alternative to both the fast food shops below in Queen's Road West and the nearby bistros and pricy restaurants of SoHo. The Lin Heung (Fragrant Lotus) restaurant is by no means the only good place to eat along Hollywood Road, but it is rightly held in high esteem by locals.

David T. K. Wong's novel The Evergreen Tea House shows the evolution of a Hong Kong entrepreneurial family after the smuggling and black market opportunities afforded by the Japanese occupation of the city. His American-educated protagonist, Xavier Chu, meets his late father's former associate, Uncle Yue, in the traditional Sheung Wan teahouse in which they were wont to discuss their borderline-legitimate financial strategies. It is Xavier's first visit to the teahouse, and is inevitably symbolic of his readiness to assume his father's position and at the same time of his deference to the traditions of filial piety, as well as his necessary respect for the values of an older generation. It seems from Wong's description very similar to Lin Heung, though as with many such fictional places it is not necessarily modelled directly on this particular one and could be a composite of several, some of which no longer exist. The novel covers several decades, but this scene is set in 1965, well before our own post-modern preoccupation with mixing conservation with self-conscious retro:

> *The Evergreen Tea House, too, seemed like a throwback to a former age. It was set in a row of two-storied tenements, each with its own outdated charm. The marble cloud patterned table top, set in a blackwood frame, had long since gone out of fashion. Four identical booths, separated by high latticed wooden panels, flanked both sides of the room. The space between was occupied by three round tables, each with six matching stools. A large brass spittoon stood next to each booth. Lazy ceiling fans made a pretence at ventilation.*

Replenished, but searching in vain for the spittoon, we walk out and direct our steps westward, following the Sun Yat-sen Historical Trail. In fact, this belated memorial tribute to one of Hong Kong's most distinguished residents (and its most significant in terms of contribution to the motherland) has numbered stages and is supposed to end in Wellington Street in Central. There is a map at this point on Hollywood Road detailing the entire trail. Sun Yat-sen lived in a number of houses in the vicinity and is reputed to have plotted the overthrow of the Manchu imperial dynasty with his fellow revolutionaries from this quarter. He went to school in Central's prestigious Victoria College, which was located just off Hollywood Road above Queen's Road West, enrolling as a student there in 1884. There is a plaque on the steps above Hollywood Road commemorating the school, which was founded as the Central School in 1862 by the missionary and respected Chinese classical text translator, James Legge. The College counts not only Dr. Sun, but also Sir Kai Ho-kai, talented doctor, legislator and jurisprudence teacher at the Hong Kong College of Medicine, which Sun also attended, among its alumni. Victoria College was later renamed Queens College and relocated to the Tin Hau end of Causeway Bay in the 1950s. It continues to flourish and has retained its prestige among the status-conscious elite of Hong Kong's secondary schools.

Under the enlightened regime of the school's first headmaster, Frederick Stewart (whose life and achievements have been scrupulously documented and entertainingly recounted by Hong Kong writers Gillian and Verner Bickley in *Looking For Frederick* and *The Golden Needle*), Chinese students were first exposed to bicultural education. This education was essentially secular rather than adhering to a particular religious creed, which was, and to some extent still is, the norm for local schools in Hong Kong. Stewart's curriculum also emphasized the equal importance of Chinese and English languages, something that the government failed to implement until long after Stewart's death. Official recognition of the status of Cantonese was only achieved in 1975 after ongoing agitation in the wake of the 1967 riots in Hong Kong.

Man-Mo Temple
One of Hong Kong's most important Chinese temples, Man-Mo Temple, is the next sight to be seen as one turns the bend. It is likely

that the distinctive scent of sandalwood incense will assuage the nostrils by the time one approaches and passes the small Museum of Stone Sculptures next door, which is targeted more at the wealthy collector than the cultural tourist. The Man-Mo Temple, by contrast, is a genuine heritage site that asserts Hong Kong's social and cultural Chinese identity more eloquently perhaps than any other single building.

The twin deities to whom the temple is dedicated can be seen as very representative of Hong Kong. Man is the god of learning and literature, Man Cheong. Formerly a loyal subject of one of the early Chinese emperors Man's outstanding virtues were recognized, and deity conferred upon him posthumously. His name also evokes a strong sense of civic responsibility and of the value of learning, and he is regarded as the patron of civil servants. Mo, on the other hand, is the martial god, usually known as Kwan Yu, the patron of policemen and antique dealers (and also, to his probable chagrin, of Triads), and a hugely popular figure in the Chinese pantheon. Taken from a real life character in the story of the Three Kingdoms, Mo, or Kwan Yu, epitomizes the qualities of steadfastness, incorruptibility and loyalty. Both gods are especially venerated here and their statues are prayed to by people who wish to do well in their careers and exams.

What is important about the twin deities is that, rather like the two sides of a coin, or like the Yin-Yang cosmogony, they symbolize two sides of a whole. In the dual image of Man-Mo the flowing sleeves of the scholar are complemented by the foreshortened cuff of the fighter, contrasting with the Western tradition which sees erudition and combat as essentially antithetical. In the Chinese cultural value system it is equally important for its martial heroes, of whom Kwan Yu is in many ways the historical prototype, to be educated *literati* also. Non-Chinese admirers of the Chinese martial arts film and literature genres often fail to realize this essential duality. We can find effigies of both gods at the back of the temple, Man dressed in red with a Chinese calligraphy brush at his side, and Mo clad in his familiar green accompanied by the model of a golden sword. Keeping these two company in the main temple is Shing Wong, the City god, celestial counterpart of the worldly city potentate, be it the foreign governor of the past or today's Chief Executive, the Catholic Donald Tsang. In addition, the visitor can see effigies of the ten judges of the Underworld at the altar and to the side of the altar, Pao Kung, the Sherlock Holmes of the gods, who as a god of justice devises ingenious methods of bringing the guilty to book, no matter how cunning their crimes. In the smaller adjoining temple reside the two most beloved female gods of the Chinese pantheon, Kwun Yam—the goddess of mercy, and Tin Hau, goddess of the sea and highly significant in a seafaring community such as Hong Kong.

The hanging coils of sandalwood incense, to which bright red votive papers are attached, burn for up to two weeks in supplication to the gods to heed prayers for relatives or to give thanks and convey a spirit of celebration. The prevailing red colour of the dedicatory papers and the poles and banners signifies, as always in Chinese tradition, good fortune and happiness. In previous times when traffic was mainly pedestrian the gods were paraded around the city in sedan chairs, which are still on view in the main temple. Also on display are the great temple bell and gong, struck to communicate to the various gods that tributes and prayers are about to be sent. Visitors can tell the date of the founding of the temple from an inscription on the bell informing them it was cast in Guangdong province in the year 1847, and the Hong Kong land records confirm this. However, as with many shrines and temples, Man-Mo is likely to have been constructed on the site of an earlier place of worship.

Man-Mo Temple played a crucial role in the development of civic consciousness among the Chinese community in what was, back in the mid-nineteenth century, in essence a frontier town. Here committees were formed to administer the Chinese community in Hong Kong and to organize not only courts of justice, but also benevolent and medical initiatives in the community. Indeed, it was from here—in the adjoining Tung Wah Virtue Court—that an initially *ad hoc* but increasingly credible parallel authority emerged, which more pragmatic colonial officers and governors recognized as being, in the words of the historian E. J. Eitel, "the unofficial link between China residents of Hong Kong and Canton". The Imperial chop beneath a plaque of recognition of Hong Kong Chinese contributions to flood relief in the motherland bears testimony (to those who can read it) to the tradition of Confucian benevolence fostered in Man-Mo Temple. Lithographs dating from not long after its construction reveal an elegant and imposing edifice and a bustling community within its environs. Today it is inevitably hemmed in by other buildings, both around and above it, making it difficult for

Man-Mo Temple, Hollywood Road

the casual visitor to appreciate its former importance. To read a most evocative reminiscence of a childhood visit to Man-Mo Temple we need look no further than Martin Booth's memoir, *Gweilo*. His encounter with an erudite old Chinese man at the temple gives the young Martin a valuable early insight into Chinese tradition. He remembered at the time speculating as to whether his friendly informant had been a "phantom" of his own imagination.

"Cat Street" and Possession Street

Leaving Man Mo Temple, we cross Hollywood Road and walk down the broad flight of steps known as Ladder Street in the direction of Queen's Road West. Yet more antique shops vie for attention, but if we observe the alley which crosses Ladder Street, designated Upper Lascar Row, we find further evidence of Hong Kong's cosmopolitan past. The Lascars were sailors of Indian-Arab origin who worked on the opium and tea clippers, which plied their trade between the coast of India and

Hong Kong on a regular basis in the nineteenth century. The street used to be a busy flea market where Lascars bought and sold second-hand goods that may or may not have been "dodgy". In Cantonese these wares were known as rat or mouse goods (*lou syu fo*) and the vendors correspondingly referred to as "cats", hence the alternative name of the street. Although more respectable establishments, mainly curio and antique shops, now predominate, there are still some street hawkers selling what might well be "rat" wares.

In her delightful book of watercolours based on the indigenous activities of the Hollywood Road denizens, *A Walk Along Hollywood Road*, Ann Beatty has evoked this sense of borderline legitimacy in the slightly shifty expression on the face of the jade seller. His case is open and he sits at ease on his stool, but he remains wary in case the special "hawker police" are making one of their periodic sweeps of the area. The green of the potted palm tree harmonizes nicely with the green pieces of jade, but, as is the case with the antiques, there is no way of knowing, unless you are initiated into the ancient lore of the jade collector, whether a piece is valuable or worthless. There are plenty of imitations of pure jadeite in quartz, soapstone or other surrogate stone, but nothing gives as much pleasure as the ownership of a genuine piece of antique jade to a cultivated connoisseur. Another of Ann Beatty's watercolours has brilliantly captured the second-hand typewriter, fan and abacus (the traditional Chinese calculator) belonging to the seller of Cat Street, who can be seen sitting or crouching patiently amongst his wares, oblivious to the danger of the precariously piled edifice crashing down on top of him. This extract from Leung Ping-kwan's 1974 poem "Demolition on Cat Street" from his anthology *Travelling with a Bitter Melon* sums up the picture neatly:

> *Hardly a foreign tourist*
> *to pick up a jade pendant*
> *and bargain*
> *only buzzing flies dusting the mottled green on copperware*
> *the cracks in glasses*
> > *and the dirt on chipped porcelain.*
> *Further back in a shop dark and dim*
> *rows of old snuff bottles*
> *each storing fragments of the past.*

Rather than returning to walk all the way down the steps of Ladder Street, we can follow Cat Street along to rejoin Hollywood Road. At the very western end of Hollywood Road lies Possession Street (*Shui Hang Hau* in Cantonese) and the small Possession Garden, adjacent to busy Queen's Road West. Timothy Mo's fictional-historical magnum opus *An Insular Possession* is aptly titled, for the planting of the British flag here in 1841 has been enshrined in the collective memory thanks to the name of the street and the enclosed Chinese-style garden. It is also recorded thus in Captain Belcher's journal: "We landed on Monday 25th January [*sic*], 1841, at fifteen minutes past eight a.m. and, being the bona fide possessors [whatever that means!], Her Majesty's health was drunk with three cheers on Possession Mount."

The fact that the street has, to date at least, retained a name so redolent to Western eyes and ears of the city's colonized past prompts two interesting observations about Hong Kong. Firstly, it is important to realize that the roman letters on street signs and names are likely to be filtered out to a considerable extent by the Chinese speaker's sub-conscious. While the English name is not quite as invisible to the Hong Kong Chinese person as the Chinese name is to the English native speaker, nonetheless places exist in the consciousness of respective ethnic groups largely through the associations inspired by the mother tongue. English proper names are usually rendered in phonetic transliteration, whilst abstract or common nouns and names of geographical features are invariably translated into their Chinese equivalents. One cannot assume that the Chinese name sounds anything like the English name.

Secondly, Hong Kong people had the tendency to co-exist pragmatically with the British, utilizing aspects of language and culture when it suited them, but paying scant regard to British imperial discourse. China always saw Hong Kong as being lent or leased to the British for an indefinite period of time rather than being ceded in perpetuity and thus belonging definitively to Britain. The naming of Possession Street can be seen in retrospect as culturally arrogant and insensitive, but it does not seem to have stirred up resentment or popular sentiment any more than naming other streets after colonial governors. Louis Dung Kai-cheung has noted this phenomenon in his *Archeology of an Imaginary City*: "This street was also the place where a watercourse entered the sea. Local people therefore called it Shui Hang

Hau, meaning 'mouth of the watercourse'. In fact, not too many locals knew that street was related to the invasion of the island." Dung observes that Professor Clark, a pre-war Professor of History at Hong Kong University, suggested changing the name to Exorcism Street to counter the more common and sinister interpretation of the word "possession". In Cantonese this translates aptly enough as *gon gwai*—chasing away ghosts and foreign devils!

In other colonized British "possessions" such as Ireland, India, or even the United States, it is inconceivable that such an apparently provocative name could survive decolonization or re-possession. Possession Garden is the rather modest and inauspicious site that marks the beginnings of modern Hong Kong. However, given the fact that Captain Belcher of HMS *Sulphur* (after which Sulphur Channel off the north-western shore of Hong Kong is named) anticipated Elliot's orders rather than acting on them, and that Palmerston and Queen Victoria were far from impressed, it is perhaps logical that no plaque or memorial should celebrate the fateful event. Possession Garden has in any case been unofficially repossessed by the local aficionados of the *siesta*, who make full use of its wide stone benches for napping purposes. Since the area was famous for its brothels in the early years of the colony yet another connotation could be read into its name. But it was also known as the Great Public Square in those early days. Nowadays the public are much less concentrated here than in the shopping precincts of Causeway Bay and Tsim Sha Tsui. After a brief nap in Possession Garden, we round the corner to cross Queen's Road West, and take full possession of our faculties once more to negotiate the traffic. A short walk along the continuation of Possession Street brings us to the back entrance of Western Market. This stylish Edwardian red-brick building, dating back to 1906, was renovated in the mid-Nineties to provide a home for the former outdoor fabric stalls of Central's once-thriving Fabric Alley.

"The Chinese Quarter"—from Tai Ping Shan to Sai Ying Pun

The area west of Central was designated "the Chinese Quarter" in the nineteenth century for the simple reason that the British colonizers wanted to reserve the central and eastern parts of the north of the island for their own military, naval and commercial activities, as well as their European-style villas and houses, and deliberately established separate communities. This explains the concentration of Chinese cultural and historical features of today's Hong Kong in this relatively small area, though much of its historical and cultural ambience has been diminished by more recent urban development. Of course, other parts of the Territory also reveal fascinating characteristics of Chinese cultural development. Parts of Kowloon and the New Territories are equally rewarding to visit from a cultural perspective, and in the case of walled villages in the latter area or the old Walled City site in East Kowloon, they date back much further.

Western District, however, retains a specifically ethnic Chinese feel today, which is partly derived from its native ghetto status on Hong Kong Island after the British developed the northern coast of the island. The oldest areas, Tai Ping Shan and Sai Ying Pun, date back to the 1840s and 1850s, when the colonial government removed Chinese inhabitants and their dwellings and market stalls from the Central area in order to clear the land for its own development projects. Although the new areas designated for them were open only to Chinese, and Europeans were barred from living in these streets, the policy was divisive. Bemoaning the lack of integration and cultural interaction between Chinese and European communities in the 1920s, sinologist Governor Sir Cecil Clementi needed to look no further than the policies of his predecessors to divine the reason. The ghetto effect created by this policy determined the present configuration of the island to a very large extent. Tai Ping Shan Street, which runs above and parallel to Hollywood Road and the streets around it, conveys the impression of an entirely different time and place by comparison with both the modern shopping malls of Central and the fast-food establishments and electronic goods shops below in Sheung Wan.

The name Tai Ping Shan literally means "Peace Hill" and is said to be derived from a sea battle in 1810 between the Qing Dynasty warships and a particularly predatory pirate fleet under "Dragon Lady" Cheng Yat and her lover Cheung Po-tsai. After they had raided the coast with impunity for years, sheltering in waters off Hong Kong, they were finally forced to surrender on equitable terms. In a typically pragmatic arrangement some of the pirates, including Cheung Po-tsai, joined the Imperial Navy and achieved rapid promotion in the service of the government, while others retired in Hong Kong and settled in the area around Tai Ping Shan Street. The peace that subsequently reigned in the region was commemorated in official references to Hong Kong Island as "Peace Mountain". The state of peace continued until the arrival of the British warships thirty years later.

Ironically, the one man whose work undermined everything the Qing Dynasty stood for is commemorated by a plaque in Blake Garden, which stands on the site of part of old Tai Ping Shan. Dr. Sun's Tong Men Hui Reception Committee established in 1900 for the benefit of revolutionary brothers who had fled to Hong Kong from China, functioned as a covert organization established for the apparently innocuous purpose of welcoming and hosting newly-arrived compatriots.

Tai Ping Shan and Ladder Streets, as well as parts of Hollywood Road, were chosen by the film director Richard Quine and his production team as the location for filming *The World of Suzie Wong*. Geographically speaking, this choice of setting to represent Wan Chai was quite inappropriate. The aim of the film makers was naturally to exoticize Hong Kong and to present it as more "authentically Chinese" than it really was in the 1950s. From another point of view, however, it was quite a fortuitous representation, both symbolically and historically. Tai Ping Shan Street, according to China mainland writer and traveller Wang Tao, writing in 1860 as a visitor of translator Dr. James Legge, was full of brothels: "gaudy houses, sporting brightly painted doors and windows with fancy curtains." Only later did the "sing-song girls" (so called because like Japanese geishas many of then were skilled singers and entertainers) gravitate to fresh areas, including Lyndhurst Terrace in Central and Shek Tong Tsui down the hill in Western on the edge of Kennedy Town. By the time they arrived in Wan Chai in the mid-twentieth century they were catering less to rich local men and more to overseas "barbarians", for whom such extra accomplishments were deemed unnecessary.

One tell-tale sign that you are in a traditional Chinese quarter is the proliferation of temples in the vicinity, three within a very small radius. Two of them were originally part of one big temple built in 1895 and dedicated to Kwun Yam, and located in Tai Ping Shan Street. The temple became so dilapidated and neglected that now, after housing development around the site, only two separated sections are left on opposite sides. In fact, these small temple halls are located in a lane just off Tai Ping Shan Street and are much less discernible to the eye of the passer-by than Man-Mo Temple, for example. The Kwun Yam Hall, the one on the left walking westwards, is small but has a beautifully carved decoration on camphor wood, called a *chai mun*, above the doorway, as well as a finely worked altar carving. The quiet and simple temple, with its hanging red banners and burnt paper offerings, is a perfect example of the preservation of deep-rooted Taoist and Confucian values in the Chinese psyche in spite of the ravages of time and city developers.

As if to emphasize the important concept of the pantheistic beliefs of Taoism, Confucianism and Buddhism co-existing happily, the third temple we come to, situated at the west end of Tai Ping Shan Street and close to Po Yan Street, is a Buddhist one. This is dedicated to Jai Kung, or the "Poor Man's Buddha". The temple was built in 1851 and was used to house temporarily the ancestral stone tablets and the actual coffins of those males who died in Hong Kong, far away from their home families and ancestral resting places. The Poor Man's Buddha confers special blessings on those who died in modest circumstances. Inside is a statue of the god, Tei Chong Wong, or "emperor of the deceased". The Baak Seng Tsz or One Hundred Surname Temple in Tai Ping Shan particularly answered the spiritual needs of those unfortunates who were left to expire in so-called "dying rooms" before the Chinese community founded the Tung Wah hospital in the early 1870s.

Descending to Queen's Road West and walking westwards along this busy one-way street, we reach Sai Ying Pun or "Western Plateau", a lively part of Western with street markets and Chinese Opera street performances on makeshift stages at festival times, especially Mid-Autumn Festival and Chinese New Year. Steep old streets ascending, respectively East Street, Centre Street and West Street, are crossed by numbered streets running east-west, namely First, Second and Third Street. Above Third Street is situated, logically enough, High Street or Gou Gai, which has many small businesses.

Going west along Gou Gai (High Street) we reach Tseng Gai (Centre Street), a delightful but steep pedestrian precinct with a commanding view over the western part of Hong Kong Harbour as one descends. This is the heart of Sai Ying Pun and the former stronghold of Cheng Yat, Cheung Po-Tsai and their pirate gang. It afforded them an excellent lookout position for scanning the western shoreline of the island for likely prey. It is in this old street that the young Xavier Chu in David T. K. Wong's *The Evergreen Teahouse* debates ideas and politics with his boy-scout comrade, Little Ho. The former champions the Darwinian concept of natural selection and the survival of the fittest in relation to the old-fashioned sugar-water shop in which they take refreshment after their day out in the hills. The smart and cynical young Xavier believes it matters little that such traditional places should go to the wall, but his friend, whose father has a humble job in Xavier's father's Goldstar Company, shows greater wisdom and a positive human spirit. The dialectic between Xavier's utilitarian attitude and the Confucian views of Little Ho anticipates and underpins the entire novel in the way it represents a fundamental Hong Kong conflict of values. The use of Centre Street and the traditional parts of Western District as locations is symbolic of Wong's implied message, that even the hardened and Westernized Hong Kong businessman needs to return to his roots at some point in his life.

Another work that evokes the spirit of place in Centre Street is Hark Yeung's and Fong So's little gem, *Our Elders* (1999). This bilingual journal depicts in English and Chinese prose and in Fong So's ink and watercolour pictures the daily life of Western District's aging population in the bustling streets below their creative studio in Centre Street:

> *I have spent most of the time over the past year in Centre Street, a steep old street in the Western district. Many old people live there. Most of them are lonely but hard-working people. It seems that they do not live with their children. Most try to keep themselves busy by finding something to do. They sell vegetables, fruit and other small items. Some really old ones even collect waste paper and sell it to the recycling merchants. There is also a hunch-backed old woman, who feeds the street cats of the district every night. For some time I have been trying to draw these from memory.*

The Battle against Disease: Chinese Medicine and Western Medicine

There are a number of places in Western District that bear witness to Hong Kong's battle against serious epidemics, especially in the last decades of the nineteenth century. It was a battle that Hong Kong was eventually to win but at a terrible cost. Bubonic plague broke out in the early 1890s, but unsanitary conditions had been festering for some time before the full extent of the crisis became apparent. Governor Pope Hennessey was opposed to the introduction of flush toilets on what might now be seen as perfectly good ecological grounds. His determination to persist with what had been, since the rapid development of the colony, an unsatisfactory and inadequate sanitation system and an unreliable public provision of safe water meant that the disaster waiting to happen inevitably occurred.

The plague, which probably originated in neighbouring Canton, broke out in the overcrowded ethnically Chinese quarter of Tai Ping Shan. Its spread was exacerbated by a deadly combination of poor sanitation and hygiene, close proximity of animals (especially pigs, cows and goats) and humans and lack of government inspection and regulation. Many of the tenements that stood in this area were cleared and destroyed, including the contents, and the inhabitants placed in isolation hospitals. The British soldiers of the Shropshire Regiment and the Government Plague Inspectors, who were detailed for this unfortunate task, were not surprisingly hated by local people, and it would not be an exaggeration to say that a residual mistrust of both authority figures and Westerners has never entirely disappeared among the older residents of the area.

The present-day, rather quiet Tai Ping Shan covers just a fraction of the original bustling community. Nearly 400 houses and tenements were simply eradicated, and the Chinese community on the island was virtually halved by bubonic plague and by migration to the mainland. The mortality rate was above ninety per cent and two and a half thousand people died in the first fifteen weeks alone. Migration, by contrast, resulted in the loss of nearly one hundred thousand Chinese residents, most of whom were fearful that new governor William Robinson would not allow their bodies to be repatriated in the event of death to enable their spirits to rest in their native villages.

The response of the Western community was to build hospitals and fight the disease at source by erecting a pathological institute in the neighbourhood to investigate the causes of the disease and try to isolate the bacillus. The institute, which was finally built in 1906—it took almost thirty years to rid the Territory of the plague following its first terrible visitation in 1894—was located in Caine Lane, just above Tai Ping Shan and a short walk down steps from the main thoroughfare of Caine Road. It is now used as Hong Kong's Museum of Medical Sciences and is significant for its central role in combating disease, functioning as a pathological institute until the early 1970s and producing vaccines to deal with outbreaks of tuberculosis, smallpox and diphtheria. The institute only came into being at the insistence of Dr. Patrick Manson, the founder of The Hong Kong College of Medicine, which Dr. Sun Yat-sen attended at the time of the plague epidemic. Manson was a distinguished bacteriologist, and not only discovered the vital pathological link between the mosquito and malaria, but also founded the internationally important London Institute for Tropical Diseases, which benefited enormously from his Hong Kong experience. Manson had also been instrumental in organizing the supply of fresh milk in the Territory from cow herds further west in Pokfulam.

By the end of the plague epidemic, twenty thousand people had died, a mortality level of over 95 per cent of those infected. Obviously the work of the institute had been to understand what caused the disease. Prevention of renewed outbreaks, rather than cure of those infected, was the main achievement of the Western medicine personnel, working hand in hand with the main authorities. Western-style surgery with its physically invasive methods was complete anathema to Chinese cultural practices, and offended against concepts of an afterlife in which the body needed to be integral. For this reason surgery was considered tantamount to eternal mutilation and not surprisingly was shunned. By contrast, the Chinese forms of medicine developed along more traditional, cultural lines, particularly the idea of harmony and balance between hot and cold and wet and dry states, a system that clashed starkly with the seemingly barbarous foreign medical practices. Based on herbal and holistic medical concepts, many of which are gaining ground nowadays in Western treatments, traditional Chinese medicine can be seen in retrospect to complement the vaccines and radical purgation and clearing practices of the "foreign devils".

A plethora of herbal medicine and health food shops purveying animal, mineral and vegetable extracts, especially in dried or pickled form, can still be seen in Western District. They are particularly prevalent in the stretches of Queen's Road West and Des Voeux Road that run parallel with the Sai Ying Pun district, and are eloquent testimony to a persistent and not unjustified faith in the virtues of Chinese medicine.

The Tung Wah Hospital in Po Yan Street had been founded in 1869 partly as civic response to the shock of discovering the existence of the "dying rooms" in the Baak Seng Tsz Temple. Without the powerful cohesive unit of the family to provide a haven for these sick immigrant workers, the Chinese community in Hong Kong needed urgently to come up with a solution, which they promptly did. The richer Chinese were willing to spend the money they had acquired as compradors or middlemen for the various trading ventures (including, of course, opium) because by this point they were beginning to see themselves as permanent rather than temporary residents in Hong Kong. Benevolence was also as much a Confucian virtue as a Christian one. Remarkably, nearly $50,000 was raised in a short space of time, enabling work to begin speedily. The success of the initiative set a precedent for the Chinese community to fund socially and educationally beneficial projects, now an accepted part of Hong Kong's idiosyncratic mix of *laissez-faire* capitalism and Confucian philanthropy.

Designated a Chinese medicine hospital from the outset, thanks partly to Governor Richard Graves Macdonnell's pragmatic recognition of the incompatibility of Western and Chinese views on medicine, the Tung Wah was the first Chinese hospital of its kind in Asia and became the model for others in the region and even for the growing expatriate Chinese community in San Francisco. The English name it became known by was simply an abbreviation of the transliteration of the words for "Cantonese people", as used in the nineteenth-century romanized script. (Present-day Guangdong was written as Kwangtung at that time.) The full name, Cantonese People's Hospital, is much shorter to read in Chinese characters, hence the abbreviation, which on its own simply means "Tung (Kwangtung) language (wah)".

Not only did the Tung Wah organization introduce a phenomenally successful vaccination programme in the years following its inception, which set the agenda for an imaginative and non-dogmatic blend of Chinese and Western medical practices, it also took a significant step in establishing a much-needed Society for the Protection of Innocent Children (the still highly active and influential Po Leung Kuk), which intervened to save youngsters being sold by unscrupulous traders into prostitution and virtual slavery. To do this they gained the approval of mercurial governor Pope Hennessey to recruit their own detective force to track down and arrest those responsible for promoting the vile trade. Those rescued from the clutches of kidnappers and traders were housed by the Society's own homes for abandoned children. In today's Hong Kong the Po Leung Kuk, now an organization in its own right, is instrumental in providing schooling and educational resources for the socially disadvantaged, particularly children of fresh immigrants. It has grown into one of the most vigorous and effective charities in the SAR, and like the Tung Wah Group is respected for an outstanding record of service to the community.

Medicine Men and Poets: the University of Hong Kong

Caine and Bonham Roads run parallel to Queen's Road from Central District through Western to Hong Kong University, which stands at the junction of Bonham and Pokfulam Road. Below the so-called Mid-Levels roads (Robinson and Conduit) but above the hurly-burly of the northern shoreline roads (Queen's Road West and Des Voeux), they both evoke a certain sense of superiority thanks to the important role they have played in the island's education. Both roads are steeped in history. Major Caine, one of the original colonials, stayed to become a draconian First Magistrate of the Colony, handing out regular floggings to both Chinese and British offenders in order to quell the criminal elements that had flocked to Hong Kong looking for easy money. Caine was a dedicated officer, though one who had no legal background or previous experience of the law to bring to bear on his senior judicial role. The Magistracy in Arbuthnot Road, Central, which was built in 1914 and is still standing, was built on the site of his temporary structure. A reputed martinet of a disciplinarian, Caine stayed in Hong Kong dispensing justice according to his lights from 1841 to 1856, when he retired to England, leaving the colony a safer place than it had been during the mid-1840s crime-wave.

Modern-day Caine Road is dotted with tutorial schools, kindergartens and churches for Mid-Levels residents. The continuation of Caine Road is called appropriately Bonham Road. Samuel George Bonham, Hong Kong's third governor, worked in close alliance with Caine during his incumbency from 1848 to 1854. Bonham Road still has a high ratio of schools, secondary, primary and kindergarten, to shops and residential buildings. It was always regarded as a suitable catchment area for the university. St. Paul's College and King's College are two of the oldest and most prestigious of its secondary schools. King's College (1879), standing a stone's throw from the university, is an impressive Victorian red-brick building, which set the tone for the scholastic ethos of this part of Western District. Hong Kong parents are generally more obsessive about education than their British and American counterparts, and have in the past had a deserved reputation for adopting Caine-like methods to induce their offspring to work hard and enter the university. The Caine approach has been mitigated in recent years by the increasing incidence of one-child families and milder attitudes to parenting among younger Hong Kong people.

The university in question has always been, of course, The University of Hong Kong. Its coat of arms bears the Latin legend, *Sapientia Et Virtus*—Knowledge and Virtue—a culturally mixed reference but one that recalls the Confucian classic, *The Great Learning*, which stressed the importance of both moral and intellectual self-development. Constructed in 1912 and by far the oldest of Hong Kong's eight tertiary institutions, the university owes its existence, not as is often presumed from its classical colonial look to the benevolence and foresight of the colonizing mother country, but to an unlikely coalition of private benefactors, most of them Chinese.

Loke Yew Hall, the oldest building and core of the original university, was designed by the architects Leigh and Orange, who were responsible for many stylish constructions of the period. Loke Yew was a Chinese-Malysian self-made man, who, like the university's most recent benefactor, billionaire Li Ka-shing, had little or no education himself but wanted to be remembered for his philanthropy in this area of human activity rather than simply his business ventures. Loke Yew Hall, with its courtyards, quadrangles and pond, its spire and cupolas and gigantic statuesque palms, was intended to be reminiscent of an Oxbridge college, and it is clear that from its inception the university saw itself as a Far East counterpart to the traditional British universities. The other donors and contributors, however, included very few Britons, who may have seen the project as inherently dangerous and a threat to British superiority in the colony. At all events apart from Governor Frederick Lugard and his wife, who forced the colonial authorities and an unwilling government to donate the land, the majority of contributors to the cause were Chinese, including donors in various cities of the newly founded Republic of China. Two other significant benefactors were the Parsee stockbroker and merchant Sir Hormusjee Naorojee Mody, who contributed nearly HK$300,000, and the great Hong Kong-Armenian entrepreneur and philanthropist, Sir Catchick Paul Chater.

Dr. Sun Yat-sen, who was something of a *persona non grata* during his stay in Hong Kong, is now considered one of the great founding spirits of the university. He is commemorated in its present-day heart, now located just above the elegant Loke Yew Hall with its permanently slow clock. Sun Yat-sen Place is a piazza adjacent to the university's well-stocked main library, from which the Sun Yat-sen Steps ascend to buildings named after other benefactors, including Shaw Brothers film mogul, Sir Run-Run Shaw and his brother Runme Shaw. Dr. Sun famously came to the university to speak to students in 1923. He attributed his revolutionary ardour and the inspiration for his fellow revolutionaries' desire for better governance in China to his Western-style education at Victoria College and the Hong Kong College of Medicine—the forerunner of Hong Kong University's medical faculty. Indeed, the inaugural batch of students in 1912 comprised a mixture of medical and engineering students, and the first buildings were primarily for medical research and teaching.

The importance and popularity of medicine as a field of study in the university's profile and the imaginative work undertaken by its research academics should not be under-estimated. The current Vice-Chancellor, Tsui Lap-chee, is noted for his ground-breaking contribution to cystic fibrosis research in the United States. Latterly, one of the world's leading virologists, Guan Yi, who works between Hong Kong University and Shantou University in Guangdong, has been engaged in research of world-wide significance into the spread and containment of modern-day killer viruses such as H5N1 (avian flu) and SARS. The past was uncannily repeated when Hong Kong's wealthiest and most powerful businessman, Li Ka-shing, donated a staggering HK$1 billion in May 2005 as an endowment to the university's medical research school, which is now known as the Li Ka-shing School of Medicine.

A less desirable type of revolutionary than the "father of modern China" addressed students here in 1933. The cheerfully iconoclastic Irishman, George Bernard Shaw, urged the students to renounce

Western imperialism and align themselves with their brothers on the mainland. "If you are a revolutionary at the age of twenty, you have some chance of being up-to-date when you are forty," he told his youthful audience. He was subsequently introduced to a courteous Sir Robert Ho Tung and his wife, who failed to register the same level of alarm as the *Hong Kong Telegraph*. In an editorial worthy of the mother country's *Daily Telegraph*, its editor opined that jail was the only corrective for a rabble-rouser like Shaw. The colonial authorities were anxious about Shaw's potential for fomenting unrest among the best and brightest of the younger generation. In the event they need not have worried, Shaw being more concerned with the next leg of his tour to China.

In spite of the innate conservatism of the look of the university and the tendency of Hong Kong's student community to be more pragmatically preoccupied than Western students with their future careers, the university has on a number of occasions been a focus for intellectual support for popular protest. In the anti-colonialist movement of the late 1960s and 1970s, many university-educated protestors helped to bring about change to the Hong Kong official language policy and subsequently after the 1989 Tiananmen Square massacre students were heavily involved in the marches and arranged for a Goddess of Democracy effigy, resembling the one on the square, to be placed in a prominent position near the Student Union. Alumni of the university include the late lyricist James Wong, one of the fathers of Hong Kong's Canto-Pop genre, who completed his doctoral degree there. Before the musical revolution and the move to Cantonese lyrics in the 1970s, spearheaded by the talented Sam Hui, pop music and student folk music had been predominantly English. Hui and another prolific Canto-pop songsmith, George Lam are both, needless to say, Hong Kong University alumni.

Another famous lyricist—although he may not have been flattered to hear himself so described—to be strongly associated with the university was prolific First World War poet Edmund Blunden. Blunden was head of the English Department from 1950 to 1960, and wrote rhapsodically of his adoptive Hong Kong home. He also recorded in his poem "An Island Tragedy" the steady incursions of the city on the idyllic pastoral environment of the university in the late 1950s (in which process the university's own growth played its part). The poem envisages a cross between a Chinese wood-god or earth god and a Tolkein Treebeard figure standing amid the trees on the hill above the university, "the steady straw-haired monarch of the wood, as one defending his demesne".

> *... There he stood, for me he always will*
> *Poor giant, poor doomed straw-hair staring down*
> *From his starved rock towards the advancing town.*

Two other buildings to visit in the university environs are Hung Hing Ying Building, a small but elegant structure facing the main building of Loke Yew Hall, and Fung Ping Shan Museum. Designed as the student union and finished in 1919, the former's mixture of English baroque and Chinese architecture, especially the glass-domed rotunda, is pleasant to the eye though much of it had to be restored after extensive damage sustained during the Japanese occupation. No longer used as the student union, it has been imaginatively transformed into a Music Department facility equipped with a soundproofed studio.

The Fung Ping Shan Museum, formerly the university library built in 1932, is located at the bottom of the steep slopes on which the university stands, just above Bonham Road. The museum houses an impressive if small collection, including early Christian missionary crosses and Han Dynasty pottery and funeral objects. Also used as an art gallery, it regularly presents fascinating exhibitions, such as the highly acclaimed photographs of the brothels of the old Western District in bygone days. Another exhibition focused on the hitherto neglected collection of 1946-47 photographs of Hong Kong by German-born modernist photographer Hedda Morrison, who spent the war years in China and came to Hong Kong not long after the Japanese surrender. Her exquisitely composed black and white photos of a forgotten era preceding Hong Kong's dramatic transformation are showcased in Edward Stokes' tribute to her work, entitled *Hedda Morrison's Hong Kong*. Morrison's feeling for everyday subjects and her sharp-focus, highly revealing camera technique convey a sensitivity and implicit understanding that come from her years in China. She is able to capture natural scenes with formal eloquence, imparting dignity to her subjects and a fitting sense of distance and perspective to her compositions. More than many Western photographers she

Hong Kong University. Staircase (1915) leading up to May and Eliot Halls.

succeeds in representing Hong Kong as a Chinese city, albeit an exceptional one.

"City of Glass": the Myths of Eileen Chang

Among the university's distinguished alumni is modern Chinese literature's most original female voice, Eileen Chang (Chang Ai-ling), who died in 1995. Prolific novelist and short story writer, Chang studied at the Department of English from 1939 to 1941 and subsequently lived in Shanghai, Taiwan and the United States. Apart from her novella, *Love in a Fallen City*, which recounts the fall of Hong Kong to Japanese troops in December 1941 and is set in Western Mid-Levels and Repulse Bay, Chang did not write, ostensibly at least, very much about her Hong Kong experience. Yet there is no doubt, as with Dr. Sun, that her sojourn here, and particularly her study at Hong Kong University, left its mark on the values and attitudes she displayed throughout her writing career. The creative rigour she brought to her writing and her spirit of modernist individualism owed not a little to her university education.

Although a number of university myths and legends have grown up around Chang's time in the English Department, a number of other "golden" boys and girls especially of the late 1960s and 1970s have been depicted in various fictional guises in stories and films set in and around Hong Kong University. The halls of residence at the university—of which the earliest, May Hall and Eliot Hall, built in 1913, are still very elegant and fronted by a plaza with white balustraded steps—played an essential role in fostering team spirit. Individual halls such as the previously all-male St. John's College and Ricci Hall (named after Italian missionary and translator of Chinese, Matteo Ricci) and the all-female Lady Ho-tung Hall (named after Sir Robert Ho Tung's wife), situated opposite each other in Pokfulam Road, acquired a mystique that was deliberately intended to be redolent of the Oxbridge system.

The 1997 film, *City of Glass*, written and directed by Hong Kong University alumni, Mabel Cheung and Alex Law, made capital of such feelings of nostalgia for a golden age, and at the same time skilfully wove a tale that evoked not just the University's past glory but present and future realities in a more brittle world. The film, which stars one of Hong Kong's biggest film and pop stars, Leon Lai, tells the story of a love-at-first-sight relationship between Ricci Hall boy Raphael (Lai) and Lady Ho Tung Hall girl Vivien (Shu Qi). Believing their first love to be simply a stage along the path of their maturity and development, they both marry other spouses after graduation, but are brought back together by fate and coincidence. The film starts with their death in a car crash in London and continues with their respective son and daughter, who are, of course, unknown to each other, meeting each other to make arrangements for flying the bodies back to their families. *City of Glass* contains some of the best shots of the university halls, especially the old Lady Ho Tung Hall, prior to its demolition and restructuring as well as some stunning scenes captured inside Loke Yew Hall.

The title of the film, incidentally, refers to the fragile quality of the lives of the idealistic generation of students who emerged in the late Sixties and Seventies, as well as to the rapidly expanding glass and chrome skyscrapers in the metropolis. Contrasting starkly with the old colonial edifices of the students' *alma mater*, the twin-towered Shun Tak Centre in Sheung Wan and other such glass palaces of the post-modern age feature significantly. The Shun Tak Centre, which also houses the Macau Ferry Terminal, was in its would-be futuristic, reflective glass-square design emblematic of much of the hi-tech look that became *de rigueur* for corporations and architects. The glass palaces represent changes that are not altogether as negative as an older generation may have imagined. Raphael and Vivien's son and daughter do not face the same pressure to conform to alumni standards of respectability in a more complex but individualistic modern world. Paradoxically, things are more transparent for them at the end of the film, although their parents' world had seemed for a while more clear-cut.

"Rouge" and Old Shek Tong Tsui: The Story of Sai Wan (Western)

> A long isle displays its splendour on the sea
> Magnificent buildings everywhere to be seen,
> Yet, outlandish are the sing-song girls
> Who put new lyrics to old tunes.

Writer Wang Tao penned these lines on Hong Kong during a visit to British sinologist James Legge in 1866, a visit that would turn into a more permanent stay in the Territory. He might have written something more sympathetic about the "sing-song girls" after longer acquaintance with them, but he was presumably too deeply engaged in his translation collaboration with Legge.

The "sing-song girls", like their cousins the yum-yum girls in Chapter Three, have also inspired some memorable works of art. Arguably none is greater than Stanley Kwan's 1987 screen masterpiece *Rouge*, adapted from a novel by Lee Bik-wah entitled *Yin Tzi Kau* (The

Red Locket). By the 1930s when the background events of the story take place, Tai Ping Shan, which was where Wang Tao met his sing-song girls, had been cleared and the entertainment district moved down to Shek Tong Tsui, the part of Western District bordering Sai Ying Pun and Kennedy Town and situated right below the university. It is hard to imagine the present-day Shek Tong Tsui, nowadays an unprepossessing area of Western merging unremarkably into Kennedy Town, as a brothel district. This urban transformation itself forms part of the narrative, as the film jumps forward in time to the late 1980s, following a superb 1930s period opening set in the Yi Hung brothel opposite Tai Ping Theatre.

The disorientated viewer is confronted by Fleur, played by one of Hong Kong's great singer-actresses, Anita Mui, in her 1930s silk *cheong-sam* and elaborate make-up, requesting that newspaper advertising sales manager, Yuen, put an advertisement in the local paper for "Master 12". There are no words in the text, only the cryptic numerals 3811. Fleur follows a puzzled Yuen to Shek Tong Tsui. Rattled at first by her anachronistic appearance and her use of archaic language, Yuen is further discomposed when she appears out of nowhere on the tram he is taking towards Shek Tong Tsui. The viewer is privileged by the information gleaned from the opening scene in which handsome merchant's son Chen (Master 12—his family status) woos the beguilingly beautiful Fleur after she has intoxicated him with her singing of melancholy lyrics in the Shek Tong Tsui establishment. Afterwards he presents her with a beautiful rouge box, which she wears on a chain around her neck as a symbol of her fidelity. Cutting forward to the less romantic but more egalitarian 1980s, it becomes comically clear to us that the modern-day Yuen has no idea that this strange woman is a ghost. Alone with her on the top deck of the tram terminating in Whitty Street in Shek Tong Tsui, Yuen's face, as the penny drops, is an absolute picture.

Subsequently Yuen and his girlfriend, fellow-journalist Ah-Chor, learn Fleur's sentimental but moving tale of joint suicide with Chen in 1934 on 8 March at 11 pm (3811). She has been permitted to return from the underworld to find Chen (played by the great Leslie Cheung). There are some great shots in the film of the streets of the area as Fleur and her new-found mortal friends wait for Chen's appearance in response to the advertisement.

In a series of flashbacks and skilful montage shots the story moves restlessly backward and forward between 1930s and 1980s Hong Kong, and in doing so underlines not only Hong Kong's urban transformation but also its often concealed nostalgia for the "good old days" and predilection for both sentimental stories and ghost stories. The now vanished Tai Ping Theatre is shown in one scene with a Cantonese Opera in full swing. Chen, playing a minor role in the hope of becoming an actor, is harangued by his prospective in-laws and agrees to Fleur's proposal to escape life's frustrations by committing suicide together. The film cuts forward to the 1980s with a desolate Fleur unable to locate Chen, seeing the Chinese Opera action in her memory superimposed on the large glass window of the nondescript store that now stands on the site of the old theatre. Yuen and Ah-Chor find her gazing in rapt nostalgia and melancholy at the modern-day street theatre version of Cantonese Opera, which for ordinary people, especially in Western District, replaced the long demolished theatres. In an intense and cinematically rich finale Fleur is finally able to locate the real-life Chen, now a shadow of the man he was.

As critic Ackbar Abbas has pointed out, Stanley Kwan's film was highly topical, metaphorically. He sees a correlation between Fleur's fifty-year constancy, transcending even death, towards a man who was not worthy of her and Hong Kong's fifty years of no-change in its post-Handover relationship. (Hong Kong is now re-wedded to the mainland after a gap of over 150 years.) The fate of Shek Tong Tsui, once a thriving "entertainment district" and focus of commerce and local political meetings, supports Abbas' view. In 1935 prostitution was banned in the colony in one of the periodic bouts of British parliamentary Puritanism, so Shek Tong Tsui's temporary pre-eminence came to an abrupt end. Like the ghost of Fleur in *Rouge* the area's affluence vanished into thin air.

The film's controlled pathos and relationship between imagination, memory and loss was heightened for many Hong Kong fans by the death of superstars Leslie Cheung and Anita Mui. They died within a short space of one another not long after the 2003 SARS outbreak, thus completing for many residents Hong Kong's unluckiest year of the new millennium. The loss of Cheung, Hong Kong's favourite son, and a loyal friend to film and pop celebrity, Mui, may well have weakened the latter's desire to fight against a debilitating combination of cancer and

Triad extortion. The tragic irony of Leslie's sad suicide at age 46 and former street singer Mui's death at age 40 only serves to make Kwan's film both more poignant and more allegorical.

Another film which uses Western District as its locale is former martial arts actor and director Ng Ma's *The Story of Kennedy Town*. In Cantonese the film is actually entitled *The Story of Sai Wan* (or Western District). Although there is a fatal heist scene set in the far west part of Western in Kennedy Town, much of the film takes place in familiar locations in the central western area around Sai Ying Pun and below the university. The film is set in the early 1960s when petty Triad activity, which had been promoted by post-war austerity, was developing into an ugly turf war, further complicated by loan-shark practices, protection rackets and local police corruption. Three *fei jai* (teddy boys) swear allegiance to each other as blood brothers, but in spite of the good faith of two of them they become caught up in a lethal game of deception and corruption, engineered by the third, Peng, who has joined the police in order to give them inside advantage. The film has judiciously selected footage of old Western District, including the Magistrate's Court and Police Station in the steeply ascending Western Street (Sai-bin Gai) and a stunning night shot of Man-Mo Temple in Hollywood Road in all its finery. Another of Hong Kong's favourite sons of the entertainment business, singer-dancer-actor Aaron Kwok plays the duped but decent Wei, who exacts revenge for Peng's cold-blooded treachery in the tense final scene.

The Story of Kennedy Town is significant for introducing the theme of high-level corruption in the police force, especially the top-down corruption instituted by the senior ranks, as exemplified by real-life Chief Superintendent Peter Godber. The scandal of Godber's and other officers' cynical and systematic abuse of power and pernicious influence on Hong Kong's police force was only partly mitigated by the arrest and prosecution of the ringleaders in 1973. Sir Murray MacLehose, the new governor replacing the embattled Sir David Trench, was forced to act in establishing the ICAC (Independent Commission Against Corruption), a body that continues to tackle corruption in the SAR. Hong Kong's purged and reformed police force went some way towards losing its reputation for endemic graft, acquiring along the way the rather facile nickname "Asia's Finest". Time will tell how well merited this more recent appellation is, but

ICAC anti-corruption swoops have continued to feature senior level figures in connection with narcotics and other Triad-related collusion. Another feature of MacLehose's period of office was a new-found determination to give young people like the three blood brothers in the film, who might be otherwise lured into petty crime, a better future through education and service.

Han Suyin and Queen Mary Hospital: a Great "Hong Kong" Writer?

Climbing the steep Water Street that runs parallel to Western Street and the Police Station and refusing to be distracted by ghosts of Hong Kong past, we regain the level of the university. If we continue up and then travel west by bus or minibus along Pokfulam Road we can see Mount Davis Road on our right and behind it the sprawl of Pokfulam Cemetery. To our left is the extremely reputable Queen Mary Hospital, which was named after the consort of George V. Among other things Queen Mary Hospital is famous for its role in a memorable Hong Kong novel by a non-Hong Kong writer.

There is a colloquially dismissive or ironically self-effacing way of describing the writing profession in Hong Kong as *pa gaak tsi* or "crawling among the squares", since squared paper is more convenient for writing Chinese than lined. Some writers, particularly the great Beijing modernist Lu Xun, author of *The True Story of Ah-Q* and many other classic tales, have come to be held in high esteem among Hong Kong's intellectuals and cultural connoisseurs. But in general it would be fair to say that Hong Kongers have often had the tendency to play down or even dismiss local artistic endeavours. Similarly, local art-house film directors such as Wong Kar-wai have had to struggle against prejudiced popular sentiment about what is viewed as the pretentious nature of their work. *2046*, Wong's sequel to *In the Mood for Love*, features a hack writer-journalist crawling among the squares to write an ambitious novel about a journey into the future. The lack of recognition for such writing, except short-term commercial gain from newspaper serialization, has probably been a stumbling-block for creative writing in the Territory. Even after 1997 it is still generally assumed that the mainland, and particularly Beijing, is spiritual home to the Chinese cultural and literary tradition—not Hong Kong. Thus, unlike filmmaking or architecture, there is no precedent for any debate about great Hong Kong writing, since the subject rarely arises.

Han Suyin's 1952 novel *A Many-Splendoured Thing* has, however, a legitimate claim to being one of Hong Kong's greatest novels, certainly among those written in English. Han Suyin was a *nom de plume* for Dr. Elizabeth Tang, a mainland-born Eurasian with a Belgian mother and Chinese father. She was originally a doctor and subsequently an acknowledged author of fictional and autobiographical works. She obtained her qualifications at London University, where she studied after the death of her husband in the civil war in China in the 1930s. She worked at the Queen Mary Hospital, a modern and relatively well equipped hospital, which had been built in the 1930s. Although many scenes recounted in this fictionalized auto-biography are set on the south side of the island, in Central or at Kai Tak airport in Kowloon, the heart of the novel is located in Pokfulam, in and around the hospital.

The story of Suyin's sojourn in Hong Kong, and in particular her "many-splendoured" love affair with the British war correspondent Mark Elliott (a fictitious name for her real-life Australian lover, Times correspondent Ian Morrison, who was the brother-in-law of photographer Hedda Morrison) is related with a searching candour and signal absence of self-pity or mawkishness. Furthermore, the novel stands as an insightful and incisive social comment on the rapidly changing post-war world. Han Suyin paints a remarkably detailed and convincing picture of Hong Kong. Even so, her aim is not simply reportage. She presents in a dialectical narrative style the conflict of values and civilizations through the conversation and experiences of Hong Kong-based friends and colleagues, of missionaries, old China hands, mediocre and blinkered colonial snobs, and above all in her soul-searching discussions with Mark. Her love affair flouts the stifling and hypocritical code of behaviour of the era, all the more so since, as a Eurasian, she is considered socially inferior and therefore acting presumptuously in embarking on a liaison with Mark. Given the repressive US and British miscegenation laws of the late nineteenth and early twentieth centuries, it is not surprising that such stratification along ethnic and class lines was still firmly in place in the early 1950s. Novels like *The World of Suzie Wong* and *A Many-Splendoured Thing* represented a serious challenge to the then status quo, hard as that may be to appreciate from our twenty-first-century vantage-point.

The greatest quality of the novel is that it is epic in scope, presenting the writer's own emotional upheaval within the larger framework of the dramatic socio-political events of the period. The novel encapsulates the uncertainty and paradoxically the growth of Hong Kong, swelled with refugees from the communist victory on the mainland. In the latter part, Han Suyin's empathy with the people of Korea, caught up in their terrible civil war, is not diminished by the eventual death of Mark in a land-mine explosion. This visionary novel's lasting legacy is its combination of unflinching honesty and quiet hope for a better world, in which respect and equality among people of different nationalities and ethnicities replaces centuries of exploitation and distrust.

Han Suyin, now resident in Switzerland, gave permission for the publication of an extract from the work in the Hong Kong anthology, *City Voices*, but distanced herself from her most famous novel, implying that for her it no longer mattered. Yet her writing on Hong Kong still matters for anyone trying to understand the complex and unique congruence of East and West that is part of the city's psyche:

> *Hongkong, excrescence off the coast of China, magnificent entrepot of commerce and appalling social anachronism, island of monopolies, where destitution is a punishable offence and refugee camps bloomed; Hong Kong, poised between land and sea, dependent on China for its birth and the existence of its sumptuous capitalist enterprise; Hongkong, the haven of many, like myself, waiting to make up their minds; waiting to let the dust settle, waiting to choose.*

Pokfulam Reservoir and Country Park, Conduit Road and Mei Lanfang

Pokfulam, or Pok Fu Lam to give it the customary three-word or syllable name in Cantonese, is one the oldest recorded village on Hong Kong Island, having been referred to in Qing Dynasty gazettes dating back to the 1720s. The village has given its name to the whole district as well as the main road. It remains a small village with its own ancestral hall and pagoda. The island's western water reservoir, actually located closer to the Peak than it is to the village of Pok Fu Lam, is called Pokfulam Reservoir. The reservoir was built in 1863 but was the subject of strong contention between fourth governor, Sir John Bowring, and the colonial surgeon, Dr. Harland, who pressed for the project to go ahead as a matter of urgency in order to deal with the serious lack of clean water for a rapidly growing population. It was connected via an aqueduct skirting Conduit Road (hence its name) to tanks above Tai Ping Shan in order to supply the Western and Central districts with fresh water. Bowring's obstructive approach to the scheme was rooted in his determination to proceed with his self-glorifying Bowrington-Victoria Praya development (see Chapter Three), and there were insufficient funds available to finance both schemes.

Behind the university and at the foot of the country park leading up to the Peak are the steep Kotewall Road and what Wang Tao would have described back in the 1860s as the Upper Ring of the European settlement on the island. This consisted of the Mid-Levels streets, Robinson Road and Conduit Road, through which Dr. Harland's water scheme for the expanding north side of the island was channeled. Hercules Robinson was Bowring's replacement. He was greeted with a sense of public relief and goodwill similar to Tung Chee-hwa's replacement as Chief Executive, Donald Tsang, in June 2005. One of this Hercules' first labours was to expedite the stalled and urgently needed water supply scheme, which explains his close association with Pokfulam and the Mid-Levels, through which the pipes passed. Fortunately common sense prevailed after Bowring's departure in 1859 and work began on the construction of the reservoir as a matter of priority. A small house was also built at the site by the government to house a permanent guard with the aim of preventing any potential poisoning attempt on the water supply.

Conduit Road, incidentally, was also associated with China's greatest modern Chinese Opera actor, Mei Lanfang, who lived here during the Japanese occupation. Famed for his interpretation of *dan* (female) roles in Beijing Opera, Mei Lanfang introduced the elevated Chinese art form in the West in the 1920s. Refusing to perform for the more culturally sophisticated Japanese officers on the mainland out of a deep sense of patriotism, he fled to Hong Kong. Here he grew a moustache as a statement of his unwillingness to entertain the enemy. He was able to count on Hong Kong's reputed lack of cultural development at this time and on a less aesthetically sophisticated variety of the Japanese officer class to ensure that he remained more or less incognito in his No.8 Conduit Road hide-out.

Writing in the 1880s about life in Pokfulam, Dr. Legge's friend from the mainland, Wang Tao, who had now settled in Hong Kong, observed: "Many Europeans have built their summer houses in the district known as Pokfulam. This picturesque neighbourhood is a fit place for those who seek solitude and relaxation." Certainly, the Pokfulam Country Park, which surrounds the area is thickly wooded and one of the greenest parts of the island. It remains relatively unspoiled by the frantic pace of development that has affected most of the northern side of the island. In that respect the area has much in common with the south side and Peak of Hong Kong Island.

Perched picturesquely in the glades above the long and winding Pokfulam Road stands University Hall, an imposing mid-nineteenth-century building, built along the lines of a fortress with turrets. It was originally the home of the Scottish Lapraik family. Douglas Lapraik became a shipping magnate after the success of his docks in Aberdeen (Hong Kong Aberdeen, rather then the Scottish city of the same name), and his steamship company gave him enough profits to build a family seat in Pokfulam, which he named Douglas Castle. One of the most interesting features of the interior is the wrought-iron interior spiral staircase. This former mansion of the would-be Laird of Douglas has been used as a Hong Kong University hall of residence since 1954. Just across the road from "Douglas Castle", or University Hall, to be more prosaic, is the former French Mission House simply called "Bethany". It acquired a reputation in the nineteenth century as a printing-house for religious texts in multiple Asian languages. Standing outside the ornate former mansion and the monastic publishing-house we seem to be a thousand miles away from the urban hustle and bustle of Western District. In the imagination of its eccentric first laird we are, of course, in the glens of Scotland. This imaginative conceit persists as we cross the delightfully shaded and thickly wooded Pokfulam Country Park, past the reservoir, in the direction of the busy waterfront of Aberdeen.

If the more arduous scenic route over the Peak is a deterrent, we can always hop on a bus along Pokfulam Road and enjoy picturesque views over the western approaches of Hong Kong out to Lantau and Lamma Island. En route we may catch a glimpse of Richard Li's (son of Hong Kong's richest tycoon) hi-tech project, the Cyberport (which masqueraded as the futuristic new Central Police Station in the last of the *Infernal Affairs* film trilogy) on the waterfront below Victoria Road. Before we explore the south side of the island, however, it might be opportune to head back up to the Peak. No visit to Hong Kong would be complete without experiencing its unique attractions.

chapter five

A FLOATING WORLD:
THE PEAK, ABERDEEN, STANLEY
AND REPULSE BAY

Rarified Air

Before she arose to the Peak
Matilda was timid and meek.
But she now condescends
To her Bowen Road friends
with a smile that is cutting and bleak.

This anonymous limerick was aimed at a lady whose name is now almost synonymous with Hong Kong's pinnacle of social climbers, Matilda Sharp. The present-day Matilda Hospital, which stands at one corner of the circular Mount Kellett Road, was named after this redoubtable Victorian lady. Matilda and her property speculator and financier husband, Granville, moved from Bowen Road in the middle-class Mid-Levels into a house part-way up Victoria Peak. The construction of the hospital was a bequest in Granville's will to commemorate Matilda, who died a few years before him in 1893 aged 64. The hospital, a handsome white-fronted building, was completed in 1907 and above the entrance is a legend on marble stone in her memory. When it opened the hospital was only available for treatment to British residents, and in any case the blatantly racist Peak Ordinance barred non-Europeans from living on the Peak. Wealthy Eurasian Sir Robert Ho Tung had inadvertently challenged the race bar by buying his house in the 1890s before the Ordinance came in to effect. As the twentieth century progressed, the stricture became gradually harder to enforce, and after the Second World War the Ordinance was repealed. Nowadays anyone who can afford the high cost of living in this "exclusive" neighbourhood and of being treated at the private hospital is admitted.

The Peak Tram: in its contemporary incarnation.

The annual Matilda sedan chair race in November, which raises money for local charities, recalls an era before motorized transport when patients were carried from the Peak Tram terminus to the Matilda Hospital by this human mode of conveyance. In fact, before the construction of the Peak Tram in the 1880s sedan chair was the only means of transport available to access the Peak for those unwilling or unable to make the ascent on foot. As a means of locomotion, the sedan chair has something in common with the rickshaw, which today has only tourist novelty value. The modern-day counterparts of the sedan-chair carriers race over a stretch of two miles to the end of Mount Kellett Road to reach the hospital. Unlike the more functional sedan chair of a bygone era, the chairs used in the event are extravagantly decked out and supported by eight runners. The occupant has to be over 16 years of age, alive and human—so at least nothing has changed in this particular!

Matilda's limerick may itself be as "cutting" as its target's smile, but it is also revealing of the close correspondence between social status and an address on Hong Kong Island's highest point. "I am never tired of the view from this house," writes Matilda's sister, Lucilla, in a letter of 1865. "We are above everyone else and look down on the blue waters of the harbour and the distant hills, while the grand old Peak rises behind us." Apart from making Hong Kong's summit sound like the Duke of York in the nursery rhyme, she puts her finger on the essence of being on the Peak—being above everyone else. Even before the advent of the Europeans, pirate Cheung Po-tsai used the place as a lookout. Then, as now, it commanded an almost-180-degree view of the waters around Hong Kong, making it easy for the pirates to spot suitable prey and to convey a signal to the fleet anchored below in Sai Ying Pun.

Matilda and her sister described the wildness of the place in their correspondence, and emphasize the necessity of being armed against the putative descendants of Cheung Po-tsai. They also refer to the occasional picnic up the Peak: "We did not go to the very top, that was too far, but about half-way, to a place called the Gap." (They were probably sitting at the point where the Peak Tram upper terminus is now located.) 'The scenery was splendidly wild and as we wound higher and higher up the Peak the ships in the harbour looked like small boats... We had to pass through wild ravines down which rushed

foaming streams. Wild flowers and ferns grew around us in profusion…
and amongst them were many of the English garden flowers. We had
several revolvers with us, for, beautiful as the scenery is, Chinese thieves
abound…"

Matilda's letters and diaries give a detailed picture of a virtually
frontier Peak that is difficult to imagine from the comfort of our own
era, in which something of the aura of places like the Peak is inevitably
lost in the process of conquering them. In one letter written in 1866 she
describes to another sister, Marian, the joy of having a piano in her Peak
residence. For the middle-class Victorian family the piano was almost
an emblem of civilized respectability, but it is likely that the capable
Matilda acquitted herself well on the instrument and was delighted for
purely musical reasons that the arduous task had proved manageable:
"Fancy moving a grand piano up a mountainside 1700 feet high. It
required twelve coolies and a head coolie to superintend them, and a
pianoforte tuner followed behind."

Timothy Mo's description of the ascent in the last part of his semi-
fictional epic, *An Insular Possession* (see Chapter One of this book) also
gives an excellent thumbnail sketch of an exhilaratingly wild and
virtually uninhabited Peak, and conveys its special ambience, as
palpable today as it was in 1841. Not only does the summit afford a
breathtaking panorama of Hong Kong and the surrounding South
China Sea, but the marked drop in temperature one experiences has
long been one of the Peak's most prized features. When the rest of Hong
Kong swelters in summer heat and humidity, the Peak provides cooling
breezes. By contrast, in Hong Kong's generally mild winter, the Peak's
micro-climate ensures that heating is switched on and overcoats worn.
In the rainy season the Peak has the tendency to be cut off, not so much
nowadays by landslides, but by the heavy damp mist that descends
without warning and lays its clammy fingers in every place.

Having said that, the superbly scenic walk around Lugard Road at
the top of the Peak, which can be done in either clockwise or
anticlockwise direction, must be one of the most satisfying and soul-
soothing perambulations on earth. To the accompaniment of birds
singing and relatively few other sounds, such as children playing, one
can get an almost unrivalled view of Hong Kong and Kowloon. Tai Mo
Shan in the eastern New Territories, which exceeds the Peak in height,
can be observed on a clear day, as can many of the outlying islands. The

great variety of trees and birds to be seen on this walk, as with many others in Hong Kong's country parks, give the lie to any notion that Hong Kong is essentially a skyscraper metropolis. Indeed, from the vantage-point of the Peak, the skyscrapers themselves enhance the beauty of the prospect. From the south side of the Peak, the view is toward Pokfulam Reservoir, Aberdeen and Lamma Island, with its distinctive power station chimneys disfiguring an otherwise pastoral panorama.

Walking up to the Peak from Conduit Road or Kotewall Road above Western District brings the walker out onto the Lugard Road walk, but the other walking route is up Old Peak Road from Central. The winding and picturesque Old Peak Road was formerly the best way to access the Peak and many Victorian ramblers wended their way up this route, the ascent being, however, equally taxing. The Peak Hotel, which was built by A. Findley Smith in the 1870s, became such a popular resort during the summer months of unbearable humidity (in the days before air-conditioning had ever been imagined) that Findley Smith decided to construct a funicular railway for more convenient access. The Peak Tram, as came to be known, was completed in 1888, ascending directly from Garden Road above Central to a point adjacent to the top of Old Peak Road and Lugard Road. From there Mount Austin Road, climbs steeply to the very summit, previously reserved for the exclusive use of the governor, which the Victorian denizens rather predictably called Victoria Peak. Built on similar principles to other trams, such as that in Georgetown, Penang, the Peak Tram climbs 1,200 feet above sea level and is 4,500 feet long. The principle by which the forces of the up-bound and down-bound trams are evenly distributed works as effectively with modern electricity as with earlier steam-power.

The present-day Peak Tram Terminal Tower only dates back to 1996 and was an award-winning architectural design. Shaped rather like an orange segment, it is supported by four concrete pillars, under which is the tram terminal, full of tourist shops. It seems deliberately constructed to appear from a distance as though it were floating in mid-air, which brings to mind novelist Xi Xi's imaginative conceit of the floating city. Its viewing platform commands an impressive view over the city, but so too does the more traditional Chinese-style lookout balcony situated close to the terminal at the top of Old Peak Road. It is worth remembering that the latter affords shade, while the former, to quote Juanita Cheung in *Hong Kong: A Guide to Recent Architecture*, "offers as much protection from the summer heat and sun's glare as an airport runway."

By the early 1950s, nearly one hundred years after Matilda and family had set the colonial precedent for living among the clouds, the Peak was still very much the preserve of the colonial elite. Long-time Hong Kong resident and novelist Martin Booth wrote in his childhood memoir, *Gweilo*, on the stark comparison between his early experiences of living on Kowloon-side and the family's subsequent move to government quarters on the very tip of the Peak at Mount Austin: "Life on the Peak had as much in common with that in Kowoon as a bowl of fish-soup at a *dai pai dong* [cheap local restaurant] had to a traditional English fried breakfast, with or without salad cream." The chapter, entitled "Living On Clouds", tells of Booth's amazement at the 180-degree panorama and the fact that there were fish to be seen in the mountain streams and even small red deer. But it also conveys his feeling of alienation, having settled in happily to a more culturally integrated life with Hong Kong Chinese neighbours on Kowloon-side during the first year of his stay. Most amusingly, he tells of a school play performance of *Toad of Toad Hall* at the Peak School near the Matilda Hospital. In the production he was reluctantly obliged to play the part of Mole, but his costume, made by the Kowloon tailor his mother normally patronized, made him appear "a mutant creature of indeterminate species and origin". When his family moved back to Soares Avenue in the Mong kok area, the young Martin was, according to his older self, perfectly happy to be back in the less rarified air of that busy environment, despite having enjoyed the natural beauty of the Peak.

Most written descriptions of the Peak, including fictional ones, represent its exquisite scenery under calm blue skies with tranquil seas spread out below. John Le Carré, by contrast, evokes a rain-lashed, fog-bound Peak in *The Honourable Schoolboy*, as the newshounds attempt to race up Magazine Gap Road and then Peak Road in order to get the inside story on the withdrawal of the intelligence staff from the fictional High Haven (which Le Carré modelled, incidentally, on the real-life house known as Stoneycroft at 28 Mt. Austin Road):

The taxi was a red Mercedes, quite new, but nowhere kills a car faster than the Peak, climbing at no speed forever, air-conditioners at full blast. The weather continued awful. As they sobbed slowly up the concrete cliffs they were engulfed by a fog thick enough to choke on. When they got out it was even worse. A hot, unbudgeable curtain had spread itself across the summit, reeking with petrol and crammed with the din of the valley. The moisture floated in hot fine swarms. On a clear day they would have had a view both ways, one of the loveliest on earth: northward to Kowloon and the blue mountains of the New Territories, which hid from sight the eight hundred million Chinese, who lacked the privilege of British rule; southward to Repulse and Deepwater Bays and the open China Sea. High Haven had been built by the Royal Navy in the twenties in all the grand innocence of that service, to receive and impart a sense of power.

Le Carré's reference to "the privilege of British rule" is, of course, shot through with his trademark irony. The novel, without a shadow of a doubt the greatest Hong Kong-London novel ever written, is deeply ambivalent about the role of the Western powers in Asia, but gives an affectionately observant and compelling portrait of 1970s Hong Kong.

Shanghai-born, but Hong Kong permanent resident, Liu Yichang, who can lay claim to being one of the city's most important modern fiction writers, depicts the Peak in plainer language in his long short story, *Indecision*. His main character and narrator, a Shanghai woman who has come to late Hong Kong to take care of deceased sister's children, is caught in two minds about whether to stay or go back to her mentally ill husband across the border. The plain narrative style underlines the fact that the narrator is a plain-speaking woman, trapped in an acute dilemma. Both her boss, fellow Shanghainese Xu Hong, and her brother-in-law are attempting to woo her. Her instincts prompt her to respond to Xu Hong but not to her brother-in-law. But her sister has entrusted the children to her care. She is invited out for dinner to the Peak by both men on separate occasions:

Hong Kong at night is really very beautiful. Looking down from here, the Kowloon peninsula in the distance is as beautiful as a painting. Actually it is even more beautiful than a painting. Lights have been switched on in thousands of buildings, and they glimmer like slivers of pearl on a piece of black velvet. The ships afloat in the harbour channel, the tall buildings in Central—they are real, but they also seem to lack the reality they should have. This restaurant is called Peak Tower Restaurant. I like it. I've been here once already…Last time, when my brother-in-law brought me here, we took the Peak Tram. That was the first time I rode in a cable car… When the tram went up the hillside I thought the scenery outside the window had tilted. At that moment I must admit that I was a bit scared. But just now, when Xu Hong drove his car uphill, while the journey was much longer and the scenery on the way was very nice, I did not feel excited.

There are various options in both the ascent and the descent of the Peak, as there are for Liu Yichang's narrator in choosing her next step, but how to get up or down the Peak is the least of her worries. If we opt to walk down the southern side of the Peak, there is a trail through the thickly wooded slopes (planted not just for pastoral beauty but more importantly for landslide prevention) of Aberdeen Country Park and past the upper and lower Aberdeen Reservoirs. Alternatively we can take the Peak Tram and catch a bus from Central to Aberdeen centre. Another path, the one that connects with Lugard Road, heads down to Conduit Road and the Mid-Levels. Do all ways lead to the Peak? For tourists certainly, and for wealthy Hong Kongers too. Increasingly, though, locals from all over Hong Kong come for both the photogenic panorama, and the shopping in the Peak Galleria shopping mall.

Aberdeen: Dragons and Dragon-boats

Aberdeen is known as Little Hong Kong (Heung Gong Jai) to local people. It got its English, or rather Scottish, name from Lord Aberdeen, who took over the Foreign Secretary post when the failing Whig government in Britain fell to the Tories in 1841, a few months after the annexation of Hong Kong. It might have been called Palmerston had that come-back specialist timed his exits and entrances a little better, but then Hong Kong might not have been what it is today, if the "mortified and disappointed" (according to his letter to Queen Victoria) Foreign Secretary had not lost office in that critical year. Both Viscount Palmerston and Lord Aberdeen accepted the *de facto* acquisition of Hong Kong less than enthusiastically. Aberdeen saw it more as a bargaining pawn than a long-term acquisition, while Palmerston esteemed it even less. Fittingly, therefore, only his Lordship is commemorated—perhaps for his greater pragmatism.

Aberdeen was settled long before the British sailors arrived, and its temples to Tin Hau, the sea goddess, attest to a long tradition of seafaring in the vicinity. Its role as a port flourished between the fourteenth and seventeenth centuries when sandalwood (*taang heung muk*) was brought here in junks from Lantau Island and the area around Sha Tin to be dispatched in larger boats up the East China coast to major cities. Clearly the *heung* (Hong) reference in Hong Kong's Chinese name is to the trade in fragrant sandalwood, which was especially useful in the manufacture of joss sticks. This local industry was killed off by the harsh scorched-earth "clearance" policy instigated by the Emperor in 1662 and aimed at depriving the pirates of safe havens on shore. Thereafter the inhabitants were Tanka and Hoklo boat-people, who made a living from the seas and spent their lives on boats in Heung Gong Jai's sheltered harbour.

Aberdeen, like many places in Hong Kong, had not really recovered from deforestation and depopulation by the early eighteenth century, when the British sailors came calling. Before the official "possession" of Hong Kong, sailors landing here in search of fresh water assumed that this was the principal place in Hong Kong, which it was—according to their charts. Lieutenant Collinson, after whom Cape Collinson on the north-east coast of the island is named, noted as much in the first full British survey: "Hong Kong Bay (called Hong Kong on the map) is the proper Hong Kong of the island and is the largest and best cultivated and prettiest in the island."

Adjoining Heung Gong Jai there was a walled village known as Heung Gong Wai, and next to it another village called Shek Pai Wan. Shek Pai Wan is now integrated into modern Aberdeen. The Tin Wan-Aberdeen-Shek Pai Wan-Ap Lei Chau cluster is located along the main road leading from Pokfulam round to the south coast of Hong Kong Island. It is home to a lively community, some of whom (especially its many seafood restaurants) are still connected to the sea. The Aberdeen district as a whole is no longer totally dependent on mariculture, as it was formerly, and the usual range of shops and businesses can be found in Aberdeen Centre.

Nevertheless a thriving boating community is still in evidence as one strolls along the waterfront, Aberdeen Praya. From the landing stages one can be ferried across to the famous floating Jumbo Restaurant, as William Holden and Jennifer Jones were in the romantic full-moon dining scene in the film version of Han Suyin's *A Many Splendoured Thing*. Han Suyin herself remembered the occasion somewhat differently from director Henry King and screenwriter John Patrick. As the author herself recounts, there were fourteen in the party, ten adults and four children, hardly an intimate *tête-à-tête*.

Twenty years later the same location is used for a panoramic sequence full of long takes and sweeping seaward and harbour-front pans in Robert Clouse's *Enter the Dragon* (1973). This was the film that cemented former child-star Bruce Lee's fast-developing reputation as an international martial arts superstar shortly before his premature demise at the age of only thirty two. As Bey Logan has pointed out in *Hong Kong Action Cinema*, "Bruce Lee's presence permeates *Enter the Dragon* from start to finish." A very different atmosphere prevails in this Aberdeen-set scene, one that is in stark contrast to the night-time serenity of *A Many-Splendoured Thing*. For one thing, the local boat-people are real people, not mere appendages to William Holden's and Jennifer Jones' felicity. The harshness of their living conditions, as caught in the revealing close-ups, is not glossed over in favour of mere spectacle. The longer shots of the busy harbour between Aberdeen Praya and Ap Lei Chau (minus its present-day high-rise middle-class housing blocks) show a seafaring community plying its trade on the familiar squat small boats known as *kaidos*, and suffering from the social privations that have long been their lot. This scene has one principal function, to express Lee's sympathy with the underdog, which lies at the heart of his own screen interpretation, irrespective of the original shooting script. The story is based loosely on the James Bond *Dr. No* narrative with a hint of Sax Rohmer's *Fu Manchu* in the portrayal of evil criminal mastermind Han, played by Hong Kong martial movie veteran Shek Kin.

The adult Lee's regrettably few films gained a new-found respect in the West among film fans of the martial tradition in Chinese culture. It was an unlikely success, for Lee's characters always express his own philosophy (Lee majored in Philosophy at university) based on Taoist and Buddhist principles, and are, unlike James Bond, contemptuous of hedonistic, fashionable pleasures. The sheer dazzling speed of Bruce Lee's personalized martial arts technique, which he called *jeet koon do*, mesmerized cinema audiences worldwide, ensuring a cult status that has never declined. As Jackie Chan has pointed out, other martial arts stars that followed in Lee's footsteps had to adopt a radically different approach to avoid paling in comparison to the master. The serious side of Lee is evident in the *kaido* scene, as he broods on the brutal and fatal attack on his sister by Han's henchmen to the backdrop of a crowded waterfront, remarkable for its relative lack of high-rises. A black American martial artist, like Lee heading by *kaido* for the bigger junk that will carry them to Han's island fortress for the martial arts competition, also reflects—in flashback, like Lee—on the racial prejudice he has encountered on his journey. A strong correlation is made between the two martial arts men and a sense of sympathy with the literally and metaphorically marginalized boat people is conveyed.

On the junk an encounter with the arrogant type of *gweilo* Lee despises, in which Bruce uses his mental ingenuity alone to humiliate the bully, strengthens the impression that Lee himself had more than a hand in script development. As fight choreographer he also exercised considerable control over the emotion conveyed in many scenes. The Aberdeen scene, in which Bruce is clearly in mourning for his sister, is attenuated by the spare, hollow-eyed look that the star had acquired in the last year of his life. Here was an apparently American film that had been skilfully hijacked by Lee to express his own message, not only about respecting Chinese culture and civilization but also about the exploitation of human drones by wealthy and unscrupulous individuals. It did not take long for some Asian audiences to see in Lee's cinematic message an allegory of relations between the East and the West and, more pertinently, between the First and Third Worlds.

Also departing from Aberdeen Praya are regular ferries to Lamma Island, to the south-west, as well as the very short journey by *kaido* to the older part of Ap Lei Chau (*chau* meaning "island" in Cantonese). The trip through the maze of boats tends to be more straightforward than it was in the 1970s when the harbour was extremely crowded. Nowadays it is still a bustling small port, but the emphasis is directed more towards leisure and tourism than in the past, although fishing boats still operate here, supplying Aberdeen's many seafood restaurants as well as other parts of the island.

Taking a short trip to Ap Lei Chau brings one into contact with the older Aberdeen maritime ethos. Not only are there marine suppliers' shops on the old-fashioned waterfront, but nearby is probably the oldest surviving temple on the island, Hung Shing Temple, built in 1770 and still in reasonably good repair. The importance of temples and religious rituals cannot be overestimated for the boatpeople of Aberdeen. This explains why the Hung Shing Temple and Tin Hau Temple in Shek Pai Wan have a long tradition as places of prayer and thanksgiving to the gods for safe return and bountiful catches. Red ribbons tied to the prow, emblems of the boatpeople's faith in the power of the gods to assist them in the pursuit of their often hazardous livelihood—especially in time of typhoons—flutter in the wind. Aberdeen is a sight not to be missed.

Dragon Boat Festival or Tuen Ng, which takes place in early June (the fifth day of the fifth moon in the Chinese calendar), is a good time to be in Aberdeen or Stanley to watch the highly entertaining boat races. The festival commemorates the suicide by drowning from a boat of a royal adviser called Wat Yuen in fourth-century BC China. Despairing of the venality and sycophancy which prevailed at court, Wat Yuen wrote poems entitled *Li Shao* to draw the king's attention to the moral corruption of his contemporaries. When these had no effect he threw himself into the river and drowned, while his attendants beat drums to frighten away fish that might otherwise devour his body. This is why Dragon Boat races are accompanied by drum-beating and furiously energetic paddling. The races have grown from humble ritual beginnings to an international sport in Hong Kong with teams from many overseas countries participating in races held the weekend following Hong Kong's own traditional races. Aberdeen in the south and Shau Kei Wan on the northern side were the original venues of Dragon Boat racing in Hong Kong, but this highly competitive event is now held in many coastal locations around the Territory.

Ocean Park (Hoi Yeung Gung Yun), standing on a rocky spur east of Aberdeen and west of Deepwater Bay, is also an exceptional place for marine life—but of an animal rather than human variety. Constructed in 1977 and financed by the Royal Hong Kong Jockey Club, it is the world's biggest oceanarium. It boasts a dolphinarium and a large open-air arena where one can witness performances by highly trained sea-lions and dolphins. Its aquarium, four tiers deep, is another of its main attractions and contains hundreds of marine species. The oceanarium is situated on the high headland section of Ocean Park accessible by cable car from the entrance below. The cable-car ride is a perfect way of enjoying the south-side panorama with spectacular views out east toward Deepwater Bay and west to Aberdeen. As one approaches the headland station, the vista over the park and the South China Sea ahead is breathtaking. The Ocean Park cable-car ride ranks with the Star Ferry and the Peak Tram as the most uplifting and magical experiences that Hong Kong has to offer.

If the blissfully peaceful cable-car ride is not sufficient stimulation to the senses, other kinds of rides including water rides and roller-coasters are among the world's longest and fastest. Below in the lower-ground section of the park are the zoo, aviary and home to Hong Kong's two pandas—not indigenous of course, but a gift of the Chinese government. There is also a spectacular aquatic amusement park called Water World. Close to Water World at the lower level is a Chinese culture theme park, called Middle Kingdom (a translation of the Chinese word for China) the more extensive Middle Kingdom takes the visitor on a journey through the China's traditional arts, handicraft and culture. It offers many theatrical and cultural spectacles, as well as arts and crafts demonstrations.

Since the low-point of the 2003 SARS scare, Western tourism has certainly begun to recover. At the same time, the introduction by the mainland government of more liberal tourism policies for Hong Kong—particularly the right of private tourists to visit, as opposed to the more strictly regimented group tours of previous years—has made an enormous difference to the economy and contributed in no small way to its speedy recovery from the Asian crash. Further evidence for this is the new spa hotel being built next to the Ocean Park site.

Assuming that we are not on a China mainland group tour, we take public transport or our own form of locomotion round a few more bends to arrive at the attractive Deepwater Bay with its picturesque eight-hole golf course and pleasant sandy beach. This is popular with local swimmers, but it has to be remembered that none of the beaches in Hong Kong enjoys international standards for cleanliness. Like most other beaches, it has a shark net and lookout platforms for lifeguards. A few minutes drive by car or bus brings us around a bend high above sea-level, from which the magnificent prospect of Repulse Bay stretches out below with the South China Sea lapping at its long sandy beaches.

Repulse Bay

According to Hong Kong legend, as we have seen, Repulse Bay was named after the rejected marriage request of a young soldier. (To make a perfect pair the legend has the young lady accept the proposal at Happy Valley shortly afterwards.) Personally one is inclined to doubt this convenient and symmetrical explanation on the grounds of implausibility: the story is too simple and neat. Another more plausible but not proven theory for the derivation of the name is as follows: the South China Sea off Repulse Bay being still infested with pirates in the early years of the colony, Her Majesty's Navy and notably HMS *Repulse* succeeded in ridding the coast of this long-time scourge. Thus the place name in English is assumed to have come from the critical role that the frigate played in this important operation. In any case, Repulse Bay is not all it seems to be. For one thing, its long golden sands, rather like fashionable young Hong Kongers' dyed blond hair, are not natural blond. The sand was imported from other beaches in Asia to help create a world-class tourist facility, a designation which Repulse Bay's superbly picturesque bay setting clearly merits.

The main southern route past Deepwater Bay intersects with Repulse Bay Road, which descends steeply and spectacularly from Wong Nai Chung Gap. Either drive (or walk) offers magnificent views across the bay and out to sea towards the scattered small outlying islands. To arrive at Repulse Bay Beach or the adjacent South Bay, one has to fork off the main road, passing through Repulse Bay on the way to Stanley. It is well worth making the detour to the beaches at Repulse Bay and South Bay, but for the cultural historian Repulse Bay Apartments—formerly Repulse Bay Hotel—is not to be missed. This was the place where the British Army made a desperate stand against the Japanese invaders in December 1941. Since an invasion from the south was anticipated, Hong Kong's ultimately inadequate defences were concentrated here, at Stanley and at other coastal emplacements on the east coast. In the event, the attack came via the northern overland route, which meant that guns stationed on the south and east coasts of Hong Kong Island could not respond to the initial waves of the Japanese assault.

Repulse Bay Apartments were erected in 1989, combining art deco-style high-rise apartments with a pastiche of the original colonial hotel of the 1920s. The effect of the stylistic fusion by a Hong Kong group of architects is surprisingly harmonious, if slightly schizophrenic. Obviously the historical significance of the original Repulse Bay Hotel justified recourse to a retro style that is rarely seen in Hong Kong, except in very recent conservation and renovation projects. Perhaps the phenomenon is less a matter of nostalgia for colonial-era edifices than a growing confidence in asserting local identity and local history. The apartments themselves, complete with a huge eight-storey-high hole right in the centre for the sake of the building's *fung shui*, reproduce the effect of modern art deco buildings with their curved façade, suggesting the form of the crest of a wave. This feature definitely enhances the *fung shui*. The inhabitants, mainly expatriates housed at the expense of multinationals in these luxury apartments, have everything going for them anyway, even without the benign influence of the *fung shui*.

The replica version of the original hotel includes shops, clinics and a clubhouse with lawn and sunshades, where the modern equivalent of "tiffin" can be consumed in reassuring retro-look serenity. It is as if the croquet players could pick up their long-abandoned game at any moment and Stamford Raffles impersonators stroll suavely in the company of poised Edwardian ladies. The elegantly *passé* ambience of the place is shattered by the prosaic reality of beachgoers and T-shirted shoppers in the vicinity of the big Welcome supermarket. Hard as it is to imagine if one looks at the site today, the old Repulse Bay Hotel was home to many celebrities of the 1920s and 1930s. One Western celebrity who stayed here many times was ballet dancing great, Dame Margot Fonteyn. Fonteyn, born in northern China, made good friends in Hong Kong and danced at the first Hong Kong Arts Festival at Causeway Bay's Lee Theatre.

Writer Eileen Chang used the hotel as backdrop to one of the most spectacular scenes in her novella *Love in a Fallen City*. The inception of the passionate love affair between the Shanghainese protagonists, playboy Fan Liuyuan and abandoned wife Bai Liusu, coincides with the onslaught of the Japanese army. Although, as we witness in director Ann Hui's 1986 film adaptation of the story, the hotel takes a severe battering, miraculously it survived and functioned as a hospital for the wounded. After the war it was patched up, and largely regained its pre-war popularity between the late 1940s and early 1960s. The film of *Love in a Fallen City*, now regarded as among the classics of the Shaw Brothers' prolific movie catalogue, was shot on location in the original hotel just prior to its demolition. It includes some impressive exterior shots of the building as well as a thoroughly authentic re-enactment of the siege from the perspective of the civilians and soldiers trapped inside.

Timothy Mo's first novel, *The Monkey King*, also uses the Repulse Bay Hotel as a fictional-factual setting to enhance the work's local Hong Kong feel circa 1953. The reluctant hero, over-cautious and status-conscious Eurasian Wallace Nolasco, is ironically identified with one of Chinese Literature's most enduring and resilient characters, the cunning Monkey from the classic story *Journey to the West*. In the Repulse Bay Hotel tea-dance scene, Wallace and his new wife May Ling are seeking allies in Wallace's worldly fellow Macanese, Mabel Yip, and his attractive and well-connected cousin Pippy. Wallace hopes that the influential Mabel will help them in their struggle for recognition in the traditional hierarchy of the Poon family. Having tea with Mabel and Pippy in the faded opulence of the ballroom is a first step to cultivating the potential alliance and raising Wallace's own self-esteem, despite the embarrassment caused by May Ling's naïve candour responding to Mabel's small-talk:

> *The cavernous, shadowy ballroom of the Repulse Bay Hotel throbbed with music and a great roar of small-talk, counterpointed by the clink and rattle of the hotel's expensive imported crockery and the rapping of teaspoons...*
>
> *As the last bar of the tango died, Mabel Yip, who had seen a thousand tea-dances at the Repulse Bay, enquired in the pause before the applause: "You would have the milk or the lemon, Wallace?"*

Wallace's imagined social *faux pas* in opting for milk in his tea gives the reader an insight into his insecurity, which stems from being considered not quite *gweilo* (a Westerner) and not quite Chinese. To add to his discomfort when the group goes for a swimming expedition to the nearby South Bay, his embarrassing brother-in-law Ah Lung dispenses with the formality of proper beach-wear and disports himself in his underpants on the grounds that once he is in the water nobody will know the difference.

The attractions of South Bay according to Mo's period description included white sand and Dairy Farm ice-cream dispensed by bicycles— "unwieldy vehicles with large ice-boxes slung from the handlebars". Much of his description is of a South Bay that has been superseded by a pleasant and commercially active market. The temple to sea goddess, Tin Hau, stands imposingly at the furthest end of the cove and with its excellent *fung shui* blends in harmoniously with the incoming waves. Although by no means the oldest temple to Tin Hau in Hong Kong, this one fringing the beach at South Bay has to be one of the most beautifully situated and most spacious. It is also one of the most open to the elements. As a relatively recent addition to the shoreline, it naturally does not feature in Mo's description of 1950s South Bay.

Stanley

From Repulse Bay to nearby Stanley is a five-minute bus or car ride, but a demanding and inevitably slow walk across rugged terrain. The views out to sea and along the shoreline from the cliffs are nothing short of exquisite. As a Hong Kong beauty spot this southern stretch winding round the bays and coves between Aberdeen and Stanley is matched only by the magnificent panoramas of the Sai Kung Peninsula in the eastern New Territories and the south side of Lantau Island. As we approach Stanley, which nestles snugly against the sheltered bay, it becomes clear why this "town" known as Chek Chue (red cliffs) in Cantonese was considered by some historians the original "capital" in preference to Aberdeen. Its red cliffs are not very much in evidence, but the second word may be a misreading or mispronunciation of another ideograph meaning "pillar", which may be a reference to another topographical feature or even a temple. Chek Chue, like Heung Gong Jai (Aberdeen), was home to a sizeable population of seafaring folk, approximately two thousand strong, and had its own bazaar or market, according to the *Canton Press* reporter in 1842. It also had a slightly dubious reputation as a pirate lair, going back to the days of the ubiquitous and irrepressible Cheung Po-tsai, who made his headquarters here for a while.

Chek Chue acquired a new name in 1842, being rechristened in honour of the Secretary of State for the Colonies, Edward Stanley, who

Main Street, Stanley

later followed Lord Aberdeen in becoming prime minister. There must be a correlation between the *fung shui* or *joss* (luck) of both places and the promotion of both men. Stanley was more disposed to support the development of the colony than Aberdeen was, and his intervention on behalf of Governor Sir John Davis, at a time when the fate of the newly acquired territory hung in the balance, proved definitive. Stanley managed to swing the balance more in favour of keeping the "fragrant harbour" and away from the option of exploring an alternative acquisition further up the coastline of China. Stanley, therefore, richly deserved the tribute. Given the fact that he was subsequently re-titled Earl of Derby, it is fortunate that his name was conferred upon the village before he was ennobled. Neither Derby Market nor Earl's Court seems to fit the place quite as well as Stanley.

Early descriptions of Stanley, or rather Chek Chue, being a well-stocked and thriving community suggest that although fishing was ostensibly the principal source of livelihood, the benefits of smuggling and piracy were not negligible in the local economy. Considering that Stanley is world-famous nowadays for its outdoor clothes market, it may not be too fanciful to see a line of development stretching all the way back to what the *Canton Press* referred to as "its very good bazaar". There is an interesting connection between the pirate plunder of Cheung Po-tsai and his associates and the "copy" merchandise sold in Stanley and elsewhere in Hong Kong of many expensive brand names. These goods are usually referred to as "pirated", in other words copied without franchise by factories across the border but increasingly well copied and well made. Stanley Market is by no means dedicated purely to the vending of pirated goods, and as in other parts of Hong Kong's "shopping paradise" it is possible to pick up real bargains, sometimes designer rejects identifiable by a neatly snipped label. We will encounter the pirate goods phenomenon again when we cross the water to Kowloon, but Stanley nowadays has an air of respectability that belies its piratical precedents.

As recently as the 1960s there were around 300 fishing boats moored off Stanley, and the village's economy was, like Aberdeen's, closely connected with mariculture, as it had always been in pre-colonial days. The radical transformation that has occurred in the last forty years may be attributed to various factors, the principal of which is tourism. Hong Kong's post-war tourism drive, like its manufacturing boom of the Sixties and Seventies, has seen a gradual re-orientation of key sites, among them Stanley, towards leisure activities as a source of generating income. The demise of the fishing industry in Stanley has been in inverse proportion to its renaissance as a tourist attraction for both local and overseas shoppers and day-trippers. The bustling market, consisting mainly nowadays of permanent shops, as opposed to mobile stalls, is self-evidently popular and appears to have survived the sharp economic downturn caused by the Asian Economic Crisis. An inane proposal in the late 1990s to raze the site and build a shopping centre on it has not been implemented to date.

West of the market is the busy Stanley Main Street, with its handful of elegant sea-facing buildings, beneath which are cafés and pubs. One or two of them bear names that are redolent of Stanley's smuggling past. At the end of this promenade along a stony seafront lies the recently completed Stanley Plaza. Its focal point is Murray House, one of the best-preserved and most handsome early colonial buildings of Hong Kong. Normally when establishments move to new locations the real business of moving is done by staff, and sometimes by the fixtures and fittings. In the case of the resplendent Murray House, built in 1845 and named after a friend of the army commander-in-chief, General D'Aguilar, the message "we are moving to a new address in Stanley" meant literally that. It was not just a leap of faith, though. The entire edifice was dismantled brick by brick in 1982 and, rather like a Lego construction kit, pieced back together onto a pupose-built concrete shell at Stanley waterfront 18 years later.

Like Lords Aberdeen and Stanley, this anonymous Murray was commemorated despite never having visited Hong Kong, so it was presumably immaterial to him where his building stood. The building now houses restaurants with superb sea views from first-floor balconies, and has become a symbol of the new-old Stanley where the lifestyle of leisure is king. It is also home to the Hong Kong Maritime Museum. To get a good impression of how Murray House dominated its former environment of Central in the early days of the colony, we need to look at one of the few Hong Kong watercolours painted by George Chinnery during his six-month stay. His middle-distance view of Murray House presents an interesting juxtaposition of two buildings: the resplendent and permanent-looking new Murray Barracks, seen in shining profile perched loftily above the temporary mat-shed church. Chinnery noted that the stark contrast between the two buildings rankled greatly with the clergy.

Close to this marker of colonial presence is a small temple to Tin Hau, which not only pre-dates colonial days but is also strongly connected with Hong Kong's favourite pirate, Cheung Po-tsai. He is reputed to have been one of the founders of the temple, and the big bronze inscribed bell and drum on display inside were used by his followers to communicate with the pirate fleet out at sea. Stretched on the left-hand wall is the rather dark skin of the last roaming tiger seen in Hong Kong, in fact thought to have escaped from a visiting circus. It was shot in 1941 by an ethnic Indian policeman named Rur Singh after it terrorized the inhabitants of Stanley. Later in the same year the inhabitants were terrorized by human agency in the form of the Japanese army. (The tigers had obviously got wind of their invasion and quit Hong Kong for good.)

Not to be outdone by Mr. Singh, Tin Hau played her part in protecting the citizens of Stanley from the Japanese shelling. Despite the danger from an unexploded bomb on the roof of the temple, the frightened villagers, many of whom sheltered here during the Christmas Day assault, were unharmed thanks to Tin Hau's intercession. The British troops and auxiliary staff, some of them Chinese and stationed elsewhere in Stanley, were not so lucky. Two other deities are worshipped in small temples near this spot. At the very end of Stanley Main Street is a very narrow temple to Wang Kung, patron of doctors and healers, and the even smaller Pak Tai temple (god of the North) is a Hoklo boatpeople's shrine right out on the headland beyond Murray House. Given their lack of acceptance in earlier Hong Kong, it is understandable that these "guests" would want their own god to safeguard their interests. The Pak Tai temple, wedged into a space in the rock-face, is sufficiently unobtrusive to have survived relatively undisturbed.

One event that one can witness today in a form not much altered from the life and times of Cheung Po-tsai is open-air Cantonese Opera, which is still performed on a makeshift stage (constructed inevitably of hardy bamboo, ideal for this itinerant form) in the playground area just above the market and below Stanley Village Road. The most likely times of the year to see performances are late September at the Mid-Autumn Festival and late January-early February at the Lunar New Year

Festival. The atmospheric productions by local groups, who promote this reputedly dying art form, are generally well attended by both locals and curious tourists. Unless one is a connoisseur (unlikely for a Westerner) the open-air performances have a very special ambience, which makes them perhaps more enjoyable than indoor shows in modern all-purpose venues. At least, that is my own experience. Other forms of Chinese Opera, or to give it a better name, Chinese traditional theatre, such as Kun, Sichuan and Beijing, are best appreciated in modern venues where good acoustics and subtitling can enhance aesthetic pleasure. By contrast, Cantonese Opera seems to thrive on the rawness of the street performance and the closer intimacy with the audience.

Back on Stanley Village Road, just opposite the bus terminus, is a building that has many historical associations, and whose walls could relate their own stories to fascinate the tourists who come there to eat. The building, now a supermarket, was formerly Stanley Police Station and Harbour-Master's Office. Built in 1859, the exterior of the building remains largely unchanged. There is a huge number 88 on the pediment above its long white columns and next to the number in smaller letters is inscribed the year of its construction. The building is now gazetted for purposes of conservation. It was here on Christmas Day 1941 that the last vestiges of British resistance were quashed by the Japanese soldiers, and fierce fighting to the death took place both outside and inside the building. This heroic but futile last-stand occurred after the official surrender by General Maltby had taken place, but word of it had not got through to the small garrison at Stanley.

Not long after this elegant police station and harbour-master's office was erected by the British authorities, the piracy problem in Stanley became so acute, and the loss of life due to fever and poor quality drinking-water (poisoned by the malevolent locals according to the testimony of some officers) so high that for a while the colonial forces decamped to the nearby Stanley Peninsula and set up a military barracks there. The Stanley Fort military facilities were considerably developed over the next century and radar equipment for eavesdropping on the mainland stood out against the bare hillside. The facility still exists, but was taken over by the People's Liberation Army following the 1997 Handover. Doubtless they found out many interesting things about themselves. Less suspicious in the post-war period, the British troops increasingly patronized Stanley Market and the pubs in Stanley Main Street, apparently without fear of consuming contaminated liquor.

Stanley Internment Camp, where the Japanese incarcerated civilians from enemy countries after the fall of Hong Kong, was located behind St. Stephen's Beach. Jean Ho Tung, a daughter of the influential entrepreneur Robert Ho Tung, was interned there while her husband, fellow-Eurasian Billy Gittins, was shipped off to forced labour in Japan, where he died. Jean survived the war and emigrated to Melbourne afterwards. Her autobiography, *Eastern Windows, Western Skies*, not only offers an excellent eye-witness account of the privations and frustrations of internment, but also an insight into the experience of being Eurasian in a society bigoted against people of mixed race. Jean writes thus of the Stanley campsite:

> Before the war Stanley had been a quiet resort where one could spend an afternoon away from the bustle of city life to enjoy the gentle breezes that came from the ocean... Rows of bathing sheds lined the beach, and weekend houses dotted the hillside below the green-tiled Carmelite convent.
>
> On a ridge rising from the peninsula end of the isthmus were the school buildings and bungalow type staff houses of St. Stephen's College. On the southern end of the ridge stood several blocks of residential flats of modern design. They were quarters for the British prison-warders and their families... Up on the ridge between the modern flats and the college buildings was an old cemetery, quiet and peacefully overlooking the boundless sea to the south and the island-studded bays on the west... Here lay the dead of Hong Kong's first garrison. Many had succumbed to malaria...

The writer goes on to describe how the guns of Stanley Fort continued to offer resistance to the last, and how a group of Japanese soldiers burst into the temporary casualty hospital at St. Stephen's after the fighting ended, bayoneting the wounded and the doctors and repeatedly raping the nurses. Ho Tung refers to it as "the most shocking of all atrocities" but it was not an isolated incident. Much the same happened in Shau Kei Wan, the coastal defence redoubt on the northeast coast of Hong Kong Island. The evidence of those who survived the massacres, either by feigning death or by miraculously recovering from their wounds, was enough to convict some of the worst perpetrators of war crimes in the tribunals held in 1946. A simple headstone in Stanley Military Cemetery showing the names of those known to have died and "unknown Chinese, Indian, Canadian and British ranks of various units" marks the infamous event at St. Stephen's College.

Away from the horrors of the wartime occupation, the day in Stanley is now structured not just around food, but also shopping, which preserves a neat balance. For the cheerful swimmers and windsurfers off St. Stephen's beach there is little awareness of the atrocities that took place here sixty years ago. Recent events to commemorate the sixtieth anniversary of the end of the war in Asia have served to focus attention on the matter of a full acknowledgement and apology on behalf of the Japanese government, for which many in Hong Kong as well as in China have long clamoured.

Tai Tam, Big Wave Bay and the Coastal Defences

Tearing ourselves away from Stanley with great reluctance and abundant purchases we take the coast road, Stanley Gap Road, which continues round through Tai Tam and the east side of the island toward Chai Wan at the extreme eastern point of the northern coastline. There are a number of places of note to observe *en route*. The first is the remarkable Tai Tam Reservoir, through which the main Tai Tam Road passes. Tai Tam Reservoir resembles European-style dams. As we pass along the narrow road bridge over the dam that transects the reservoir and take in the tranquil and picturesque view across what appears a man-made lake, we could almost be in Lancashire or the Lake District, were it not for the Asian-looking trees and vegetation fringing the red-brickwork at the waterline.

Today Tai Tam Reservoir is a beauty spot in its own right, but visual aesthetics were hardly the main priority in its construction. The Pokfulam Reservoir had reached capacity almost immediately after its 1863 completion, thereby necessitating the urgent construction of another large source of fresh water for the island's inhabitants. Idiosyncratic governor John Pope Hennessey had, like his predecessor Bowring, objected to the provision of fresh water. However, a newer, less reactionary generation had emerged in mid-Victorian Britain, from which Osbert Chadwick, the man given responsibility for the reservoir project, emerged. Arriving shortly after the retirement of the eccentric, though well-meaning, Hennessey in 1885, Chadwick threw himself energetically into the project. He designed the new reservoir and oversaw the building of the pumping station, which stands to this day. Unfortunately for Hong Kong the scheme was not completed until 1918, due to slowness in generating funds. By that time the population had been exposed to the horrors of cholera, smallpox and plague epidemics, with the armed forces particularly vulnerable.

When Tai Tam Reservoir eventually started supplying fresh water to the island's inhabitants in the 1920s, the growth in the population of Hong Kong over the forty-year period of its construction ensured that it was already inadequate for the needs of the city. The chronic shortage of water, especially during periods of low rainfall, continued right up until the 1960s. After water rationing and severe restrictions had to be introduced in 1963 the government was forced to search for alternative solutions. Extra reservoirs hurriedly constructed in the New Territories and a desalination plant also proved inadequate, and in 1977, following the collapse of the Cultural Revolution and the death of Chairman Mao, a deal was struck with the administration in Guangdong to pipe much needed water across the border. As we pass Tai Tam we should spare a thought for the pre-colonial village of Tai Tam Tuk. Today there is a newer village located on the site of the older one, which was inundated when the reservoir was being built.

After Tai Tam we have a choice of continuing along the east road until we reach Chai Wan, on the north-east side of the island, or making a detour past Cape Collinson (named after the naval engineer responsible for the first topographical survey of Hong Kong) toward two beautiful beaches, Big Wave Bay (Dai Long Waan) and Shek O. The latter is a delightful spot, possessing one of the pleasantest and best-kept strands in Hong Kong as well as some quaint houses and agreeable *al fresco* dining establishments. At the former bay, a popular spot for wind-surfing, one of Hong Kong's earliest traces of prehistoric habitation was discovered in the form of a Neolithic cave drawing as recently as 1977.

From the long peninsula on which Big Wave Bay is sited back to the main road to Chai Wan is a long but rewarding journey. It is possible to appreciate that, although its deep anchorage and the narrow eastern Lei Yue Mun approach made Hong Kong a desirable port, its extensive, rocky coastline also made it difficult to hold against determined forces of invasion. To understand the coastal defence system of Hong Kong, both under the Ming and Qing Dynasties and later under British colonial rule, a visit to the Sai Wan Museum of Coastal Defence (close to Shau Kei Wan on the north coast, also a former pirate stronghold) is essential. This building, constructed on the site of the Lei Yue Mun Redoubt and downhill from the old Sai Wan Fort was part of the eastern coastal redoubt, defending the main harbour approaches. It was built as the centrepiece of a complex of defences in the 1880s, at a time when tension between the British and the Russian empires was acute.

The skilfully concealed gun emplacements and pillboxes were more than adequate to deal with an expansionist threat from Russia that never materialized. Instead, their antagonists in the Russo-Japanese War of the early twentieth century developed imperial ambitions of their own, for which Hong Kong was fatally unprepared in 1941. Most of the big guns were not even pointed in the right direction, and the Japanese bombardment of Hong Kong's island defences, following the inevitable capitulation of the British forces on Kowloon-side, proved lethal. Japanese ingenuity in disguising some of their troops as innocuous Chinese coolies proved another decisive factor. Taken unawares, many of the defenders were slaughtered in close combat. Those who surrendered, in a brutal scenario that was to repeat itself elsewhere, were bayoneted by an army that had little time for the niceties of the Geneva Convention, and were in any case not signatories to it.

It is not only surviving army veterans like Jack Edwards, Osler Thomas and Arthur Gomes (all of whom have recounted their wartime experiences), who have been understandably anxious to prevent the historical erasure of such crimes. Older Hong Kong and Chinese people suffered terribly at the hands of their fellow Asians, whose atrocities were committed paradoxically under the aegis of the "Greater Asian Co-Prosperity Sphere". Many of them are unwilling to simply forgive and forget without a sincere formal expression of recognition and remorse on the part of Japan. It should be noted that this attitude among older Hong Kongers is offset by the strong interest in Japanese culture among younger generations, for whom Japan holds no negative associations. Disney's Mickey Mouse or Winnie the Pooh, for example, will have their work cut out attempting to compete with the phenomenally successful Hello Kitty cat logo, which, despite being a Japanese cartoon brand, is a virtual symbol of Hong Kong's "cutesy" self-image. Much depends for the future on how the Japanese government proceeds with its tentative policy of apology and reconciliation, which has been undermined in recent years by renewed China-Japan tension and the resurgence of Japan's small but vocal nationalistic right-wing. Doubtless Hong Kong will continue to live with its contradictions in dealing with things Japanese—appreciating cultural contact, but deploring official hypocrisy.

chapter six

ACROSS THE FRAGRANT HARBOUR: THE NINE DRAGONS

Kowloon: an Introduction

The Kowloon peninsula had been a small but important centre for salt mining in China as far back as the Sung Dynasty in the eleventh and twelfth centuries—long before the coming of the British. As mentioned in Chapter One, legend has it that the name Kowloon or "nine dragons" is derived from a smart but sycophantic remark from the boy emperor's adviser to the effect that, in addition to the eight dragon-shaped ridges separating the peninsula from what later became the New Territories beyond it, the young emperor himself represented the ninth dragon. The figure of the dragon has always enjoyed a positive symbolism in Chinese culture, so the name ought to have been auspicious. After the Ming Dynasty counter-piracy clearances, however, few villages were left, and only a very small number of indigenous people returned to live off the land. The population at the time of the British takeover of Hong Kong was negligible. It expanded very rapidly thereafter, becoming a focal point for receivers of stolen goods, casual labourers and general ruffians, wishing to participate in the potential gold rush that the foreigners' presence appeared to have precipitated.

Between the years 1841 and 1860 as the British occupation of the island was ratified by the Treaties of Nanking and the Bogue and then strengthened by the Treaty of Tientsin, it became obvious that Hong Kong Island itself was not adequate for the defence of a community now consolidating its gains. The proximity of the China mainland, though in some ways advantageous, was also potentially dangerous. Less concerned about Chinese government hostility, which had largely abated, the British worried about incursions by Russia in the wake of the Crimean War. From a military perspective it was vital to control the peninsula and the Lei Yue Mun channel. The strategic point of Lei Yue Mun, or Lyeemoon as the British called it, lay opposite the Lei Yue Mun Redoubt on the Hong Kong Island side. Lawless cross-harbour escapades were becoming more frequent and the British authorities were concerned about what William Mercer, Colonial Secretary and John Bowring's effective deputy, described as "this objectionable settlement". According to Mercer, the crude settlement became identifiable as the village of "Teem-Cha-Tsuy" about 1853.

The name Tsim Sha Tsui (a more phonetically accurate rendition of the Cantonese word than Mercer's) actually means "sharp sand-spit", and serves to remind us that here, where according to the imaginative account in Timothy Mo's *An Insular Possession* the colonizers played a very *ad hoc* game of beach cricket, there were originally sandy foreshores. The dilapidated fortifications of the Celestial Empire's meagre garrison were evidence of the lack of interest in the area, since the Emperor's attention had been seriously distracted by the southern China uprising, known as the Taiping Rebellion. The initial negotiations were carried out by the 31- year-old secretary and emissary of Bowring, Harry Parkes, who had arrived with the missionaries as a 14-year-old and done well for himself. In Mo's version the devil-may-care Parkes is seen by his elders as potential gallows material, but he survived to gain a knighthood for his decidedly *gung-ho* efforts in initiating the acquisition of Kowloon.

Parkes thought he had bought Kowloon for the sum of 500 taels of gold from Governor-General Lau at Canton (Guangzhou). Embarrassingly for the British Foreign Office, the lease was made out in both Parkes' and Bowring's names. They communicated their willingness to purchase Parkes' share of the "Cowloon Peninsula" (the earlier anglicized spelling of Kowloon), but the Arrow Incident (see Chapter Three) and the attack on Peking nullified Parkes' earlier deal. Parkes was not destined to be the model for all latter-day Tsim Sha Tsui speculators wishing to make a quick profit on the resale of their property. Under the Treaty of Tientsin the British were bought off, and the cession of Kowloon to the Crown was included in the raft of trade demands.

After the Kowloon peninsula was acquired, military fortifications and barracks were established at Tsim Sha Tsui on the site of the present-day Kowloon Park—Whitfield Barracks, as they were called. In addition the Marine Police Headquarters, a handsome blue and white building on a hill overlooking the harbour, was constructed in 1884 to control the waters between Hong Kong and Kowloon-side. Debate continues about the preservation of this historic building which stands on a prime piece of real estate. In its former days of glory the Marine Police Headquarters, renowned for its excellent *fung shui*, commanded an uninterrupted view of the peninsula and the isthmus that used to lie behind it, where there are now hotels. What is certain is that historic photos of Tsim Sha Tsui taken a hundred years ago—or even those taken fifty years ago—bear little relation to what can be seen today. Houses with front gardens, avenues lined with trees and grassland have all inevitably given way to concrete, glass and chrome high-rises.

One rather amusing feature of early Tsim Sha Tsui was that the original town planners' street names tended to replicate the Hong Kong-side names, with little thought for the confusion this was likely to cause to posterity. This was corrected in 1909, when Robinson Road, Elgin Road, MacDonnell Road and Des Voeux Road were altered respectively to Nathan Road, Haiphong Road, Canton Road and Chatham Road, all important thoroughfares that have become closely associated with contemporary Kowloon.

As historian Frank Welsh has pointed out, in the fifty years following their acquisition of Kowloon the British never expanded much further than the present-day boundary of Tsim Sha Tsui and Jordan, which are the first two stops on the Kowloon Mass Transit Railway (MTR) after the under-harbour crossing at Admiralty. Indeed, until the advent of the over-ground railway known as the Kowloon-Canton Railway (KCR) in the early years of the twentieth century, Hong Kong-side European residents assumed that nobody who was anybody would live there, with the exception of the military garrison, who had no choice in the matter. However, when Parsee merchants as well as Portuguese and Indian residents started to break the mould and settle in Kowloon, it was still considered eccentric and suspicious for any *gweilo* to do so. In my early years in Hong Kong in the late 1980s and early 1990s I found that the same bizarre prejudice persisted, although by that time there were many who, like author Martin Booth, positively preferred Kowloon to the "little England" mentality that tended to prevail on Hong Kong-side. After the acquisition of Kowloon, the addition of further land in the form of the New Territories in 1898 (this time leased for one hundred years as opposed to being ceded in perpetuity) provided the spur for further development of Kowloon peninsula.

The Star Ferry and Victoria Harbour

The Star Ferry, today one of the most famous forms of public conveyance in the world, had rather modest beginnings. Parsee resident Dorabjee Nowrojee, who worked his way up from humble origins to become a very successful entrepreneur and hotelier, instituted the ferry service for his immediate circle of friends. His hotel, the King Edward, and his other businesses were located on Hong Kong-side, but his home was in Tsim Sha Tsui on Kowloon-side. Not wishing to move home to the vastly more expensive side of the harbour, he had little choice but to provide himself with transport. His first launch, the *Evening Star*, was in frequent use, so he commissioned a second launch, which he dubbed the *Rising Star* (both boats owing their names to a rather sentimental Tennyson poem), and the Star Ferry Service was born. At this stage Indians and Parsees travelled free, whereas Chinese and Europeans had to pay. Nowrojee's Star Ferry did not become a regular public service until the 1890s, but by this time Kowloon was beginning to be developed. The cheap and convenient form of cross-harbour transport proved extremely popular, and the present-day design is still based on the 1923 double-ended ferry. This model enabled ferries to reduce crossing time by avoiding the necessity to turn about for the return trip across the harbour. The Union Dockyard of the Hong Kong and Whampoa Dock Company in Hung Hom, where the launches were built, was one of the first employers to operate a policy of egalitarian working practice among Chinese and Caucasian employees.

Although the skyline may have changed substantially from the days when Nowrojee ran his own personal Star Ferry, the boat itself has not changed dramatically. It remains one of the most pleasant and best value-for-money forms of transportation in the world. Still costing only HK$2.2 for the upper deck and $1.50 for the lower, the magic of the journey across to Kowloon (or in the reverse direction) lies in its relatively short duration—approximately seven minutes on average nowadays. It is enough time to take in the fabulous view of Kowloon peninsula and the island of Hong Kong, as well as the eastern view towards the old Kai Tak airport and the western view towards the container port at Kwai Chung and the broadening South China Sea reaches beyond nearby Stonecutter's Island and Lantau Island in the middle distance. It is also time enough to immerse oneself entirely in

Star Ferry sign, Tsim Sha Tsui.

the experience, enhanced by the distinctive smell of engine oil and the cool breeze against one's cheeks.

The Star Ferry features in the arresting openings of both book and film versions of *The World of Suzie Wong*. In the original book version protagonist Lomax meets the jauntily self-confident Suzie on the ferry from Tsim Sha Tsui to Wan Chai, and is deceived into thinking she is the privileged daughter of a rich businessman. The film's representation of the scene does not give us much impression of the view, since the camera focus is very much on William Holden as Lomax and Nancy Kwan as Wong Mee Ling, with the latter boasting about her father's many houses, her forthcoming marriage and her virginity. The book effects the introduction as the two are waiting at the Kowloon ferry pier and includes a good description of the embarkation:

> The ferryboat came churning alongside and the crowd moved forward. We jostled together up the gangplank—and chose one of the slatted, bench-seats on the covered top deck. The ferries were Chinese owned and run, and very efficient, and we had hardly sat down before the water was churning again, the engines rumbling,

the boat palpitating—and we were moving off busily past the Kowloon wharves past anchored merchant-ships past great clusters of junk... We rounded the tip of the Kowloon peninsula heading slantwise across the channel for Wanchai, the most populous district of Hong Kong's eastern flank. I turned to look at the girl beside me...

Larry Feign, cartoonist at the *South China Morning Post* for many years, produced a delightful spoof on *The World of Suzie Wong*. His "cross-cultural cartoon love story" *The World of Lily Wong* depicted a hapless *gweilo* named Stuart attempting to date a demure and winsome Hong Kong girl (Lily), who coyly but calculatingly resists his advances. The cartoon story which appeared in short episodes in both the *Post* and *The Standard* in the late 1980s is not only dryly amusing, but a glorious snapshot of an era in which such trans-cultural relationships were still comparatively rare in Hong Kong. That situation was to change dramatically in the 1990s. At the end of the first series Lily's family is set to immigrate to Canada, threatening the future of their very slowly developing relationship. After saying a robust farewell to Stuart, Lily is depicted waiting for the Star Ferry back to Kowloon and reflecting on what it will mean to leave Hong Kong behind. Shakespeare's Henry V eve-of-Agincourt speech is humorously juxtaposed with the image of Hong Kong and its harbour as "This sceptred isle, this other Eden, this precious stone set in the silver sea... This blessed plot, this earth, this realm, this Hong Kong." Feign ends "with apologies to W.S.". Feign still works in Hong Kong but writes freelance nowadays, having seen his vein of mordant cultural and political satire fall from favour with editors in the more politically correct years immediately after 1997.

In an entirely different vein from Mason and more akin to the spirit of Larry Feign, Hong Kong writer Nury Vittachi, undisputedly one of the wittiest pens in the Hong Kong SAR, places the Star Ferry centre stage in his story *Mysterious Properties*. The title is a neat pun on Hong Kong people's predilection for both real estate and geomancy (or *fung shui*). During a journey from Central to Tsim Sha Tsui, Bilton Au-Yeung asks the great *fung shui* sage, C. F. Wong—hero of Vittachi's whimsical *Fung Shui Detective* series, from which this story is taken—what is so special about the Star Ferry:

"No magic," said C. F. Wong. "Good fung shui... The harbour and the Star Ferry are the fung shui centre of Hong Kong. It is not the map centre. It is not the geography centre. But it is the true centre. Hong Kong island on this side, 10 times smaller than Kowloon peninsula on that side. But Hong Kong island has very great ch'i energy. This balances the ch'i energy of Kowloon, also very strong... Here there is balance. It is not perfect but it is quite good... This is why many people feel strong when they are on the Star Ferry..." It was dusk and the neon lights of the Hong Kong cityscape were flickering into life around them. The purples, reds and yellows of the neon logos were reflected as long shimmering streaks in the water...

Lorette Roberts' beautiful watercolour of Victoria Harbour in her collection of Hong Kong sketches, *Sights and Secrets*, captures Vittachi's evocative description perfectly, especially in her choice of colours. However, the fictional Bilton's description of a lovably old-fashioned and slightly down-at-heel Star Ferry may soon be out of date. There are plans to move the Tsim Sha Tsui Star Ferry concourse and pier to a new site west of the present one and also relocate the bus terminus that has stood adjacent to the entrance at the very tip of Kowloon's Salisbury Road for nearly a hundred years. Inevitably the Central-Wan Chai waterfront development scheme will also change the look of the Hong Kong-side terminus, although the controversially relocated Central Pier is designed as historical pastiche to recreate the authentic look of the original Star Ferry terminals.

While it remains unchanged the best views of both terminals, and indeed the entire harbour, are probably to be had from the open car-park at the Marco Polo Hotel outside the sixth floor. Simply take the lift to the sixth floor, walk in the direction of the bar and continue through the glass door (not automatic, please note). As you turn you will obtain a stunningly close-up view of the ferry below, the harbour, Hong Kong-side and the outlying islands. This vantage point is also recommended for the spectacular fireworks displays that take place on the waterfront at Tsim Sha Tsui every 1 October to mark China National Day and every 1 July to commemorate the 1997 Handover. Such fireworks displays make the harbour every bit as magical as Vittachi's characters suggest, but you would have to ask a real-life C. F. Wong whether it enhances the *fung shui* or not.

The Cultural Centre, the Clock Tower, the Star Ferry and the harbour.

One notable musical evocation of the harbour and waterfront of recent years was a piece by leading Hong Kong-born composer Clarence Mak Wai-chu entitled "Sentiments in the Wind". This piece is not a hymn to the powers of *fung shui*, but a musical portrait of the wind blowing on the waterfront in the composer's boyhood memory. Mak's intention was to write a commissioned work for the Hong Kong Sinfonietta which would convey the dramatic and turbulent effects of the harbour and at the same time the soothing breezes on the boy's face by using both Asian and Western musical elements, resulting in a highly textured and colourful tone poem. The premiere of this musical depiction of the ever-changing moods of wind and water was in October 2004 at City Hall. In his programme note Mak tells the audience how the impressionistic piece relates to his recollections of the fresh breezes from the harbour when he was a boy in the Sixties:

The street is still there and the wind is still blowing but accelerated because of tall building blocks. It blows with dust and the traffic noise. And now it is impossible to see the harbour on the street because of the new land and new community. Something that the boy loved no longer exists—except in the man's memory of it.

Modern Tsim Sha Tsui

Standing at the Star Ferry terminal in Tsim Sha Tsui is to put oneself figuratively in the sharp beak of the mythological bird, the meaning of which is also connoted in the written Chinese name. This point represents the Land's End of the land mass containing China and stretching all the way west to France and Spain. In fact, the overland rail journey on the Trans-Siberian Railway to Moscow and on to Paris and London was in its early days seen as a fast alternative to the more leisurely sea route, taking a mere three weeks, as opposed to six on the boat. If the present-day urban renewal scheme is implemented, the changes to the very point or tip of the peninsula will be as radical as those made in the post-war period when the colonial-style Kowloon-Canton railway terminus was demolished and shifted to Hung Hom near the present-day central harbour tunnel. Today all that is left to remind us that it was possible for intrepid inter-continental travellers to board here in Tsim Sha Tsui next to the Star Ferry is the stately-looking 150-foot red-brick clock tower. Its ever-punctual electric clock dating from 1920 is for many Hong Kongers a local and smaller version of London's Big Ben. It is now an inalienable part of the Tsim Sha Tsui skyline, and an unmistakable landmark.

Immediately behind it is the Hong Kong Cultural Centre (Man *Faa Jung Saam*), standing where the station concourse used to be. Construction was completed in 1989 and, like the Academy for Performing Arts, it has no harbour-facing windows, doubtless for *fung shui* reasons. Initially compared to an artificial ski slope on account of its concave roof (and also, less flatteringly, to a giant public toilet), the building seems to have grown into its role as the principal venue for cultural events, including the Hong Kong Arts Festival, the Hong Kong International Film Festival and the New Vision Festival. The Cultural Centre, sharing the role with Hong Kong-side's City Hall, is home to the SAR's increasingly admired orchestras, Western and Chinese. These are the Hong Kong Philharmonic under the baton of the renowned

The Clock Tower, Tsim Sha Tsui Waterfront.

conductor, Edo de Waart, the Hong Kong Sinfonietta with its popular local female conductor, Yip Wing-sie, and the Hong Kong Chinese Orchestra (playing traditional Chinese instruments and sometimes culturally mixed programmes) under its Artistic Director Yan Huichang. The Hong Kong Ballet under the guidance of former dirctor Stephen Jeffries has become a critically acclaimed international company in the last ten years with highly successful overseas tours.

For the time being, the Cultural Centre is to all intents and purposes the government's flagship venue. Its distinctive roof and rosy-hued ceramic wall tiles are by now familiar features on the Tsim Sha Tsui waterfront skyline. Indeed, it has now become a meeting point for many locals and tourists, especially on New Year's Eve, which tends to be celebrated *al fresco*. Perhaps when the planned West Kowloon Cultural Hub eventually opens in 2014 (if, in the event, it doesn't turn out to be put on hold indefinitely!), Hong Kongers may entertain warm and nostalgic feelings for the building formerly thought of as a convenience.

The proximity of the Registry Office in the adjoining administration building ensures that there are frequent throngs of photograph-takers in the immediate vicinity. In addition to the 1,700-seat grand theatre (in which large scale productions such as operas, musicals and traditional Chinese theatre performances take place) there is also a circular-shaped concert hall and a flexible studio theatre space. Performances of various descriptions are also held in the spacious foyer as well as in the exterior space close to broad, sweeping steps that command a view of both performers and the harbour. Beyond this area is the harbour-front promenade with its "Walkway of the Stars" imitating Hollywood's original conception by which tourists and locals can trample on famous faces underfoot. By no means all the Hong Kong stars represented here will be familiar to the average tourist, but Bruce Lee and Jackie Chan will always be household names.

The various venues attract nearly a million paying customers per annum and many others who make use of its facilities—including free public toilets. Two interesting modern sculptures catch the eye and help to define the building's ethos. Outside the harbour-side entrance stands a work by French sculptor, César, donated to Hong Kong by the Cartier Foundation in France. This Icarus-like bronze depiction of the Flying Frenchman appears poised for flight, but the figure's single wing symbolizes to those who read such meaning into it Hong Kong's aspiration for greater political autonomy. Dominating the interior is a vast gold-coloured metallic sculptural relief by Hong Kong artist Van Lau. Entitled "The Meeting of Yin and Yang" (based on the Chinese principle of complementary opposites), the sculpture shows two figures, a male and a female, with arms and wings outstretched. Not unlike Inca depictions of the sun-god, the two stare fixedly ahead, co-existing without interacting. An allegorical representation of One Country Two Systems (the post-1997 Hong Kong-China relationship) according to the insights of art critic and Fine Arts professor David Clarke, the frosty relations can also be seen in its temporal context as a veiled metaphor for Hong Kong's fear of China in the wake of the 1989 student massacre.

Integrated into the same cultural complex on the site of the former railway station are the white-domed Space Museum and the Hong Kong Museum of Art, which boasts six galleries, educational facilities and conservation workshops. The Museum of Art features regular exhibitions on tour from the China mainland, with retrospectives on Chinese pottery and archeological artifacts, some of them dating back to the dawn of Chinese civilization. The museum has also presented exhibitions of Western art, including a phenomenally popular exhibition of French Impressionist paintings in 2005. There are collections of historic pictures of Hong Kong and a Chinese Antiquities Gallery that contains hundreds of exhibits dating back to Neolithic times. Like the theatre venues, the Museum of Art has started to flourish after a sluggish start in the early 1990s when local people were still resistant to what at the time seemed to some a white elephant. Now with the hi-tech, multi-billion-dollar West Kowloon Cultural Hub being planned, there is the same process of soul-searching and scepticism in relation to cultural needs and identity in the city as occurred when the Cultural Centre was under construction. What is at stake is Hong Kong's success in reinventing itself as a culturally vibrant "world city", as opposed to a strictly commercial enclave in which culture plays second fiddle.

Directly opposite the Cultural Centre in Salisbury Road is a pink-topped cluster of buildings, built in 1907, which were formerly the fire station and the Tsim Sha Tsui post office. The low but elegant 1952 building located adjacent to it, squatting defiantly and incongruously amid the skyscrapers, was formerly a welfare handicraft store specializing in traditional locally made arts and crafts. Across the busy Kowloon Park Drive is the rather smart YMCA building and beyond it stands the Peninsula Hotel, Hong Kong's most famous existing hotel. The latter, with its original colonial façade and grand entrance supplemented by a thirty-storey modern angular structure looming up behind the classy main entrance, is another Hong Kong institution. The hotel dates back to the 1920s when Kowloon was expanding rapidly. Designed as a railway hotel for the Kowloon-Canton railway terminus, the building first housed the garrison reinforcement sent to maintain order in the turbulent year of 1927 on the South China coast. The Peninsula Hotel was officially inaugurated in 1928 and opened its doors to a stream of illustrious visitors. Charlie Chaplin, for example, who stayed here during the making of his 1967 film *A Countess from Hong Kong*, did not actually go anywhere else in Hong Kong during his brief sojourn, which is a recommendation in its own way.

The hotel has always been owned by the Kadoorie family, which has a long history of entrepreneurship in Hong Kong. The family fortunes were made by the judicious broking activities of Ellis Kadoorie, a Jewish merchant from Baghdad who came to Hong Kong from Bombay in the 1880s to try his luck. Their interests also include Hong Kong's major power company, China Light and Power. The Peninsula is famous for its afternoon tea (partly because of the price), which can be enjoyed in the neoclassical-style hotel foyer to the soothing accompaniment of live musicians. The elegant décor and delicate bone-china tea services provide a pleasant sense of a bygone age. When the bill arrives, however, the illusion of living in a distant era is swiftly dispelled. In his 1950s memoir, *Gweilo*, Martin Booth recalls the experience of tea at the Peninsula:

> *Known locally as the Pen, the hotel was considered one of the best in the world. We sat in the grandiloquent entrance lobby, surrounded by gilded pillars and serenaded by a string quartet. Silver pots of Indian, Earl Grey or Jasmine tea, cradling over methylated spirit lamps, were served with wafer-thin sandwiches and delicate little cakes. The bread and butter came with four different jams. My mother was in seventh heaven. To her this was a film star's existence. When the bill was discreetly presented she blanched...*

Booth's mother engineers their escape without paying, but they return the next day to pay what they owe, whereupon the *maitre d'* insists on offering them tea on the house for the second time. You can find out for yourself whether or not this ploy is effective nowadays. As you make good your escape, pursued by a burly doorman past the refreshing forecourt fountain in the direction of Nathan Road, you may like to reflect on the fate of British Commanding Officer, General Maltby, and wartime governor and Commander-in Chief, Sir Mark Young. Having surrendered here to the Japanese army on Christmas Day 1941, they were incarcerated for two months in the hotel before being sent to prison camp in Formosa (Taiwan).

Arriving slightly out-of-breath in Nathan Road, named after Hong Kong's only Jewish governor, you will see a straight and busy thoroughfare that could almost have been constructed by the Romans. In Matthew Nathan's short tenure (1904-7) extensions to this 1860s road formerly known as Robinson Road and initial works on the Kowloon-Canton railway were considered a waste of money. The Nathan Road and Kowloon-Canton development project was contemptuously dismissed by snooty Hong Kong-siders as "Nathan's Folly". Today Nathan, originally an officer in the Royal Engineers, can have the last laugh as Nathan Road has become a highly prosperous tourist attraction, often referred to as "the Golden Mile". It is one of the most frequented and commercially dynamic areas in Hong Kong, famous for its camera and computer shops.

The best bargains are not to be had here, however, but in Mong Kok, much further up this road that extends over several miles. The Tsim Sha Tsui shops rarely display prices, but the higher rents of this busy and fashionable section of Nathan Road plus the dearth of local shoppers in these electrical goods emporia indicate that the canny visitor should exercise caution. Newer shopping precincts such as the post-modern-looking Park Lane Shopping Boulevard have reinvigorated the Tsim Sha Tsui end of Nathan Road. In fact, this whole area with its teeming shops on the east side in streets like Cameron Road, Granville Road and Carnarvon Road, is the main reason that Hong Kong in the first place acquired the "shopping paradise" tag (a phrase first put into print by author Han Suyin, who placed more than a dash of ironic emphasis on that word "paradise"). Nathan Road retains its up-market image, however, by comparison with the hurly-burly of these cut-price side streets.

Probably the most famous commercial building in the busy final stretch is the emporium-cum-cheap guest house known as Chungking Mansions. This former select apartment block built by a wealthy entrepreneur became distinctly down-market after its Sixties heyday, and acquired fame as a haunt for prostitutes entertaining American sailors in the latter stages of the Vietnam War. It then transformed itself into intricate network of cheap units for backpackers interspersed with Indian and Pakistani restaurants, most of which serve authentic and inexpensive food, especially curries. According to Hong Kong cultural historian Patricia Lim, the main reason that this anomalous and idiosyncratic edifice has survived the wrecker's ball is that there are too many individual owners for the government to trace and issue compulsory purchase orders to. Be that as it may, the building has acquired its own movie star status thanks to Wong Kar-wai's quirky 1993 classic, *Chungking Express*. The opening sequence of the film involves a cool and stylish Brigitte Lin (Taiwanese by birth and one of Hong Kong's most talented film actresses) playing a mysterious and single-minded female assassin topped by a strawberry-blonde wig, who is seen making deals and then hunting down the double-crossers in Chungking Mansions. The roving fisheye camera lens provides a wonderfully atmospheric glimpse into the building's labyrinthine interior. Of course, it affords an equally illuminating look at the moody and impressionistic direction of Wong and the compelling cinematography of his creative collaborator Christopher Doyle. Proving that life imitates art, one of the adjacent shops rejoices in the name Chungking Express.

Another artistic work of the Nineties to feature Chungking Mansions is by Hong Kong-born Indonesian-Chinese writer, Xu Xi, a prolific creative and critical writer and anthologist of Hong Kong English language writing. In Xu Xi's story entitled simply *Chunking Mansion* we are treated to recollections of narrator Ai-Lin's childhood in Sixties Tsim Sha Tsui. The story follows the then nine-year-old's fascination with an orange-haired young lady (sophisticated-looking to the narrator but in fact only a few years older than she) waiting for US sailors outside Chungking Mansions. The story provides an atmospheric and accurate depiction of the Tsim Sha Tsui of that era, when Nathan Road stood on the waterfront. It also presents the mundane truth and daily hypocrisies of adult life through the eyes of an innocent child to powerful literary effect. Imaginatively written from the child's perspective, *Chungking Mansion* offers a wonderful guide to a Nathan Road and environs that are still recognizable, if substantially altered. Part of the enjoyment of reading the story is in imagining the locale as it once was, with its network of short-cuts and its direct harbour-front view:

> *I like Tsimshatsui and our flat which has two floors and an interior connecting staircase. From our verandah on the seventeenth floor I can watch the Kowloon-Canton Railway trains pull into the station and the grey U.S. battleships in the harbour. The sweep of the island's hills is like a picture frame for the buildings dotting the hillside and the waterfront. At night the neon lights go on. My favourite is the one on the top of the low building in the middle with the three red Japanese characters, which Dad says is an advertisement for monosodium glutamate. It isn't lonely in Tsimshatsui, or quiet and scary.*

Bordering the west side of Nathan Road is the forty-acre Kowloon Park, Tsim Sha Tsui's lung that enables it to cope with exhaust fumes and the constant hum of human activity. In a previous existence the park had been Whitfield Barracks, but was subsequently handed over by the army for civil use. It was not built as a park until the 1980s, complete with sports facilities recreational spaces, bridges, paths, Chinese gardens and shaded sanctuaries for peaceful contemplation. There is also an open-air sculpture space which includes works by various artists including Eduardo Paolozzi and the ubiquitous Van Lau. Coming out of the park onto Nathan Road one is struck by the elegant and imposing Kowloon Mosque and Islamic Centre with its graceful matching minarets at the corners. The mosque was completed in 1984 on the site of the original 1896 edifice, built primarily for the benefit of Indian servicemen of the Muslim faith.

Religion has always played an important part in Hong Kong's architectural, as well as cultural and educational, development. Indeed, the symbolic co-existence of various religions in Hong Kong, as evidenced by the close proximity of places of worship of very different creeds, is a good example of the possibility of religious harmony and tolerance. The Muslim, Hindu and Sikh communities played a vital role in Hong Kong's commercial and administrative life from the early years of the colony and their presence in Tsim Sha Tsui lends this area a strongly multicultural ethos.

Opposite Kowloon Mosque and a little further up the road on the east side, is its Christian counterpart, the serene St. Andrew's Church, dating back to 1906 and looking for all the world as though it has just been transplanted into Tsim Sha Tsui from a London suburb. Likewise Edwardian is the low-rise, bright-red Antiquities and Monuments Office next door to St. Andrew's, standing in sharp contrast to the chic Park Lane shops on the opposite side. This centre has the challenging task of promoting awareness of Hong Kong's heritage. In a city where old buildings have until recently been valued as much as yesterday's newspapers, getting the conservation message across to the public has not been easy. At least its Gothic-style neighbour, as a listed historical building, appears to have a secure future. So too do the two-storey, colonnaded Hong Kong Observatory building, located up the hill adjacent to the Antiquities and Monuments Office, and the nearby Blackhead Signal Tower in Minden Row, behind the Mariners' Club. Designed to provide early warnings of typhoons and to enable mariners to check the accuracy of their chronometers, these still imposing listed monuments are a powerful reminder of Hong Kong's seafaring traditions.

Just off to the left beyond the former naval headquarters in Chatham Road is the separate area of Tsim Sha Tsui East. Two more museums are to be found in this cluster: the stylishly designed Museum of History with its special permanent exhibition, the Hong Kong Story, which is a must-see, and the Museum of Science. The latter is also well worth a visit, both for its exhibits including the story of the dinosaur and its imaginative modern architectural design In addition to its higher cultural profile, this area is the playground of the affluent and fun-loving among the Chinese community who generally shun the *gweilo*-oriented Lan Kwai Fong in Central. Tsim Sha Tsui East has a plethora of hostess bars, karaoke lounges and slightly dubious massage parlours, as well as some opulent modern hotels. Club B- Boss, its most celebrated disco, is periodically raided by Hong Kong's vice squad and revels in lurid publicity in the local Chinese press, which the English-language *South China Morning Post* and *Standard* studiously ignore.

One of the most evocative film depictions of the streets of Tsim Sha Tsui, especially those between Nathan Road and Chatham Road, is

Johnnie To's stylish masterpiece PTU (meaning Police Tactical Unit). The film shows another side of Tsim Sha Tsui during the early hours of the morning when only police patrols and potential criminals are on the streets. The dark atmosphere, laconic wit and unflinching depiction of the seamy side of the city and of police practices make this a movie to appreciate only after you have experienced the streets of TST in full daytime and evening swing.

Beyond Tsim Sha Tsui East is a strange looking, spaceship-like building adjacent to the Kowloon-Canton Railway terminus at Hung Hom. This building is in fact not a reminder of one of Hong Kong's close encounters with aliens, but a huge concert arena. Dubbed the Hong Kong Coliseum, the 10,000-seater hall hosts Hong Kong's Canto-pop acting-singing megastars such as Andy Lau, Eason Chan, Kelly Chen, Leon Lai, Faye Wong, Jay Chou, Joey Yung and The Twins (Charlene and Gillian), as opposed to lions-versus-Christians contests. It is usually packed out for a whole week of performances. By comparison, international acts playing here only manage a couple of nights at best. When Hong Kong's singing superstars Leslie Cheung, Anita Mui and Teresa Teng were alive they could command even bigger audiences, and the ticket demand was intense.

If the performers need to get to Guangzhou (Canton) fast for their next show, they can simply hop on the Kowloon-Canton Railway (KCR), which operates both the over-ground Kowloon to New Territories route stopping at all stations and the express through-train to Guanghzhou. Crossing the border at Lo Wu-Shenzen on the through-train is an experience not to be missed, and in the past was somewhat akin to the Checkpoint Charlie crossing in Berlin.

The Markets of Yau Ma Tei

Nowadays the urban sprawl of Kowloon makes it hard to discern lines of demarcation between one built-up area and another. Walking north up Nathan Road, following the MTR line, one comes to an area known as Jordan, after the road that traverses Nathan Road, leading to the Jordan Road Ferry. Continuing northwards we find that the streets of Jordan shade into Yau Ma Tei, and those on the western side are of particular interest. Here on Temple Street the celebrated Kowloon Night Market reigns supreme from early evening (starting around 18.30). The late Hong Kong superstar Anita Mui began her singing career in street opera here. Singing Cantonese street opera is far less glamorous than it sounds. In common with most people who live and work in this working-class district, musicians find that the street life, lack of sleep and lack of privacy all take their toll. Anita Mui's gruelling concert and film schedules were predicated on this stamina-building adolescent experience.

When Yau Ma Tei, meaning "sesame seed ground", is in full swing it is impossible to imagine it as the fishing village it once was. Sesame seeds, among other wares, were exported from here in the days when Yau Ma Tei stood right at the seafront. Waves of land reclamation, as the name of Reclamation Street confirms, have ensured that Yau Ma Tei's waterfront, its busy typhoon shelter and steam ferry terminal have all receded into the distant collective memory of residents. With the loss of immediate proximity to the sea came a rapid development in markets, so what was a loss to the district in one sense became a gain or at least a re-emphasis in its commercial livelihood. The Tin Hau Temple, standing on the intersection of a network of original Kowloon streets including Public Square Street (Jung Fong Gaai) and Temple Street (Miu Gaai) and not far from the throbbing Nathan Road, attests to Yau Ma Tei's earlier maritime credentials. Indeed, there are many photographs, especially aerial ones from the pre-and post-war eras, showing Yau Ma Tei at the heart of a district that was both closely connected with the waterfront and also linked by the long Waterloo Road thoroughfare, which begins here, with the rest of Kowloon. The shelter, incidentally, like the one at Causeway Bay on Hong Kong-side, was always packed with boats when a typhoon struck. It was completed in 1915 as a response to the fierce 1906 and 1908 typhoons, which devastated the important shipping industry locally. The latter one left approximately 10,000 dead in and around Victoria Harbour.

Tin Hau being the patron goddess of seafarers, it is clear from the substantial size of this temple complex that the seafaring community has a long history in Yau Ma Tei. According to a stone tablet in the temple grounds commemorating restoration work in 1870, the original temple on the site dates back to when Yau Ma Tei was developing as a community, a long time before British rule. The temple committee, the *kai fong*, rather like the Man-Mo Temple committee, has always been highly active in promoting community life and development. Not only is the temple cluster (four temples and a community hall) prominently located, but it also continues to function as a central point in an area that retains its unique flavour, despite the constant threat of encroachment from nearby Nathan Road.

The large enclosed forecourt in front of the temple vindicates the name, Public Square Street. In addition to shops selling religious items for temple worship there is an open space for walking and relaxing as well as for inevitable exploitation by street vendors. The space comes alive in the evening when Yau Ma Tei's markets are in full flow. Inside the temple complex is an impressive shrine to Tin Hau, guarded by stone lions and containing an altar and a number of icons of the goddess. The adjoining motherhood temple (named Fuk Dak, meaning "blessing and virtue") contains statues of twelve model mothers as well as the presiding deity of mothers and babies, Lady Kam Fa. The Earth God and Harvest temple and the City God (Shing Wong) temple complete the complex. Though perhaps not as well-known to visitors as the Man-Mo Temple in Hollywood Road, nor as significant for Hong Kongers generally as the Wong Tai Sin Temple in central Kowloon, this is in many ways the most aesthetically pleasing and suitably located of all Hong Kong temples.

A stone's throw from the Tin Hau Temple on Public Square Street stands one of Yau Ma Tei's sought-after markets, the Jade Market, which is actually located underneath the flyover for another very busy Kowloon thoroughfare, Gascoigne Road. Yau Ma Tei's jade market is indisputably a major attraction for tourists, especially those with Chinese lineage. Jade stone, available in different colours—green, white red and black—is one of the most powerful connotative emblems of Chinese culture and civilization. Green is probably the most popularly worn and desired colour. According to Chinese tradition dating back to the days of Confucius, high quality jade signifies graceful, aesthetic qualities and purity for ladies and scholarly, gentlemanly, benevolent virtues for men. It is commonly set in rings and necklaces, although pieces of jade are often worn on pendants to invoke good fortune. Good quality jade is highly prized in Hong Kong as in other Chinese societies, but the Jade Market is probably not the place to buy very valuable jade, as it is easy to be duped into paying more than the market value, if one is not an expert. The lively and well-lit market is, on the other hand, an excellent place to browse through the many stalls looking for attractive and relatively inexpensive pieces.

It is perhaps reassuring to know that Yau Ma Tei's market is situated under the protective eyes of the Tin Hau Temple and the old grey and blue-fronted Yau Ma Tei Police Station, which was originally set directly on the waterfront when it opened for business in 1920. Still an imposing but genteel-looking building, the police station has featured in a number of films set in Yau Ma Tei that evoke the colonial era. The older style tenements of Yau Ma Tei dating from the 1940s and 1950s also provided imaginative inspiration for the Hong Kong company G.O.D. (a cleverly ambiguous acronym, signifying not only the English "Goods of Desire" but also a homophone of the Cantonese name, Jee Ho Di, which translates as "live better"). G.O.D. is Hong Kong's popular home-grown designer brand. The company likes to use the memorable image of old building exteriors as a design motif on bags and even sofas. Local retro chic it may be, but the Hong Kong chain seems to have struck the right chord with local consumers judging by the proliferation of outlets. Unfortunately there is no such shop in Yau Ma Tei, which seems anomalous, though there is one in Tsim Sha Tsui.

Right opposite next to a housing estate is a more modern building, highly popular with Hong Kong's younger film aficionados. The Broadway Cinematheque, built in the 1990s, has become a magnet for art-house film lovers who have proliferated in Hong Kong following the success of the thirty-year-old International Film Festival. Showing an imaginative blend of local, regional and international films not considered sufficiently "commercial" to earn a decent run in other cinemas, the Cinematheque has delighted film audiences with its range and its enlightened policy. The Kubrick film centre and cultural bookshop next door, a haven for browsing or attending cinema-related talks, is a further reason to patronize this flourishing arts cinema complex. Not far from here at the intersection of Waterloo Road and Shanghai Street, close to the bustling Yau Ma Tei fruit market and wholesale vendors, is Yau Ma Tei's first cinema, dating from 1925. This theatre, a carbon copy of many early European cinemas, is now under renovation following years of neglect. Happily, the theatre, with its stylish white façade, is to be preserved as a local heritage centre.

Mong Kok: "The Most Densely Peopled Place on Earth"

Continuing on foot northwards up Nathan Road, the main artery of Kowloon, you soon come to the place that superseded Yau Ma Tei in

Sai Yeung Choi Street, Mong Kok

importance, not necessarily in terms of markets but as a trade and shopping hub. As with the transition from Jordan to Yau Ma Tei, it is not clear on Nathan Road at what point one is actually no longer in Yau Ma Tei and suddenly in Mong Kok. The crowds, however, become denser and one is soon aware that Mong Kok's reputation as the most heavily populated square mile on earth may not be as exaggerated as it sounds. Long before the meteoric rise of Mong Kok to become one of the trendiest places for young people in the modern-day city, there was simply a small village here surrounded by farmland. Development started in the 1910s with the construction of a ferry pier linking Mong Kok Tsui with Hong Kong Island. There was a main road running through the village, known as Shanghai Street, connecting Yau Ma Tei with Sham Shui Po Village. This road still runs through both Yau Ma Tei and Mong Kok parallel to Nathan Road, but in earlier days it was the main thoroughfare.

Looking at the maze of streets, the forest of neon signs, the endless traffic, both human and petrol-fuelled, the never-ending buying and selling of hi-tech and low-tech products, it is virtually impossible to conceive of this place as a once-upon-a-time quiet village. The fact that it is now a distinctive yet indistinct part of the Yau-Tsim-Mong (Yau Ma Tei-Tsim Sha Tsui-Mong Kok) municipal sprawl is testimony to the phenomenal success of twentieth-century road planning on the Kowloon peninsula, especially between the Star Ferry at the southern tip and Kowloon Tong and Lion Rock at the northern boundary.

One interesting feature of Mong Kok is the strangely different pronunciations of its initial sound in English and Cantonese. The Cantonese name is pronounced Wong Gok whereas the English language version uses an "M" for the initial consonant. The words "mong" and "wong" in Cantonese both can mean "busy", and the overall meaning of Mong Kok sounds like "busy meeting point". Mong Kok was originally a fishing village, like so many other places, and the word "mong" also means "fishing net". After land reclamation separated Mong Kok from the waterfront and the area thrived as a commercial centre, the consonant shifted from "mong" to "wong" in local usage, implying a place of prosperity. A different but plausible explanation is that the name derives from the "mon" grass that originally proliferated here. Nothing is simple in Hong Kong place-name etymology!

Like Yau Ma Tei, the Mong Kok area has long been noted for its street markets. The oldest of these (specializing in flowers) is located in Flower Market Road near Mong Kok Police Station just off one of the area's oldest main roads, Prince Edward Road. This main east-west Kowloon artery is named after the Prince of Wales of the early 1920s, not Queen Elizabeth's youngest son. Prince Edward is virtually indistinguishable from the rest of Mong Kok nowadays, but it was formerly on the edge of the Kowloon cession to the British in 1860. Boundary Street, just north of here, marked the boundary with Chinese territory. Today's busy but ordinary road was simply the path that ran alongside the high bamboo fence separating Kowloon from China. Even the fence did not deter the flower sellers who brought their wares down to Mong Kok to sell in what rapidly became a thriving market.

The range of flowers sold in the market, in which permanent shops have become established to replace the temporary stalls, is amazing. Not only are international species of plants and flowers on sale, but importantly for Chinese cultural tradition those that signify wealth and happiness at auspicious times such as Chinese New Year are essential items: kumquat, narcissus, orchid lotus, chrysanthemum, plum and peach blossom among many other varieties of plants and flowers. Prices vary, especially around Chinese New Year and on other significant dates such as St. Valentine's Day, according to the pragmatic laws of supply and demand.

Caged birds have long been popular for their song but also for their symbolic characteristics in Chinese mythology. Keeping songbirds in cages has always been considered a sign of good birth and gentility and is strongly rooted in traditional Chinese culture. Bird Street, now moved to the area between Prince Edward Road and Boundary Street, used to be in the heart of Mong Kok close to the main market. It was originally one of the busiest and most famous streets in Mong Kok and Hong Kong's many bird fanciers would congregate here, the vast majority of them middle-aged or older men. The original street was narrow, crowded and dark but in its new environment in Yuen Po Street the bird market is at more spacious and airy. Older men taking their caged birds for a walk is a common sight in Kowloon generally, and especially in this area.

Another kind of market is depicted in Madeleine Marie Slavick's poem "Mong kok Market", which appears in her 2004 poetry and photography collection, *Delicate Access*. There is a network of street markets to be discovered around Fa Yuen ("Flower Garden") Street, famous for its nearly authentic designer clothes and cleverly faked designer accessories. These include the Ladies' Market, the vegetable market and the fish market, all on Tung Choi ("Hollow Vegetable") Street and Sai Yeung Choi ("Watercress") Street. Slavick depicts the instant slaughter one cannot avoid witnessing at the live meat and fish stalls. This practice is deeply embedded in Chinese culture as a means of ensuring the daily freshness of fish and poultry:

Blood at the neat hand
Shout
Buffet for the quiet eye
Wide
Sweet leaves of heaven
Sing...
Brown feathers are pulled silent from a young hen
the small body a single organ
a fallen star
Cold tofu blocks stand in formation like frozen corporals
then are sliced
and wilt
into a white blubber stomach...

Mong Kok and Tai Kok Tsui, its north-west extension, provide an exciting and evocative backdrop for locally made films. Perhaps the most internationally famous of all is John Woo's 1986 *A Better Tomorrow*, a bloody tale of cops and double-crossing gangsters which launched the careers of Woo as a director and, more significantly, the cool and charismatic Chow Yun-fat as an actor. Scenes of stylized bloody fights between heavily armed gangsters are played out in the dingy waterfront locale between Yau Ma Tei, Mong Kok and the more industrialized Tai Kok Tsui. The area is also favoured by director Johnnie To as a haven for Triads in his film *Election* (2005), a skilful and implicit allegory about election processes and mainland interference in Hong Kong's affairs using succession struggles among Triad figures, portrayed by Simon Yam and Tony Leung Ka-fai, as his more explicit subject matter. The yellow sign (equivalent to "red-light") district of Portland Street is the locale for director Yip Wai-man's fascinating vice-and-Triad themed movie

Portland Street Blues with its tough heroines played by Sandra Ng and Shu Qi. In Derek Yee's 2003 film *One Nite in Mong Kok* contemporary heartthrob actor Daniel Wu plays the hero on the run in a rather hostile and menacing late-night Mong Kok.

Giving a completely contrasting impression of Mong Kok is the elegantly up-market Langham Place and Langham Hotel development close to the Mong Kok KCR train station. This luxury complex indicates a brighter, smarter future for the whole of Mong Kok twenty years or so from now. On the other hand, it is precisely the cheap, practical down-to-earth ethos of Mong Kok that many Hong Kongers like and are comfortable with, so perhaps there will be firm pressure on the urban planners to preserve some of Mong Kok's colourful character.

One district they are doubtless eying for its potential is the low-rise residential Kadoorie Avenue, a short walk eastward from the busy centre of Mong Kok, which looks pretty much today as it did in the 1950s. This was when Lord Kadoorie developed the hillock behind his still-standing art deco-style headquarters of China Light and Power in Argyle Street and created a leafy Finchley-like suburb near the heart of Mong Kok. Kadoorie Avenue is one of those great Hong Kong anomalies. It simply should not be here, and one could easily miss it, and yet there it is asserting its Fifties retro-chic style. The reason for its survival was that it lay directly under the flight-path for Kowloon's now obsolete Kai Tak airport.

Another great Kowloon survivor, standing at one of its busiest road junctions with a traffic flyover careering overhead, is the 1932 church of St. Teresa. In old photographs the church's stately white spire dominates a peaceful suburban skyline. Today the rather Italianate and now more weathered structure still stands out for its slight but unmistakable resemblance to a Disney castle. Yet it has been effectively reduced in stature by the implacable urban development of Kowloon, where every square inch is in demand and potentially under threat. Like St. Teresa's, the red-brick fortress of Maryknoll Sisters' school and convent, standing a little further north on the opposite side of Waterloo Road, makes a strong case for religious education in the city. Many schools and hospitals owe their founding to the dedication of religious denominations in looking after the interests of the young, the old and the sick. It was not until more reform-minded and public-spirited representatives of the Crown arrived in Hong Kong following liberation from the Japanese after 1945 that Hong Kong's education system started to develop along centralized lines. Up to that point religious groups such as the Carmelites and the Jesuits, as well as Chinese religious associations, assumed responsibility for educating the young, while the rest of Hong Kong got on with the business of making money. Hong Kongers have always had a firm belief in the value of self-help, but there is no doubting the important role played by religious groups of all shapes and sizes in the life of the Territory.

The Lion and the Tomb: Kowloon Tong and Sham Shui Po

Kowloon Tong, Shek Kip Mei and Sham Shui Po, which lie directly north of the Mong Kok-Prince Edward district, were not part of the original post-1860s Hong Kong territory. Prior to their inclusion as part of the acquisition of the New Territories in 1898, Boundary Road at the northern edge of Mong Kok had delineated the end of British territory. The so-called New Kowloon area lay in the shadow of the natural boundary between Britain and the land of China beyond formed by the hill known as Lion Rock. In fact, Lion Rock is only one of the series of ridges that run east-west between Kowloon and the New Territories. Today a traffic tunnel, together with the Kowloon-Canton Railway tunnel, connects the two sides, but before they were constructed Lion Rock and the other hills constituted a solid and formidable barrier to the traveller. In pre-Second World War times tigers roamed the hills, so although there were known paths and roads, the journey could be a perilous undertaking.

The name Lion Rock does not actually strike the visitor as particularly apt until it is viewed from a suitable angle on a clear day. Broadcast Drive, home to RTHK (Radio Television Hong Kong), offers one such prospect. You can see the majestic leonine shape reclining on its front paws with the head and mane clearly delineated against the skyline. On a clear day the craggy weathering of the Lion Rock comes alive with its uncanny verisimilitude. The hills of Kowloon may have suggested eight dragons to the young Emperor's advisor, but the most prominent of the eight has definitely transformed itself into a lion over the intervening centuries.

Lion Rock and the range of hills dominate the view, and for many both on Hong Kong Island and in Kowloon it seems as though China itself rather than the New Territories has always lain beyond, which of course was the case prior to 1898. Kowloon Tong, Lok Fu, Shek Kip Mei, Sham Shui Po and other areas lying in the lee of Lion Rock were not developed until well into the twentieth century. Before then there was only agricultural land and small intermittent hamlets. It is hard to appreciate this transformation today when the whole of Kowloon is seamlessly joined in what appears continuous urban development.

Below the Lion Rock was the name of Hong Kong's most popular and longest-running television drama series. Beginning in the 1970s when poverty was still common and the city was utilizing its huge influx of refugees for the manufacturing industry, the grittily realistic series followed the lives of a working- class family in the Shek Kip Mei government housing estate. As a result of devastating fires in the squatter encampments that had sprung up below Lion Rock to house the increased population (and particularly the great fire of Christmas Day 1953), the government embarked on an urgent building programme. As the television series made clear, the new housing estates were hardly idyllic. Indeed, the cramped flats were basic and spartan, with many sharing sanitation and washing facilities. Better than any other series *Below the Lion Rock* captured the period and is a fascinating piece of social documentary as much as a drama. Socially conscious movie director Ann Hui and other talented directors and scriptwriters cut their teeth on this three-decade long series. One of Hui's episodes dealing with police corruption (the Godber affair) was actually banned by a nervous government in a period of unrest. *Below the Lion Rock* became synonymous with Hong Kong people's lives, in general and the Lion Rock a benign local emblem for Hong Kong and Kowloon, not just Kowloon Tong and Shek Kip Mei.

The Kowloon Tong area is distinct from the surrounding high-rise estates for a very simple reason: it was in the flight-path for Kai Tak airport, which was started before the war and completed afterwards. Many of the streets in Kowloon Tong bear the names of English counties: Dorset Street, Oxford Road, Essex Crescent, Cornwall Street, Hereford Road, Somerset Road, etc., and there are still many graceful two-storey houses with gardens to be seen in this neighbourhood. Jackie Chan has his business headquarters in a converted former town-house on Waterloo Road in Kowloon Tong, for example. One thing conspicuous by its absence, however, is the type of clothing and stitching factory ("Imperial Stitching") that American writer Paul

Theroux envisaged as the setting for his entertainingly written but grossly caricatured novel *Kowloon Tong*. The kind of factory that Theroux had in mind was plausible east of here in Kowloon City and Kwun Tong, even in 1997 when this ham-fisted Handover novel is set, but definitely not on Waterloo Road in Kowloon Tong.

A far more authentic portrait of the Kowloon Tong area is depicted by Xu Xi in her novel *Hong Kong Rose* (1997). Rose and her boyfriend Paul look for escape from Rose's interfering mother to satisfy their passion in public parks, of which there are many in the Beacon Hill vicinity where the fictional Rose lives. Maryknoll, Rose's (and Xu Xi's) old school is mentioned in an early chapter because it is such a distinctive landmark. Like many good writers, Xu Xi's fictional world acquires credibility partly because her characters and situation have much in common with a world she knows, which is patently not the case with Theroux's conception of Kowloon Tong.

Another Xu Xi tale, one of the short story collection entitled *History's Fiction* (2001), is about a boy from a housing estate in nearby Lok Fu who becomes obsessed with the new "underground iron"—to use the Cantonese slang expression for the metro, the MTR. The period is the late Seventies at the time of the completion of the gleaming new underground train system linking Hong Kong and Kowloon and richer areas with poorer ones. The boy is able to travel to Kowloon Tong for the first time in his life and on subsequent visits a fatal fascination for a world unknown to him and outside the sphere of his miserable family life takes hold. This beautifully simple, downbeat story shows the kind of disparities that are inevitable in Kowloon, where more affluent streets and blocks are near neighbours with functional public housing estates.

As Hong Kong's most controversial rap group, LMF (short for LazyMuthaFuckaz) have spent more than a decade exploring the urban alienation that comes from the experience of growing up on public housing estates. Most of the ten band members come from that background but their resilience and good fortune in meeting like-minded, would-be musicians helped to keep them out of the Triad trouble that may otherwise have been their lot. Their lyrics are vituperative, occasionally whimsical and frequently littered with expletives. Nevertheless, there is something life-affirming about the band in performance despite the fact that according to their documentary video, *Dare Ya!*, they are avowedly bone idle and dysfunctional in basic life skills such as eating. Another great Hong Kong band that was spawned in the housing estates of Kowloon was early 1990s group, Beyond. The urgency of their sound seemed to epitomize the mixture of anxiety and anger felt by Hong Kong youth in response to the uncertainty of life in the increasingly affluent but insecure Eighties. After the death of their iconic lead singer Wong Ka-kui in a tragic stage fall during a concert in Japan the group never recaptured the spark of their early popular appeal.

What comes through the raw but engaging music of both these groups is the kind of direct attitude and teenage restlessness and tension that are also perceptible in the grittily compelling films of maverick director, Fruit Chan. Two Chan masterpieces, *Made in Hong Kong* and *Hong Kong Hollywood* (not Hollywood Road in up-market Hong Kong-side, but the squatter area in front of Plaza Hollywood in Diamond Hill, close to Lion Rock) exemplify the unpolished, urgent and laconic style of this deceptively avuncular doyen of Hong Kong's independent movie scene. One of the LMF group members played the lead in Chan's urban poem of a movie, *Made in Hong Kong*, with great aplomb and conviction. To get a good idea of life in a Kowloon-side housing estate in the Nineties, a Fruit Chan film is the closest thing to actually staying in one.

Back in the 1970s when memories of squatter encampments were still strong, one of Hong Kong's most popular and successful movies, *The House of Seventy Two Tenants*, directed by Cho Yuen for Shaw Brothers, evoked an era when refugees from the mainland were crammed together in overcrowded housing and made to pay extortionate rent. The film locates the tenement of the title in the Sham Shui Po area, well within view of Lion Rock, and brings it up to date with mocking and self-mocking humour, the latter a Hong Kong Cantonese speciality. With topical references to grasping landlords, severe water rationing and corrupt police commissioners, it struck a contemporary note, but managed to convey the straightened circumstances of the early 1950s Hong Kong immigrants at the same time. Its comic but heart-warming romantic dénouement was both populist and popular and the film ran for a record number of performances, as did the earlier play on which it was based. Stephen Chow also used the basic narrative as a vehicle for comedy in his smash hit 2004 movie, *Kung Fu Hustle*. It seemed somehow appropriate for

Hong Kong's version of this old Canton drama to be set below the Lion Rock in the Shaw Brothers film, and for it to be relocated to Canton in Chow's farcical, special effects spoof.

Today Sham Shui Po (the name meaning literally "deep water bank"), north of Prince Edward and not far from the more up-market Kowloon Tong, is another very busy working-class district. It was the site of British army barracks built on levelled and reclaimed land in the 1920s, as the further parts of Kowloon became integrated into the British "possession" and dubbed "New Kowloon". These military barracks, which used to command a sea-view, were used as an internment camp by the Japanese army during the occupation. Strolling in today's Sham Shui Po, possibly for the purpose of acquiring cheap and unethical software or hardware in the Golden Computer arcade, it is hard to imagine what occurred there less than one hundred years ago. It is harder still to grasp that in the midst of this vibrant concrete jungle lies one of Hong Kong's most significant archeological finds. The 2,000 year-old Han Dynasty Tomb (circa 90 AD) was discovered by accident in 1955 by workmen excavating the Lei Cheng Uk site in Sham Shui Po ahead of a big urban resettlement programme. It also contained many artefacts, including bronze bowls, pottery and mirrors. Subsequently it was preserved as an archeological site and is now managed by curators from the Museum of History. Lei Cheng Uk Han Tomb was believed to have been built as the cenotaph of a Han Dynasty official, according to some experts, and as that of a southern Han empress according to others. A museum was opened at the site in 1957 and a Han Dynasty classical-style garden added. The protective roof built after the discovery and excavation of the tomb to combat water seepage is now being replaced with a more hi-tech canopy.

McDull—a Kowloon icon

Another enormously popular work of the imagination set in the central Kowloon area and featuring the Lion Rock is the award-winning film animation, *McDull*. An all-Hong-Kong creation with characters designed by director Brian Tse and screenplay writer Alice Mak, the first film, *My Life as McDull* introduced the anthropomorphic young pig who lives with his mother in a housing tenement area between Kowloon Tong and Kowloon City. The district seems to be based on the busy real-life streets of To Kwa Wan. He goes to a cramped kindergarten where he and his classmates, including best friend McMug, are taught by the earnest Ms. Chan and lectured to by the pedantic and cliché-dependent headmaster at school assembly. The depiction of the concrete jungle of Kowloon's heartland is brilliant, partly because the cartoon portrays another Hong Kong of green open spaces, which is easy to find if one takes a bus eastward toward the dazzlingly beautiful Sai Kung and Clearwater Bay Peninsula. There is a wistful, nostalgic quality about the way the old Kowloon and Hong Kong buildings and streets are depicted in the (to date) three *McDull* films.

Tongue-in-cheek and full of ironic throwaway Hong Kong humour, the animated films can be appreciated on different levels by children and adults. They have more in common with the Shrek animations than with Disney, but are more oblique and sophisticated in their humour. McDull has inevitably been commercialized in various forms of merchandise for Hong Kong people but not particularly overseas because the lovably "un-cute" pig is somehow a quintessential product of Hong Kong culture. In this writer's humble opinion, he is an infinitely more fitting icon for the city than those crassly unsubtle interlopers, Hello Kitty and Mickey Mouse, could ever aspire to be. Not that there will ever be a money-grubbing McDull-land in Hong Kong. That is just not his style. But the self-effacing and earnestly well-meaning McDull qualifies as a new dragon, not just for the commercial acumen of his creators, but for the inspired way the animation captures the spirit of the city and its people.

As if underlining the independent ethos of To Kwa Wan and Kowloon City, the former government abattoir-turned arts colony of Ngau Paang or Cattle Depot, located near the former city airport of Kai Tak, has become a Mecca for experimental visual artists and theatre groups. This remarkably agreeable complex of low-rise, colonial red-brick buildings, formerly used to slaughter cattle, is now a vibrant artists' village, attracting both locals and overseas visitors who want to explore the outer limits of the Hong Kong arts scene. Nestling snugly if incongruously against the local Towngas gasworks, the artists' commune houses theatre groups Zuni Icosahedron and On and On Theatre and a cluster of visual arts practitioners, including exponents of installation and performance art. In some ways it is Kowloon's idiosyncratic alternative to the Hong Kong Fringe Club.

From the Walled City to Kai Tak

Going down Junction Road, which as its name implies joins Kowloon Tong and Kowloon City, one can easily get to some of the most historically significant and architecturally interesting buildings in Kowloon. One of the sites, the Walled City, is now a commemorative park and one has to use one's imagination to glimpse its historical role. When the British occupied Hong Kong Island in the mid-nineteenth century and Tsim Sha Tsui was still an uninhabited sand-spit, the Chinese Qing government decided to reinforce the small garrison that had controlled the salt trade in the area since the Sung Dynasty emperors as far back as 1000 AD. The modest fortifications that had been established in that era were strengthened and more troops were sent. In 1847 by order of the emperor fifteen-feet-thick stone walls were added to existing fortifications as well as watchtowers and heavy gates.

Despite some disruptions during the Taiping Rebellion in the following decade, the garrison continued to expand. In 1860, after the British acquisition of Kowloon, the Chinese government insisted on maintaining the five-and-a-half acre Walled City, as it was now known, as sovereign territory not to be included under the foreigners' jurisdiction. The consistent Chinese refusal to cede this enclave to the British represented not only a thorn in the side of British authority, but suggests to the unbiased observer that the cession of Hong Kong and most of the Kowloon Peninsula under duress in periods of political weakness was never intended to constitute a definitive and irreversible surrender of sovereign territory. The successive enforced treaties were seen as coercive and illegitimate by the Chinese side. Margaret Thatcher failed to understand this when she pressed an adamant Deng Xiaoping to yield on Hong Kong's retrocession in the 1982 negotiations in Beijing. Some thought that when she took her historically symbolic tumble down the steps of the Great Hall of the People, Heaven was punishing her for her arrogance.

The Walled City continued to flourish despite the development of Tsim Sha Tsui and Yau Ma Tei in the latter decades of the nineteenth century. Yet after the New Territories were ceded to the increasingly demanding British occupiers in 1898 by a Qing government tottering on the brink of collapse, the writing was, so to speak, on the Wall. Plans to invade and reclaim Kowloon had come to naught and the garrison was demoralized. At the height of British jingoism the British Volunteer Force, and more bizarrely the Welsh Fusiliers, occupied the Walled City and set up the Union Jack on the walls. The Chinese garrison left having offered very little resistance, and from this point the Walled City remained an historical and political anomaly.

In 1942 during the Japanese occupation it lost its defensive walls and ramparts. They were torn down by the prisoner-of-war labourers to serve as foundations for the extension of Kai Tak airport's runway. By now a ruin in which desperate Kowloon people foraged for materials, the Walled City would never be the same again. After the war it could not be incorporated into Kowloon because the Chinese communist government never acknowledged British sovereignty. As a result it became a ghetto of packed tenements and makeshift utilities, inhabited by lawless elements including drug pushers and users as well as Chinese medical practitioners, who were not licensed to pursue their livelihood under the Hong Kong health system. The Walled City became an insalubrious slum that would have been unrecognizable to its 1850s commander, General Chang, who made it a more civilized environment and whose calligraphy adorns the walls and buildings that were fortunate enough to escape the ravages of time and man. The Walled City was eventually demolished in 1994, three years before the Handover, after the Chinese government under Deng Xiaoping let it be known they would not oppose the move, as they had steadfastly done up to that point.

A few years before its demolition, I went inside the Walled City, as one was allowed to do at one's own risk. The overall impression was of medieval-looking, dark and narrow alleys (without the light quality of European medieval towns) and an inevitable stench of poor sanitation and garbage disposal. Yet this bastion of self-determination and Triad infiltration had seen a marked social improvement after the unlikely intervention of a Christian missionary named Jackie Pullinger. This remarkable woman arrived in Hong Kong from Britain in 1966, and after experiencing the hopelessness of Kowloon City's drug addict and prostitute population, she proceeded to set up an organization to convert and give hope to those who had none, leading by her own indomitable example. Pullinger's Hong Kong experiences are recounted in her down-to-earth memoir *Chasing the Dragon*, written in 1982. Against all odds, she succeeded in mobilizing charitable and religious organizations and even the government to rehabilitate an astonishingly high number of addicts and petty criminals, who as Walled City residents had been the flotsam of society. Pullinger's faith seemed to protect her even against the Triads for whom her activities ought to have been anathema. In the Kowloon Walled City Park, which stands on the site of the former Walled City, a rock with an inscription commemorates the work of this exceptional and dedicated lady.

Talking of dedicated ladies and British ones to boot, one of Hong Kong's most redoubtable social activists and legislative councillors chose a similar course to that taken by Dr. Pullinger. The young Elsie Elliott (no relation to Charles) arrived as a young teacher but was so disgusted by the prevailing culture of complacency and inertia on the part of bureaucrats toward poor children's education that she set up a free school for children in neglected East Kowloon. Her struggles to establish the school in the face of official obstruction and her subsequent plucky campaign against endemic corruption in the Hong Kong system are recounted in her autobiographical memoir. Elsie Tu, as she later became after marrying former mainland Chinese colleague Andrew Tu, stayed on to become a symbol of change and a tireless campaigner for the rights of the many disenfranchised working-class people. When limited democracy was introduced in the MacLehose era this feisty lobbyist, by then a   member of the Urban Council, joined the Legislative Council, officially representing the people of Kwun Tong and East Kowloon. Tu's third memoir, *Shouting at the Mountain* (2004), details the gradual changes that occurred throughout the 1970s and 1980s, as the struggle for a better deal in terms of education and housing began to bear fruit. The mountain of the title refers in part to the peaks of Kowloon, which literally oversaw the lives of the community in an era when relatively little travel within Hong Kong was possible for low-income families..

Inside the Walled City Park, built in imitation of the classical Suzhou and Hangzhou style, a large and ancient rock commemorates the re-establishment of Chinese sovereignty. One older building, the administrative centre and court called the Yamen, has survived with General Chang's so-called "fist calligraphy" still intact on its walls. Old photographs of the interior of the Walled City in Cheng Po Hung's and Tung Po Ming's record, *A Century of Kowloon's Roads and Streets*, bear witness to its rich history with wonderful pictures of its ramparts and rusting cannons. By the 1920s it had become a tourist attraction. In the foreground of some photographs, facing the Walled City and closer to the waterfront, one can see the Sung Wong Toi Rock (the Sung boy emperor's terrace) which today stands in Sung Wong Toi Garden. What was the Walled City is now once more a tourist attraction but at the same time a recreational area for local people with giant chess boards and viewing spots. After its 1,000-year vicissitudes the place belongs once again to the people of Kowloon.

So too does the Kai Tak airport site which lies opposite Kowloon City's busy streets overlooking the harbour. Today the decommissioned airport, its terminal building now demolished, is used as an occasional market, a venue for open-air concerts and a roller-skating rink. Kai Tak's extensive site has an almost ghostly appearance and eerily old-fashioned-looking arrival and departure signs are still clearly visible from the street.

The story of the development of Kai Tak airport, named incidentally after the distinguished nineteenth-century jurist, legislative councillor and founding member of Hong Kong University, Sir Kai Ho-kai, is compelling reading. Gavin Young tells the story of Kai Tak's and Cathay Pacific's emergence in the post-war years after the fledgling airport was taken over by the invading Japanese forces in his book, *Beyond Lion Rock*. Five years before the Japanese occupation the first London-Hong Kong flight had taken place, landing in 1936 at a very rudimentary Kai Tak. The significance of Young's title is certainly worthy of comment: the Lion Rock was a major obstacle to low-flying aircraft and the descent into Kowloon was so tricky that Kai Tak was considered one of the world's most dangerous airports. New pilots were only allowed to fly in and out after many hours practising on a simulator.

The open airport tarmac with stunning views of the hills and the harbour—from which well-wishers could wave to arriving or departing friends and loved-ones—is well depicted in the two 1950s Hollywood Hong Kong films, *Love is A Many-Splendoured Thing* and *The World of Suzie Wong*. Indeed, the barrier of the eight dragon hills behind the landing strip is particularly well shown. It does not take much imagination to see that pilots had little margin for error. One China Airlines (Taiwan) pilot overshot the tarmac and the passengers had to be hauled out of the harbour, unprepared for their combined landing and instant harbour tour. Before the new airport opened at Chek Lap Kok on Lantau Island in 1998 the great landing story of those Hong Kong-bound passengers with window seats always focused on what could be seen on TV in the flats of Kowloon City residents, or the contents of the washing lines (or poles) jutting from their balconies.

Seen from above, it is clear that there are several interesting but (at ground level) easily overlooked temples in the vicinity of Kowloon City. One of them is the nearly 300-year-old Sung Dynasty-style building known as Hau Wong Temple off Junction Road and close to the Walled City Park and to Kowloon City. The present temple pre-dates British rule and was built on the site of the original one in 1730. Nestling picturesquely among trees on the fringes of Kowloon City, it is dedicated to one of the protectors of the city whose name is redolent of both fact and myth. Yeung Leung was the loyal bodyguard to the two Sung Dynasty princes who died near here. He gave his life trying to engineer their escape from the implacable Mongol forces and was posthumously made a Marquis with the name Hau Wong—a generic name for steadfast and well-respected mandarins. His memory continued to be venerated in the Kowloon City temple built in his honour by Sung loyalists and traditionalists in Kowloon.

Wong Tai Sin Temple: Hong Kong's Refugee God

Heading east from Kowloon City and Kowloon Tong in the direction of the eastern residential and industrial areas of Choi Hung, Kwun Tong and Lam Tin, two buildings stick out like sore thumbs. This is simply because they are neither modern skyscrapers nor industrial blocks, but temples. One is perched on a hill above Diamond Hill (Gin Sek Shan) near the garish Plaza Hollywood and is known as the Chi Lin Nunnery. This serene and attractive complex, juxtaposed incongruously with the unlovely shopping centre (see Fruit Chan's film *Hollywood Hong Kong*) like Beauty and the Beast, is a recently constructed replica of a Tang Dynasty Buddhist nunnery. It includes all the features of Buddhist monasteries and nunneries, including symbolic lotus ponds which are connected with the concept of reincarnation, columns containing Buddhist scriptures, images of the Buddhas and the Immortals and authentic classical-style Chinese architecture. Lord Buddha's birthday on the 8th day of the 4th Chinese lunar month is the most important festive occasion in the life of the nunnery.

The second is more down-to-earth, literally so. Wong Tai Sin Temple is on lower ground set back from the main highway, Lung Cheung Road, which runs east-west and is easily missed unless one knows where to look. Today it is almost swallowed up by the housing blocks and commercial buildings that surround it. The MTR station and the locale itself take their names from the 1921 temple founded on this spot. In the early years few people came here to worship because the area was largely rural and the terrain before the post-war development of the area was hilly and difficult. The reason why the god Wong Tai Sin is worshipped in this part of Kowloon is itself fascinating and the subject of an excellent study entitled *Wong Tai Sin: the Rise of a Refugee God* by Graeme Lang and Lars Ragvald. Wong Tai Sin is a traditional Taoist god, but at the time he was introduced into Hong Kong in 1921 he was a rather minor one. His name is a reference to his great wisdom (literally Great Sage Wong) and he was a shepherd of the Jin Dynasty around 300 AD. He studied Taoist enlightenment under a master and then became a hermit and lived in a cave on a mountain in Zhejiang Province. Later his name became associated with a family in Guangdong Province, south of Zhejiang. Descendants of this family, the Leung family, brought his picture with them first to Macao and subsequently to Hong Kong in 1915. The temple is supposed to have been founded according to the specific instructions of the god at an exact spot located so many paces from the waterfront and so many from the foothills of Lion Rock.

After a number of structural developments, Wong Tai Sin's fortunes, which had been unspectacular following the founding of his temple, suddenly improved. A major reconstruction project in 1973 put this previously out-of-the-way temple at the heart of a new community, mainly refugees in a resettlement area. Gradually Wong Tai Sin, himself a refugee god from the Shanghai region, assumed symbolic importance in a community largely composed of fellow refugees relocated in ever greater numbers. More and more people began to visit the temple at Chinese festivals, especially at Lunar New Year, to have their fortunes told. In spite of a colonial government move to requisition the land for public housing Wong Tai Sin's lucky charms prevailed, and the temple survived to become more and more popular.

Today it is quite simply the largest and most frequented temple in the whole of Hong Kong, and, as well as being run as a charitable

Wong Tai Sin Temple, Kowloon.

institution, is authorized to hold marriage services according to Taoist tradition. The god is believed to communicate with his supplicants through a medium in a similar way to that employed in Western spiritualism. His image, the original picture brought to Hong Kong by the Leung family, can still be seen on the altar of the main hall. Fortune telling by sticks is the most popular method of prognostication used in the adjoining fortune telling house, which is continuously patronized on festivals.

Beyond Wong Tai Sin and Kowloon City three more of the Sung boy emperor's dragons rise impressively over the cityscape. The view from any of them is amazing even in this built-up era and each of them offers an almost uninterrupted panorama across the Kowloon Peninsula toward Hong Kong Island. Kowloon Peak and Fei Ngo Shan (Flying Goose Hill) are on the border of East Kowloon and the New Territories in the direction of the spectacularly scenic Sai Kung.

Further east at the straits of Lei Yue Mun, the narrowest crossing point of Victoria Harbour, the so-called Devil's Peak (Pau Toi Shan) looms up behind the village and beach of Lei Yue Mun. This was the site of the British and Indian forces' Dunkirk-like evacuation from Kowloon, as a valiant rearguard of Indian Rajput troops held the emplacements on Devil's Peak against vastly superior numbers, while troops were being ferried across to Hong Kong Island on small boats. The evacuation was a triumph of fortitude and timing, but of course it was all to no avail when Hong Kong Island was itself overrun. Devil's Peak earned its name not from this life-and-death encounter but from earlier ones between ruthless pirates and the passing ships they were able to prey on from such a perfect vantage point. At this history-soaked outpost of Kowloon there is still a handsome old temple to the sea deity Tin Hau with sacred inscriptions dating back to the pre-colonial days of the early Qing Dynasty.

The Alternative Emperor of Kowloon

From Sung Dynasty boy emperors to British monarchs and monarchs-in-waiting such as Prince Charles, royalty seems to have continued to exercise a sense of fascination on the average Hong Kong denizen. Prince Charles, of course, made his mark symbolically speaking at the Handover ceremony across the water on Hong Kong-side. Over in Kowloon, however, a very different kind of royal personage, the so-called King or Emperor of Kowloon, has been leaving his calling cards in the area for several decades.

This emperor, as he styles himself, is graffiti specialist Tsang Tsou-choi, who has defied both colonial and post-colonial authority to share his frank opinions with his fellow citizens for many years. This latter-day emperor's calligraphic inscriptions have adorned flyovers, walls, bus stops, bridge struts, post boxes and other public utilities and are instantly recognizable. This is partly because unsociable Hong Kongers do not normally deface buildings; they simply drop litter, which is much more time-efficient and cost-efficient. Tsang's calligraphy has always had a point, inasmuch as it is rooted in social protest. Although locals tend to consider him a bum and mentally unhinged, some in the arts community have championed his work as vital and subversive. One of his principal supporters, owner of the Blue Door Jazz Club in Central, where jazz guitarist virtuoso Eugene Pao sometimes performs, has added to the club's ambience by featuring Tsang's work in the club's interior décor.

Like the Kowloon City which is his heartland, Tsang never accepted the validity of British rule, and his assertion of his right to "colonize" public space through his demotic art form always made for a visibly powerful form of social protest, derived some say from the dispossession of his ancestors' land by the British. Since the 1997 Handover, however, his strategically placed calligraphy suggests that he does not accept Beijing's rule either. The emperor's voice has always been eloquent and direct and his bold style of calligraphy, while certainly not aesthetically elevated, is undeniably communicative and effective. Already in his eighties, Tsang's work, despite being exhibited in galleries in recent years, is best appreciated at its most direct on the street. Perhaps in his own way he has been an older LMF-style rebel. His period of tenure has been longer than that of the Sung boy emperor, but all empires fade in time.

chapter seven

"SOMEWHERE BETWEEN HEAVEN AND EARTH": FROM THE NEW TERRITORIES TO THE OUTLYING ISLAND

The "New" Territories: an Introduction

Like many places rejoicing in the moniker "new"—the Pont Neuf (New Bridge) in Paris and New College, Oxford spring readily to mind—the New Territories is a total misnomer. This area, comprising 286 square miles north of the Kowloon border in 1898 when the British acquired the land, is older and more traditional in character than anywhere in Kowloon or Hong Kong Island. Here one can find strong evidence of a flourishing walled village system which, though part of the Xin'an ("New Peace" County) administrative region before the advent of the British, enjoyed a high degree of autonomy. Most of the inhabitants were farmers, fishermen or their dependents. The central part and western side of what became the New Territories were peopled mainly by Cantonese-speaking settlers of Han Chinese lineage known as Punti (from the Cantonese word for local or indigenous) who cultivated rice. On the more hilly eastern edges the non-Cantonese Hakka and Hoklo tribes eked out a more precarious existence, while the Tanka boatpeople (or "eggheads"—a rather derogatory way of describing them because of their head-wear) relied mainly on the fruits of the sea for their subsistence.

The routine existence of all who lived in the rural area to the north of Kowloon, cut off from the city by high hills and mountains, was varied by religious festivals and clan ritual observances. Rarely, if ever, were hazardous journeys made to the foreigner-controlled city area. For one thing, tigers still roamed the hills. For another, the villagers had their own markets and could obtain most of what they needed in their immediate environment. In the uncertain city areas they would inevitably be regarded rather disdainfully as hicks or yokels. People needed to be tough and resilient as there was little access to medicine to

The Giant Buddha on Lantau Island

protect them from regular and unwelcome disease visitors such as malaria and typhus. The inhabitants of these villages prided themselves on their self-sufficiency and adherence to local tradition and custom. They were well organized at local level into a three-tier administrative system of *heung* (group of villages), *dung* (sub-committee or literally "cave") and lastly the village's internal representation or *chuen*. Subsequently, when the British were trying to gain the trust and co-operation of the villagers under their administration, this system proved a useful model to work with and endorse. The strong clans had good links with imperial mandarins further north, who in any case tended to adopt a policy of non-intervention in rural areas. Indeed, many of the powerful New Territories clans sent their sons to compete in the imperial examinations for mandarin posts in Canton.

The year 1898 changed the lives of the natives of the area irrevocably. Following the ailing Qing Dynasty's loss of territory to predatory foreign powers, the British in Hong Kong, who had long regretted their somewhat modest demands for extra territory in the Kowloon peninsula under the 1860 treaty agreement, saw the perfect opportunity to exploit China's weakness. They pressed for concessions that would have included, if granted in full, British control of the village of Shum Chun (Shenzen) across the Shum Chun River. The line of control of the area leased after negotiations turned out to be south of the river. Had it been further north, the throbbing metropolis of modern-day Shenzen (as it is pronounced in mandarin Chinese, which is commonly spoken there) would not have come into existence. Intrinsic to the agreement was the provision that the swathe of land under negotiation was being leased for 99 years only, not in perpetuity, as had been the case with Hong Kong Island and Kowloon.

On this clause the future of the whole of the Territory was subsequently to depend. The year 1997 (when the lease expired) was a date with destiny that neither the British nor the Chinese, nor for that matter the inhabitants of Hong Kong itself, could ignore. While the British could argue—and Margaret Thatcher did—that manifestly unequal treaties guaranteed British rule in perpetuity over Hong Kong and Kowloon, there was no escaping the inevitability of the New Territories resuming Chinese sovereignty after 1997. Without the co-operation of China in providing food, water and electricity, Hong Kong and Kowloon had no conceivable chance of going it alone. Thatcher's predecessor, Edward Heath, was more realistic in accepting the inevitable and in attempting to negotiate, as Patten and others were to do later on, more favourable conditions for Hong Kong in the transfer of power.

A year after the 99-year lease was granted by the Qing government, the British took over the area in April 1899, following a comprehensive survey and report by Stewart Lockhart, the Cantonese-speaking colonial secretary (after whom the busy Lockhart Road in Wan Chai is named). During the early years of British control communications were radically improved, with the construction of two major roads linking Kowloon and Tai Po over the central hills and Kowloon with Castle Peak in the more accessible west. Tai Po Old Road and Castle Peak Road continue to be used to this day. Matthew Nathan's more ambitious and visionary Kowloon-Canton railway project, connecting Hong Kong and Kowloon with the China mainland via the New Territories, was to have an even greater impact on the eventual development of the latter.

The last forty years of British presence transformed the appearance of the New Territories more dramatically perhaps than the previous thousand had done. The satellite towns of Tsuen Wan, Sha Tin and Tuen Mun came into existence in the late 1960s and 1970s and they were soon followed by drastic urbanization programmes in more traditional communities such as Tseung Kwan O (Junk Bay), Yuen Long, Tai Po, Sheung Shui and Tin Shui Wai. Taken together with the ongoing transformation of Lantau Island, site of the new Disney amusement park and Chek Lap Kok airport, and large-scale infrastructure development, including the spectacular road and rail link, the Tsing Ma Bridge, it is evident even to the eye of the newcomer that the New Territories are no longer a rural backwater. Indeed, Hong Kong's cosmopolitan status and size can be compared with other "world cities" like New York, London and Tokyo precisely because the New Territories are now effectively part of the city itself. Now that the New Territories have become irrevocably linked with the destiny of Hong Kong and Kowloon, the city has benefited enormously.

For the New Territories it has been a mixed blessing. Ugly and unrestrained development has blighted previously bucolic landscapes in the area. Industrial emissions from the economic powerhouse of Shenzen, situated right across the border, have reduced visibility and air quality alarmingly in the border sector. Container depots and sprawling car-breakers' yards with endless corrugated iron-fencing are simply an eyesore, suggesting minimal environmental planning or sluggish enforcement of existing inadequate restrictions. In some less inhabited areas abandoned and derelict houses are a visible reminder of the break-up of the traditional pattern of village life. In others the population consists predominantly of elderly residents. Without economic resources apart from their land, they have been forced to sell off land and watch their environment become degraded through uncoordinated development. Fortunately, the many leafy and hilly country parks, where such despoliation is prohibited, provide a welcome contrast to this negative picture.

The fact remains, however, that the rapid urbanization of the New Territories has come at a heavy price to its former rural environment. The mass emigration of able-bodied men from the area to the city beyond the Lion Rock in earlier years, and later directly to London and in even greater quantities to other Western cities to serve the expanding Chinese restaurant and fast-food industry, was more of an effect than it was a cause. Original subsistence agriculture in the New Territories had been supplemented by commercial farming as the New Territories became Hong Kong's vegetable garden in the first half of the twentieth century. The Japanese occupation from 1942 to 1945 had a devastating effect on the fragile balance between subsistence and commercially viable agriculture and mariculture, making subsequent changes even more inevitable. In the 1980s, post-Cultural Revolution stability and pragmatism in China and bilateral agreements between China and Britain opened up the way for fruit and vegetable imports from the mainland. New Territories people had no option but to diversify their economic activities and make use of the valuable commodity of space in their natural hinterland between Hong Kong and Shenzen.

Yet as this chapter will show, culture dies hard in communities like the New Territories, as it does in similarly tough, close-knit traditional communities all over the world faced with the encroachment of the third millennium's global mono-culture. Many of the walled and un-walled villages in the New Territories and the smaller towns in both the New Territories and the Outlying Islands have stubbornly clung to the vestiges of their tradition, especially as manifested in their temples, ancestral halls, genealogies, burial customs and religious festivals.

Fung Shui, Feuds, Festivals and Food: New Territories Tradition

It is true to say that the character of the New Territories people, especially those who trace their lineage back to the pre-colonial era, is proud and resilient. Under the able leadership and organization of the Tang clans, they stubbornly resisted the British takeover of their homeland in 1899. Indeed, they have continued to organize themselves effectively despite the problems of being integrated into the British administrative and judicial system, which has largely survived the Handover. One area of inevitable conflict has been inheritance issues, since the traditional social code of the New Territories is fundamentally patriarchal. Only as recently as 1994 did women become eligible to inherit following a legal ruling – all in the teeth of bitter opposition on the part of the conservative Po Leung Kuk organisation. In the past respect was paid to cultural differences and New Territories villagers could have recourse to either British or traditional Chinese laws to settle disputes. Nowadays, deeply enshrined Chinese clan values do not always sit well with modern metropolitan opinions.

Austin Coates' entertaining memoir of his period as a District Magistrate in the New Territories in the 1950s and 1960s, *Myself a Mandarin*, offers insightful and amusing examples of the culture clash, not just between East and West but between rural and urban value systems in vivid and almost novelistic prose. Coates, who lived in Hong Kong for many years and after retirement became a novelist living on the island of Cheung Chau, recalls his first case involving a dispute over what appears to be an errant cow infringing village grazing rights. The villagers seeking redress from their new magistrate come from remote villages in the north-eastern part of the New Territories. As he probes the case more deeply through the medium of an experienced government interpreter, it becomes apparent to the magistrate that what is really at issue is a case of hurt pride on the part of the first or legitimate wife (*git faat*). This woman, who owns the cow and has made it available to both her husband and the village elder, has had her position usurped by a younger number two wife or concubine (*yi leung*). The real cause of grievance turns out to be the concubine's success in giving birth to a son, in stark contrast to the first wife, who has only conceived daughters. An impossible, culturally intricate dilemma is resolved when the magistrate is advised by his local interpreter—who had been testing out his new boss from the beginning—to give all of them a good old-fashioned moralistic sermon. Surprisingly, this seems to do the trick. Coates reflects whimsically:

> *I walked back slowly towards my desk, and a final incongruity struck me. Before me, between two windows looking out on a small tree-covered hillock, was a portrait of Her Majesty the Queen. What more simple example of the strangeness of Hong Kong could there be than the scene this room had just witnessed? There we had been, beneath the beneficent gaze of our Christian sovereign, quietly engaged in promoting harmony among concubines.*

Coates is not the only expatriate to become intrigued by the New Territories' customs and traditions. The area has been a goldmine for anthropologists studying Chinese rural society, especially from the 1950s to the 1980s when such places in China were closed to foreigners. Chinese language and culture academic, Hugh Baker, and administrator James Hayes have both written authoritatively about their experiences of living in the New Territories, and Hayes started writing about its rich literature of inscriptions and documents back in 1962. His latest book, *The Great Difference*, is about the relationship between New Territories people and those on the mainland and in Hong Kong. He has also collected and studied calligraphy and poetry and investigated ancestral tablets and honour boards of those who distinguished themselves in the imperial examinations. Coates, too, was commemorated as he wryly reminisces in the final chapter of his memoir. His name was inscribed along with many others on a new bridge which was built thanks to the efforts of New Territories villagers. The Chinese inscription, however, simply recorded him as "foreigner" because according to clan traditions, he did not have a proper name that could be recorded for posterity, as they did.

In many ways the New Territories have retained a vital link with tradition, lost to a considerable extent due to invasion, wars, internal politics and modernization in China. The clan social structure, which is still significant in the walled villages, is partially responsible for this phenomenon. Admittedly, non clan-members, particularly those outside the clan gentry with their scrupulously kept genealogies, were gratified to find the greatly-resisted British rule to be something of a social leveller. For one thing, all were equal before the law, which had not been the case before 1898 when the gentry were not accountable to their social inferiors. In many respects, though, not much changed, and British rule pragmatically recognized existing structures and practices.

Tight control over right to own land and houses in a village has long been exercised through the power and prerogative of clan elders. Residency did not entitle outsiders to membership or village decision-making rights. In recent years, however, the idea of having a non-indigenous representative or village leader as well as an indigenous one has become more widely accepted, albeit reluctantly at first. This policy has even resulted in one *gweilo* becoming the non-indigenous representative in his village, which must have horrified the spirits of the village ancestors. One village tradition that dates back to feudal practices was that of keeping *ha fu*. The word refers to a lower caste of bonded labourers who served the wealthy clan families over generations. These people had no rights at all and were regarded as family chattels to be inherited and disposed of as the masters saw fit. Children born to such a slave family could be divided among the heirs when the master died. They were stigmatized by the rest of the community, much as the "untouchable" caste was in India. Purchased bondmen, concubines and family servants were common before the onset of modernization, but with the decline of feudalism in China more egalitarian values permeated into the northern New Territories. This was aided by stricter Hong Kong laws about practices such as polygamy, which was banned only in 1974.

Amazingly, many old village houses in the New Territories were built according to an architectural model that can be traced back thousands of years in China, as unearthed evidence of miniature houses contained in ancient burial tombs has revealed. Many of the people who settled in the New Territories centuries ago were descended from Tang or Sung Dynasty families and sympathizers of the Ming Dynasty. They were determined to maintain cultural traditions in the face of what to them were the barbarous Manchu customs of the usurping Qing Dynasty. Not surprisingly, they continued to place heavy emphasis on their links with a tradition that elsewhere was being gradually eroded by the advent of modernity.

A number of important traditions connected with houses and villages are visible in the New Territories. One of the most prominent is *fung shui* or geomancy. In order to promote the flow of the *chi* or life force and ensure a comfortable and favourable position, villages were usually built with their backs to elevated wooded areas with an open plain or fields in front and preferably facing the sea or water. These age-old principles of harmony with the environment and of natural balance can be seen as common sense rather than mere superstition when one contemplates the situation of such villages. *Fung shui* actually makes a lot more sense as evident in villages in the New Territories and the Outlying Islands, since the observer can perceive it in the type of context for which the principles were originally designed. Vulnerability to typhoons and flooding or to droughts and alien attack could be reduced by following the basic *fung shui* concepts.

To enhance the protection afforded by appropriate *fung shui*, walled villages (usually those villages whose names end in the word *wai*) had a narrow gatehouse entrance, high walls and in some cases moats. Villages also had their own store of weapons and occasionally their own cannons, one of which can still be seen at the Tang Clan Hall in Ha Tsuen Shi. The houses themselves have narrow doors and small windows to maintain coolness as well as tiled, upwardly curving roofs to provide shade and rainwater channels. The door gods designated in calligraphy on either side of the entrance and often in the design of the decorative door panels, as well as the mirrors angled down from above the lintel, protect dwellers from the intrusion of evil spirits and ill fortune. In fact, the visual representations of door gods date back to a Tang Dynasty emperor who was ravaged by dreams of intruding ghosts. Preferring the protection of his martial and extremely red-faced generals to that of ordinary sentinels, he slept more securely knowing they were guarding his door. When the generals began to wilt from lack of sleep, he had the ingenious idea of having their fierce effigies in full battle-dress painted on the door. Obviously the malign spirits in question were bamboozled into thinking they were the real thing, and door gods became hugely popular. The Tang Clan ancestral hall in Fan Ling, not far from the border, has well-preserved likenesses of these two rubicund warriors on its doors.

Despite cultural similarities and political affiliations between many of the clans long resident in the New Territories such as the Liu of Sheung Shui and the Tang of Kam Tin, there was also occasional distrust and conflict among various communities. In periods when they needed to gather together for protection against the common enemy of bandits and pirates, inter-clan feuding was rarer. Yet by the mid-nineteenth century such feuds were becoming more common. In one territorial conflict between villagers in Shing Mun near present-day Sha Tin and the former village of Tsuen Wan, many young men from both villages died. Even when Austin Coates was magistrate to the New Territories in the 1950s there was the ever-present possibility that disputes might lead to bloodshed if villagers decided to invoke precedent and take the law into their own hands. Timothy Mo lampoons this clan-based feuding somewhat caustically in the second part of *The Monkey King*, the section set in an unspecified New Territories village. Protagonists Wallace and May Ling are temporarily exiled to Mr. Poon's remote home village near the north-eastern border to escape the threat of prosecution over that patriarch's dubious dealings. The sequence is not only wryly amusing; it also provides a wonderful period description of the pre-industrialized New Territories. It includes an exorcism to correct village *fung shui*, a brilliant recreation scheme for generating much-needed income masterminded by Wallace and the obligatory inter-village feud:

> *The invariable state of affairs between neighbouring settlements was rivalry; each had its particular feuds. The village had been engaged in a vendetta, started by an irrigation dispute somewhere around the time of the Tai Ping rebellion, the details of which were lost in time, against a Hakka settlement seven miles up the valley. The Hakkas, 'guest people', had arrived in the area a few centuries ago. Shortly before the colonial authorities had assumed control of the area, an exceptionally sanguinary battle had been fought in which men of the Hakka village had laid hands on an ornamental cannon, harnessed water buffaloes to it, and fired fearsome home-made grape-shot into the village.*

Bloody conflict is avoided thanks to Wallace's innovative idea of a hockey match to resolve differences between the two villages. The farcical (and violent) free-for-all that follows ends with honours even and face saved on both sides.

The New Territories annual calendar has from time immemorial revolved around festivals. Most of the rituals and their local earth gods and shrines can be traced back to the shamanism of early religious groups in China, which was assimilated by later Confucian and Taoist beliefs. The best-known of these festivals today are Lunar New Year in January/February, Hungry Ghost Festival (*Yue Lan*) with burnt offerings for the roaming spirits in late August, Mid-Autumn Festival in late September and Dragon Boat Festival in early June, as elsewhere in Hong Kong. Many other local festivals that have little significance for Hong Kong urbanites are also celebrated in the New Territories. Some of them, organized by groups of villages on a ten-yearly basis (known as *ta tsui*), have their origins in big purification rituals designed to keep the area clear from disease and to exorcise malign spirits. The cost of these two-week long events is paid for by subscriptions and trust funds and can climb to almost HK$1 million.

The "Wishing Tree" Festival in the Lam Clan Village is one of the better known local events, but others dedicated to Tin Hau and Kwun Yum and Buddhist festivals throughout the New Territories and on the Islands are numerous and strictly observed. The Festival of Che Kung, for example, is peculiar to the New Territories, although it is technically part of the Lunar New Year celebrations. Che Kung was a Sung Dynasty general credited with special powers to ward off pestilence and provide protection to inhabitants of what became the New Territories. One reason to place his festival on the third day of Chinese New Year (*chor saam*, as it is called) is that this day is inauspicious for meeting friends and relatives. Formerly a trip to the New Territories would be a way to avoid meeting many people one knows.

At festival times the traditional Lion and Dragon Dances that can be observed in most Chinese communities are often staged in more elaborate, ritualistic ways in villages, and in the Hakka culture the Lion dances are replaced by Unicorn dances. While the dragon and lion are both potent yang (male) symbols, the unicorn connotes benevolence and gentleness. In some celebratory dances all three are represented. Food and banquets are a vital component of such occasions, and large sums are often expended on special menus. Sticky rice wrapped in lotus leaves is a typical symbolic festival dish. Others, especially types of cakes, are served because they have names that sound like words associated with luck and fortune. Numerology is likewise important at festival time, with the numbers eight and eighteen, signifying riches, especially popular. Superstition applies to many occupations at these moments, so that fishermen and sailing folk avoid turning over the fish they are served as others normally do, since the action suggests a boat capsizing.

Finally, some local festivals are celebrated with lengthy Cantonese Opera performances in makeshift open-air bamboo theatres. The origins of Cantonese Opera lie partly in ritual and religion, and performances are given to celebrate the festivals of local deities and to enhance purification rites. Spirits, ghosts and gods were the primary audiences of the performances. At the same time, they served to enact historical events and inculcate moral teachings among villagers many of whom in earlier days were illiterate or semi-literate. Brightly coloured costumes, vibrant, attention-grabbing music and singing and stage physicality all made traditional theatre very appealing to human audiences in the past. Younger Chinese do not generally share the enthusiasm of their elders for this art, and there are concerns that this part of Hong Kong's (and even China's) heritage could be lost to future generations.

Ping Shan Heritage Trail and Kam Tin (Yuen Long)

The oldest surviving settlements in the New Territories are those around Ping Shan (*shan* meaning hill) and Kam Tin, where the powerful Tang clan set up their base nearly a thousand years ago in the Sung Dynasty. In particular, the monastery known as Ling To founded by the Buddhist monk and later abbot Pui To (Pei Tu in Mandarin) near Ping Shan in 424 AD is the oldest recorded place of worship in the whole of Hong Kong. There is still a monastery on the site, although not the original. A few years later, Pui To built another retreat further west in what is now called Castle Peak. Subsequently the Tang Dynasty fortified and settled this part of the New Territories. Several original buildings dating back the earlier centuries of Tang clan pre-eminence during the Sung and Yang Dynasties have survived. These include two Tang ancestral halls and a pagoda (Hong Kong's only one) as well as a Tin Hau temple between Kam Tin and Pat Heung with a memorial stone bearing the legend "800 years from Sung to Qing".

Hong Kong's Antiquities and Monuments Office established the heritage trail of Ping Shan in order to promote awareness of historical roots which were fast being eradicated by industrialization and commercial development. The Ping Shan Trail, which is well served by public transport including public light rail and bus, is a treasure-house of visual information on the pre-British way of life in the New

Territories in general and offers an illuminating insight into village life. There are two Tang villages, Hang Mei Tsuen and Hang Tau Tsuen, and a number of historic buildings can be seen in both of them. These include the Kun Ting Study Hall, two temples and two ancestral halls where the lineage is commemorated. Close to the next village, Sheung Cheung Wai, is Hong Kong's only pagoda known as Tsui Shing Lau ("picking stars pagoda"). This three-storey eight-sided structure dates back to 1486 and was built by seventh-generation Tang clansman Tang Yiu-tung. Originally it was seven storeys high (hence "picking stars") and auspiciously located facing Castle Peak and the sea, intended to enhance the chances of success of young clansmen in the imperial examinations. The upper floors may well have taken a battering in typhoons, with the result that the clans decided not to rebuild them and left the edifice in its present condition.

Further along the Ping Ha Road and a mile or so from Ping Shan is the village of Tung Tau Tsuen, which has an impressive temple dedicated to Hau Wong, the Sung princes' loyal bodyguard. The temple was built in 1811 by Tang clan descendants of those who founded the village in the fourteenth century. It is one of the best preserved temples in the New Territories and boasts excellent carvings and paintings in its interior. Adjacent to the main building is a smaller temple in honour of Mandarins Chou and Wong who finally succeeded in persuading the Qing Emperor in 1662 to reverse his draconian and damaging policy of clearances in the South China coastal regions. Further still along Ping Ha Road and turning off to a small village called San San Tsuen, we find the monastery built on the site of Pui To's original Ling To institution in the secluded and peaceful surroundings that made it an ideal retreat for Buddhists. It was also a retreat for those seeking refuge from the occupying Japanese soldiers, who were too intimidated by the spiritual ambience of the place to force their way into the monastery.

Like Ping Shan, the ancient ten-village group of Kam Tin is also close to Yuen Long. Kam Tin was actually settled before the Ping Shan area in 1069 by Tang Fu-hip, son of Tang Hon-fu, and other members of the Tang clan who established their presence here in a hamlet called Tsz Tong Tsuen. This was the place where the Tang Dynasty princess sought refuge and eventually married after fleeing civil war further north. The descendants of her marriage to the son of general, Tang Yuen-leung, consolidated the aristocratic credentials of the Tang lineage in the New Territories. In that era the cluster of villages was known as Shum Tin and was only changed in the sixteenth century when according to some sources the Tang village elder donated rice to a famine-stricken county in the region. As a result the village group was dubbed Kam Tin or "Golden Fields" in recognition of the benevolent deed, a very euphonious name for the source of the gift. However, the modern Chinese character for Kam signifies 'brocade' or 'tapestry', so perhaps a tapestry gift was made in recognition of the elder's benevolence. Whatever the reason, Kam Tin has stuck!

One of the most interesting surviving parts of Kam Tin is the walled and moated village of Kat Hing Wai, which can be translated as "Good Fortune Village". It dates back to the mid-fifteenth century and has gun emplacements and watch towers built for the purpose of repulsing pirates and bandits. Its strong village gates have their own story to tell. When the village, having rejected the idea of British rule in 1898, was besieged by British soldiers, the gates were ripped off (both literally and colloquially). Governor Henry Blake purloined them and had them shipped back to his native Ireland. Twenty-five years later, however, they were returned to the village after a successful search was ordered. Then Governor Sir Reginald Stubbs made a powerful plea to the Colonial Office in London endorsing their restitution. Looking at them today, one may reflect that it was as well they had not been donated by Blake to the British Museum.

Ironically one of the British barracks in the New Territories, complete with airstrip, was built a stone's throw away from Kat Hing Wai in nearby Shek Kong. Nowadays there is little sign of the small PLA (People's Liberation Army) contingent stationed there. Many tourists, who visit this interesting but rather run-down example of a walled village, like to have their photograph taken posing with the local older women in their black, broad-brimmed hats. A financial sweetener is necessarily involved in this intercultural transaction, it should be observed.

Satellite Towns—Yuen Long, Tuen Mun and Tsuen Wan: Three Weddings and a Crocodile

The western part of the New Territories, as well as having strong historical associations with the early development of the area, is home to four out of its six new satellite towns. Yuen Long and Tuen Mun in the north-west both have a distinguished heritage dating back well before the colonial era. While Tuen Mun (meaning "garrison channel") was a small port and the major settlement in the Hong Kong area during the Tang Dynasty of the seventh and eighth centuries, Yuen Long was established as a market town in 1670 during the early Qing Dynasty, with its own calendar dates for big open-air markets. The Tang family from Kam Tin controlled the market as they controlled much of the Yuen Long plain, and had become extremely wealthy as a result of their activities. In the early twentieth century, however, they lost their monopoly of the lucrative market to private companies with shareholders. While many of the market stalls were still run by indigenous people with clan affiliations, more and more shops and new stalls were being opened by new immigrants. When the markets sold local produce, especially the high-quality rice from the area, the well-established feudal system worked effectively. But when the New Territories' agricultural way of life began to be eroded by development, the structure proved inadequate to resist pressure for change.

The Yuen Long crocodile must have had more mixed feelings about his new surroundings in 2003 when he was spotted in the Yuen Long River and tempted with appetizing bait by humans attempting to capture him. The clever animal resisted all attempts, even those by a real-life "Crocodile Dundee" croc-hunter from Australia, who went home with his tail metaphorically between his legs. In the end Pui-pui, as he was dubbed, was caught and consigned to comfortable captivity in a Yuen Long reserve.

Hong Kong writer Alan Jefferies has also captured the crocodile rather well in his imaginative reconstruction of the story for children and adults, entitled *The Crocodile who Wanted to be Famous*. In Jefferies' version of the tale, which is enlivened by Mariko Jesse's wonderful line drawings of both crocodiles and the city, the fictional crocodile named Crafty sees images of Hong Kong on television, and makes up his mind to go there. Leaving his family in their mainland "crocodile village", he arrives in Hong Kong, encountering detritus and polluted waters, and becomes a media celebrity. The real crocodile, Pui-pui, unlike his fictional counterpart, only made it as far as Yuen Long. Crafty, being smarter than his real-world *alter ego*, evades his would-be captors and returns to his family, having found that the city is not as enticing as it appears to be. Thus Jefferies' environmental moral tale, which is designed as a parallel Chinese and English text, has a sting in the tail. Hong Kong parents reading what appears to be a simple children's tale find that there is a strong underlying anti-pollution message and a salutary warning for the city's polluters. At the end Jefferies envisages a miraculous transformation of the city following Crafty's snap visit:

> *But the people of the big city never forgot the young crocodile, and from that day onwards, they started taking better care of the river. School children worked day and night to clean up the rubbish that had polluted the river for so long. Trees were planted and beds of flowers appeared along the riverbank.*

Both Yuen Long and Tuen Mun have become high-density, high-rise towns, as has Tin Shui Wai (formerly a walled village). Indeed, modern Tuen Mun is now the most heavily populated of the New Territories new towns. Before the development of the early 1970s, the Castle Peak Bay area on which Tuen Mun was built consisted of villages constructed on stilts with rudimentary walkways. With the massive influx of refugees from the mainland, the population became essentially an immigrant one without the tight clan affiliations of those in the villages. Not surprisingly, there are social problems arising from the dense living conditions in the satellite towns. Better communications systems, including the Westrail link to Kowloon, Lantau and Hong Kong Island, have improved quality of life in the new millennium.

Close to the busy new town of Tuen Mun is Hong Kong's second-oldest Buddhist monastery, established by legendary founding father Pui To in 428 AD. It lies slightly to the north-west of Tuen Mun but is easily accessible by taxi or on foot from the Light Rail Transit system that runs between Tuen Mun and Yuen Long. The Tsing Shan Monastery is located on the slopes of Castle Peak (Tsing Shan in Cantonese means "green-mountain") and is approached by steps and a walled entrance constructed in 1917 on the site of the original. The monastery features a beautiful roof ridge with symmetrical dragons that long predates this reconstruction. There are many legends and stories associated with Pui To that have remarkable parallels in Christian hagiography, and his journey to Tunmen appears to have been ordained by higher powers. He arrived by boat, as legend has it, or rather in his wooden drinking vessel, miraculously transformed into a sailing vessel, and founded the monastery with his acolytes. A pavilion and a statue of Pui To on the rocks above the rebuilt monastery commemorate the abbot. Among his exploits were visits to the local markets to buy fish. The fish were then released back to the sea from these high rocks overlooking the Pearl River. The fish that died were interred in a tomb, since for Buddhists all life is sacred. Thus Hong Kong, or to be more specific, Tuen Mun, may well lay claim to having formed the first animal rights activist movement.

Tsuen Wan, the oldest of the New Territories new towns, is in many ways the most connected to the Hong Kong-Kowloon conurbation. It is the terminus of the MTR line running from Central through central- and west-Kowloon via the industrial complex of Kwai Chung and Kwai Fong. Much of the industry is linked to the gigantic Hong Kong International Container Terminal at Kwai Chung, on which Hong Kong's prosperity has relied to a considerable extent. Lying on the western side and not far from Tuen Mun, via the winding and scenic Castle Peak Road, Tsuen Wan developed from clusters of villages. The original inhabitants were boat-dwellers in the bays and land farmers, most of whom were non-indigenous Hakka. Early village settlements like Hoi Pa ("sea-wall") and Sam Tung Uk became incorporated into the town centre of Tsuen Wan as heritage centres after their inhabitants had been resettled. Sam Tung Uk is particularly well presented as a museum, showing exactly what life was like in a Hakka walled village of the mid-eighteenth century. One or two others like Kwan Mun Hau ("mouth of the sluice gate") retained more independence as communities.

For most Tsuen Wan dwellers life was harsh, since malaria and other diseases were prevalent. The area was notorious for being poverty-stricken prior to the twentieth century, and there was a folk saying: "If you want to prosper, go to the Golden Mountain (California). If you want to die, go to Tsuen Wan." This advice does not reflect the state of affairs in modern-day Tsuen Wan, although it is busy, noisy and often shrouded in traffic fumes, being an important transport hub. Today the town is primarily residential and commercial in nature, and although there is an industrial estate, it is no longer composed predominantly of factories. Tsuen Wan's earliest factories in the 1920s reversed the cycle of poverty that had blighted the area and brought welcome revenue to its inhabitants. This industry focused on the production of sandalwood joss-sticks (joss is not, in fact, a Chinese word but a variant on the Portuguese word for god, *deos*). The fragrant powder produced by grinding bark from the *heung* or sandalwood trees and mixing it with glue and water before pasting it on the end of bamboo sticks represented the sweet smell of success for Tsuen Wan. The joss-stick mills, of which there were over twenty located in and around Tsuen Wan, were simply reviving one of Hong Kong's age-old industries, although not one native to Tsuen Wan itself. Before the clearances of the 1660s joss-stick production based on the ample wood sources of Lantau had been a major source livelihood. Hong Kong owes its name, of course, to this valuable trade.

The Tsuen Wan area was probably populated before the coastal clearances, but there is little remaining evidence. Yet on the hills above Tsuen Wan (chosen for their favourable *fung shui*) is a tomb dating back to the year 1100, the late Sung Dynasty. This contains the earliest known Tang clan ancestor, the imperial mandarin Tang Hon-Fu, who first landed in the New Territories roughly where Tsuen Wan is now. On that occasion he is supposed to have continued on his mission, but returning with his son he set up his home and thus his important lineage in the New Territories. Not surprisingly, the clan descendants have continued to pay homage at his tomb and successfully resisted a colonial government plan in the late 1970s to relocate the tomb in order to make way for an extension to the MTR line from Tsuen Wan. There is also a Ming Dynasty tomb dating back to 1637 on the island of Tsing Yi, which is close to Tsuen Wan and well linked by roads and bridges.

Mai Po Wetlands and the Border: A Foot in Both Camps

The border between China and Hong Kong has long exerted great fascination on both residents and visitors alike. In spite of the 1997 Handover the border has been maintained in its original configuration, with a gradual loosening of restrictions for mainland Chinese visiting Hong Kong as tourists and for Hong Kongers travelling to formerly closed parts of China. There is, however, a closed area in the northern New Territories running from San Tin in the west to Sha Tau Kok in the east, forbidden to all but those with special permits. Beyond lies the border crossing to the former village and now large city of Shenzen on the China mainland side. The main crossing nowadays is not by bridge across the Shenzen River, as it was formerly, but by train through the Lo Wu KCR border station. Travellers descend at this station and walk through the immigration control on the Hong Kong side, beyond which lie the mainland China immigration desks. Having shown one's travel documents (and visa if one is traveling on a non-Chinese or Hong Kong travel document) one walks through into a bustling Shenzen, by contrast with which Hong Kong is almost sedate. Alternatively, one can take the so-called "through-train" from Kowloon's Hung Hom terminus to Guangzhou, which enables travelers to glide across the border from a quiet, relatively rustic northern New Territories into the glitzy metropolis beyond without interruption. Other crossings are for heavy goods vehicles and buses, but the most common way of getting overland into China is through Lo Wu. One can only access Lo Wu if one has valid China travel documents. If one does not, then Sheung Shui is the station at which one alights.

In the 1950s, the border was far tenser than it is today. The closed areas are still policed to prevent IIs (illegal immigrants) slipping across the border. However, in the period shortly after the collapse of the Kuomintang and the communist takeover, and especially during and after the Korean War, the area was on high alert and the border, which had been open prior to 1949, was then closed completely by 1952.

One of the other land crossings into China is at Lok Ma Chau. Close to Lok Ma Chau and to the old village of San Tin where the Man clan—the last of the original five clans—settled, is the awe-inspiring bird reserve of Mai Po. On the shores of Deep Bay and facing the high-rise buildings of Shenzen across the bay, it is home to thousands of wild birds, many migrating from the colder climes of Korea, northern China and even Siberia. To get a good impression of Mai Po the documentary by Evans Chan, *Journey to Beijing*, is worth watching. The Mai Po episode is only part of a well-crafted and unusual documentary on the 1997 reunification. In the interview, which contains wonderful shots of the birds at rest and in flight on the bay, the management at Mai Po expresses hopes and concerns about the fragile ecology of the area, calling for a partnership between the mainland and Hong Kong to protect the ecosystem of these unique wetlands. A major threat to the sanctuary, which has been a popular weekend destination for Hong Kong's enthusiastic bird-watchers and also for school parties, is the avian flu virus. It has been pointed out that no human deaths have been caused by contact with wild birds, and Mai Po remains, at the time of writing, free from infection. Every January the bird population at Mai Po swells to a maximum of more than 50,000. The reserve is easily accessible from the Yuen Long Highway and is highly recommended.

Monitoring the border, like monitoring the birds at Mai Po, is a difficult task. Smuggling has long been commonplace, and the proliferation of bays and small islands on the peninsula make the job of the marine police in Deep Bay and in Mirs Bay, on the opposite eastward side of the New Territories, well nigh impossible. Guarding Hong Kong's territorial waters was a bigger issue before reunification, but as many Hong Kong gangster and Triad movies have indicated, it has always been comparatively easy for well-organized gangs to materialize on the streets of Kowloon and melt away under cover of darkness into coastal waters. With increased cross-border co-operation between Hong Kong and Mainland police, border policing both on land and at sea is more effective than before.

The border village of Sha Tau Kok, right up in the north-east corner of the New Territories, presents an entirely different problem. It is in the closed border area and people living or working there require a permit. What makes life a little more complicated than elsewhere in Hong Kong is that the border at Sha Tau Kok, the northernmost point in the New Territories, runs right down the middle of the main street, Chung Ying Street (literally Chinese-English Street). Before 1997 one could stand in the street and have a foot in China and the other on British territory.

Before the 1898 treaty Sha Tau Kok was a fishing port and a flourishing market town and had access to economically valuable salt fields. Its inhabitants were mainly Hakka people, originally from the north of China. There was a strong local association known as the *sap yeuk* (the alliance of ten), which administered the community of villages in the north-east. Sha Tau Kok's port and market, the latter established in the early nineteenth century, increased the village's wealth and importance in the area and enabled the clan alliance to retain independence from the other clans of nearby Fan Ling and Tai Po. A boundary splitting their village in two was possibly the last thing they needed, but that is what they got after the British lease (along with a road and other services as compensation). During the colonial period the villagers had freedom of access to both sides of the divide. Not surprisingly, they had many affiliations with their compatriots on the Chinese side of the border, but when access to Shenzen was closed down in the early 1950s the community's local economy went into sharp decline. Many Sha Tau Kok males migrated to London and worked in restaurants during the late 1950s and early 1960s.

Tai Po and Sha Tin: Modern Towns, Old Communities

The modern town of Tai Po, with its industrial estate and residential high-rise blocks, does not look much like a place of any historical interest. Appearances are deceptive, though, because Tai Po's history, like that of Tuen Mun, can be traced back to the Tang Dynasty and to its garrison of soldiers stationed here to monitor the imperial pearl-fishing industry. In this period oysters were abundant in the seas off Tai Po. The process of collecting them was extremely hazardous to the locally employed pearl-fishers, many of whom drowned for the sake of the emperor's passion for pearls used to embellish his palaces. Some imperial advisers succeeded in petitioning the emperor to put a stop to this costly practice, but it was revived in the Yuan Dynasty and the imperial monopoly only ended in the Ming Dynasty. The pearl industry declined but there are still oyster beds in the north New Territories, not for the extraction and cultivation of pearls, but for the consumption of oysters which are a popular dish in Hong Kong. Tai Po also became famous for its tigers, which roamed the nearby forests and caused travellers to quicken their pace in order to reach the safety of the settlement. Tai Po means "big steps" in Cantonese, which is presumably what the anxious travelers were inclined to take.

At this time it is certain that there was a market and settlement in Tai Po, which developed into a network of villages, of which Tai Po was the centre under the control of the Tang clan. Tai Po Old Market, as it is known, was built on this site in 1672 during the Qing Dynasty, and even today a market continues to flourish. The Old Market was a focal point of resistance to the British forces in 1898 when the Union Jack was raised on 16 April. The mat-shed bamboo structure built for the transfer-of-power ceremony was burned down by local rebels. Inspired by both anti-Qing and anti-British sentiment and mobilized by the tight Tang clan organization, these militias proved a thorn in the side of the new masters. They actually launched a frontal attack on the British forces' camp in Tai Po before being repulsed by surprised but superior forces. The Old Market remains but the original shops were demolished and the market is no longer the focal point it was over many centuries. One other building worthy of note in Tai Po is the former Tai Po Market KCR station, built in 1913 and now used as a railway museum with old Kowloon-Canton Railway steam engines and other train memorabilia on display.

The Wishing Tree at Lam Tsuen, the group of villages in a pretty valley to the north of Tai Po, is an attraction for locals for one major reason; the tree is reputed to make wishes come true. The legend surrounding it, far from being ancient, only dates back thirty years, when a boat-dweller prayed in front of the tree and then recovered from a debilitating disease. Since then the tree has become Hong Kong's equivalent to Lourdes, and local and overseas Chinese make pilgrimages here after praying in Tai Po's Tin Hau temple, especially at Chinese New Year. Supplicants used to throw oranges wrapped in prayer messages at the tree. If, according to superstition, an orange lodged in the branches, the thrower's wish would be granted. After being quite literally over-burdened with wishes, the tree collapsed and died and an adjacent banyan tree was designated the new wishing tree.

Between Tai Po and Sha Tin, overlooking the long Tolo Harbour inlet, is the Chinese University of Hong Kong, also built during the 1960s. This institution, situated on an extensive and attractive campus with its own dedicated railway station, was conceived as a more China-oriented university than the more British-style Hong Kong University. The Chinese University has achieved high academic standards during its three and half decades. One of its former English academics, Andrew Parkin, anthologized a collection of English and Chinese poems (translated into English) about Hong Kong. The anthology is entitled *From the Bluest Part of the Harbour* and includes some memorable poetic evocations of the area. Laurence Wong's lyrical poem of homeland nostalgia, "Autumn Thoughts", offers perhaps the best overview of Tai Po and Tolo Harbour:

> *Now once more, Tolo Harbour shows*
> *Its gentle ripples while the eagles fly on high.*
> *Languid white foam*
> *Fringes the harbour's scatter of islets...*
> *From the bluest part of the harbour*

A few white gulls take off.
The soft mists in Ma On Shan and Wu Kai Sha
Are blown away beyond Chik Mun Channel...

To listen on the dam of Plover Cove to the solitary sounds of
Autumn
To sit and lean languidly on the bench at University Station
Not caring if the diesel train arrives on time,

The New Territories' first new town was not surprisingly Sha Tin, since it had been part of the closest village cluster to Kowloon. It is situated just across the natural border provided by Lion Rock and is accessible via the KCR railway tunnel or the Lion Rock motor vehicle tunnel. Modern-day Sha Tin was designed in the 1960s as a new town in the mould of British new towns of that brash era. It was built like much of Hong Kong's newer development on reclaimed land, at the confluence of the Shing Mun River and Sha Tin Harbour. The Shing Mun River flows, thanks to artificial diversion, through the centre of the town. Although the river is now rather polluted, it still gives character to an otherwise characterless town when the lights are dancing on the water at night. Sha Tin was a collection of small villages for most of its history, which dates back to the sixteenth century and the Ming Dynasty. This network of villages includes adjoining Tai Wai, originally a walled village but now virtually a suburb of Sha Tin New Town. The alliances of families and even of Cantonese and Hakka villages, known as the alliance of nine, made it one of the most tribally integrated areas of the New Territories.

The Shing Mun villages, dotted across the hills above Sha Tin which separate it from Tsuen Wan in the west, were conversely renowned for their quarrelsome disposition and inter-village clashes. More recent conflict took place here during the Second World War. Shing Mun Redoubt, located in modern-day Shing Mun Country Park close to the dam and reservoir, was dubbed the Gin Drinkers' Line, after a bay of that name, which was reclaimed in the development of Sha Tin, and not because gin was the preferred military tipple. These fortifications saw fierce fighting when the allied forces tried in vain to hold Kowloon against the inexorable advance of the Japanese troops in December 1941,

There are a few places worth visiting in Sha Tin. The most significant is probably the handsome, yellow-roofed Hong Kong Heritage Museum, situated close to Sha Tin in a green valley area with good *fung shui* and attractive views towards the hills to the north. This museum houses permanent exhibitions of, among other things, local Cantonese Opera traditions and New Territories food rituals. Another place to see is the amazing Ten Thousand Buddha Temple, located close to the KCR station of Sha Tin. Built on the hillside in 1951 with money raised from donations, the Ten Thousand Buddha Temple actually contains nearly 13,000 small Buddha figures. Not that the numerical discrepancy matters much. Ten thousand (*maan*) in Chinese numerology is simply equivalent to a very high number.

High above Sha Tin on a promontory overlooking much of the east New Territories and northern Kowloon is the counterpart of the Lion Rock. Seen from a certain perspective, especially the rear, the Amah Rock looks uncannily like the figure of a woman holding a child and gazing longingly out to sea. The legend is embedded in local folklore and her story has been passed down in folk songs. She is said to be waiting stoically for her fisherman husband to return, braving the cold "strong like stone or iron" as the folk song puts it. In time the waiting woman turned to stone, according to the legend. The stone formation is remarkably life-like and has inspired many local stories.

Further down the Shing Mun River, near where it flows out into what was Sha Tin Harbour before it was reclaimed in the 1970s, stands Sha Tin's impressive racecourse. Built by the Hong Kong Jockey Club in the 1980s, this magnificent modern racecourse hosts race meetings at the weekend by contrast with Happy Valley, which only has meetings on Wednesday evenings. It has its own KCR branch station, which only opens on race days.

The Sai Kung Peninisula: Rugged Beauty

Close to Sha Tin and the racecourse is Hong Kong's tallest peak, Tai Mo Shan (3,150 feet). This commanding spot, affording panoramic views over the whole of Hong Kong, is a focal point for hill-climbers especially at Chung Yeung Festival on the ninth day of the ninth month of the lunar New Year. It is customary for some people take to the hills on this day—a public holiday—since, according to Chinese tradition, the hills are the only safe place to be on an inauspicious day. Ma On

Shan is also a central point of the MacLehose Trail, established in 1979 and named after governor Sir Murray MacLehose. It crosses twelve country parks and runs east-west across some of the New Territories' most scenically spectacular terrain. Every year in November there is a charity marathon walking event known as Operation Trailwalker, set up to raise money for a raft of charities both local and international, and organised initially by the British Army.

To the east of Ma On Shan lies the Sai Kung Peninsula, without doubt the loveliest location in the whole of Hong Kong (although some residents of the Outlying Islands may argue with that verdict). The Sai Kung district consists of Sai Kung Town and Country Park, the beautiful Clearwater Bay Peninsula and approximately seventy small islands, some of them inhabited. The area has retained its pristine beauty largely thanks to its isolation and the hilliness of the terrain. Its population is small and many of its scattered villages comprise fewer than a hundred residents. Even busy Sai Kung Town retains its slightly antiquated feel despite the restaurants, coffee shops and modern facilities that add to its resort ambience. Lorette Roberts' evocative painting of the harbour at Sai Kung gives one a glimpse of what is so special about Sai Kung, and the small flotilla of sampans, junks and rowing boats moored in the natural harbour simply enhances the effect. The vista of bays and islands from Sai Kung's extensive waterfront is among the most beautiful in Asia.

One of the most historically important and scenically impressive sites in the area is the Tin Hau Temple at Fat Tong Mun (Joss House Bay as it is known in English), originally built in 1012 by two brothers named Lam who survived a shipwreck off the Sai Kung Peninsula. Their descendants rebuilt the temple in 1266 in recognition of the gracious intercession of Tin Hau in preserving their family. Even today fishermen and boat people, who traditionally made up the majority of Sai Kung's residents, come to worship Tin Hau every May on the occasion of her supposed birthday. The temple has been rebuilt many times. Behind the building is an inscription on a rock dating from 1274. It concerns the visit of a Sung Dynasty official who came here shortly before the collapse of the dynasty probably accompanying the boy emperors.

Clearwater Bay (Tsing Shi Waan) remains one of the most delightful tourist spots in the whole of Hong Kong, its relative remoteness ensuring a high degree of environmental conservation. Its beaches are excellent and its water amply justifies the name. The pleasant waters of Clearwater Bay are not just attractive to local swimmers; sharks are known to include these bays in their annual itinerary, normally in early summer. Few attacks have actually occurred, but there are warnings and shark nets to be seen.

The other type of shark to be found in the area is the movie and television mogul. Clearwater Bay Studios is the home of one of Hong Kong's great institutions, the Shaw Brothers film studios. This prolific movie empire, at one time referred to rather simplistically as "the Hollywood of the East", produced over ninety films between the 1960s and 1980s. Many of these were directed by highly respected martial arts directors such as Chang Cheh, King Hu and Tsui Hark. Jackie Chan and other Hong Kong martial arts stars like Sammo Hung graduated from the rigorous Hong Kong martial arts school run by *Sifu* (Master) Yu Jim-yuen, which originated in Chinese Opera's martial and acrobatic techniques. They also owed a considerable debt to seminal action stars such as Kwan Tak-hing, who became immensely popular for playing the legendary nineteenth-century, real-life hero, Wong Fei-hung, a sort of Chinese Robin Hood. Then, sensing that the Kung Fu martial arts genre had run its course internationally, the astute Run Run Shaw started his own TV channel, which became TVB Pearl, and devoted his attention to this more lucrative medium. The Shaw Brothers studios with their spacious facilities in Clearwater Bay, including extensive sets and sound stages, dominated the Asian market for a long time.

The Outlying Islands: Between Heaven and Earth

In 1888 Rudyard Kipling on his sea approach to Hong Kong described the islands thus in his travelogue, "From Sea to Sea: Morning gave us a new world—somewhere between Heaven and Earth. The sea was smoked glass; reddish grey islands lay upon it under fog-banks that hovered fifty feet above our heads. The squat sails of junks danced in the breeze and disappeared, and there was no solidity in the islands against which the glassy levels splintered in snow." On clear days one can see across to Lantau Island, the biggest of Hong Kong's islands, from the western side of the New Territories. On more smoggy days, when the mixture of Shenzen's (approximately eighty per cent) and

Hong Kong's own (twenty per cent) pollution cocktail is particularly bad, Kipling's first impression is easily replicated.

Nowadays, though, one no longer needs to make the journey by boat. The majestic Tsing Ma and Ting Kao suspension bridge interlink spans the channel between the New Territories mainland, crossing the adjacent islands of Tsing Yi and Ma Wan and touching base on the north-eastern tip of Lantau Island. At over 7,000 feet the Tsing Ma Bridge is the longest integrated road and rail span in the world. The view from the bridge, or even better from the Tuen Mun Highway approach to it, is nothing short of breathtaking, especially on a clear day with sunny skies. Completed in 1995, work began on the construction in 1992 with components from Britain and Japan assembled in China, which gives the bridge an international character entirely consistent with its major function as the transport link with the international airport at Chek Lap Kok on North Lantau. As one approaches the bridge by road, the conventional aeroplane logo on the road sign adjacent to an unnerving pair of giant ears indicates North Lantau's twin attractions of Chek Lap Kok airport and Disneyland. The purely graphic information on the signage appears to convey the message: "Beware low-flying giant mice," but no sightings have been recorded to date.

Hong Kong's role as a gateway to southern China and as a small but vital commercial hub of the Asia Pacific Rim has been greatly enhanced by its award-winning airport, which is, remarkably, the size of London's Heathrow and New York's JFK airport combined. The migration of services from Kai Tak in Kowloon to Chek Lap Kok took place literally overnight in 1998, and despite one or two teething problems the new airport has gone from strength to strength. One cannot help being struck by the airport's light and airy design (Norman Foster's elaboration of a blueprint used for London's Stansted Airport) as well as its calm efficiency. Between 2004 and 2005 HK$3 trillion worth of business passed through Chek Lap Kok. Built on the reclaimed and formerly isolated island of Chek Lap Kok, the airport complex is apparently the second most highly visible object seen from outer space after the Great Wall of China.

Whether or not Hong Kong's new 311-acre Disneyland at Penny's Bay (cost: US$3.2 billion) on the east coast can be observed by aliens is also difficult to verify, even if it has been visited by hordes of them since its grand opening in September 2005. China mainland passport holders

Hong Kong Internation Airport: Ancient and Modern.

encouraged by the lifting of visa restrictions, as well other Asian and Western visitors, have flocked to the Disney Corporation's latest contribution to global monoculture. There have, however, been allegations that terms and working conditions in Hong Kong Disney fall far short of American and European norms.

Before road and rail access to Disney was feasible, the ferry from Central to Mui Wo (Silvermine Bay) was Lantau's most direct connection with the metropolis. Lantau's name really means "broken head", a reference to its fragmented shape in the northern part. (The island is known in Cantonese as Dai Yue Shan or Big Island Mountain.) Fifty-five square miles in area, Lantau is approximately twice the size of Hong Kong Island and even more rugged and mountainous. Its two highest points, Lantau Peak (3,093 feet) and Sunset Peak (2,851 feet), are higher then Hong Kong's Peak and almost as high as Tai Mo Shan in the New Territories. There is evidence of a stable population on Lantau as far back as 2000 BC and of agriculture for nearly as long. The Yue (or Yao) indigenous population of the island died out, to be replaced by Hakka and Tanka people.

Prior to the advent of Disney, Lantau's great tourist attraction was the Po Lin ("precious lotus") Buddhist Monastery and its spectacular and imposing 85-foot outdoor bronze Sakyamuni Buddha (meaning Lord of the Sakya tribe, the name for the Buddha, Siddartha Gautama), the largest of its kind in the world. The monastery and effigy are situated 45 minutes from Mui Wo on the Ngong Ping Plateau. In the autumn of 2006 the direct cable-car link between the Ngong Ping Plateau and Tung Chung MTR station was completed, simplifying access for tourists considerably by offering a panoramic alternative to the long and winding bus route to the lofty but isolated attraction. The cable-car ride is likely to become a quintessential Hong Kong experience for visitors, thereby boosting the popularity of Po Lin as compared to Disney.

The Buddhist retreat here was founded in 1920 and a monastery built on the site. The present-day monastery, built in 1970, is located close to the Big Buddha and consists of two halls. In the main hall of the temple are three gold-painted wooden Buddhas and a smaller temple where the monks pray. In the complex, at which vegetarian meals are served to tourists, an atmosphere of serenity seems to reign, even on busy days. For a superb filmic representation of the Big Buddha and Po Lin Monastery the second part of the Hong Kong blockbuster *Infernal Affairs* is required viewing. The stunning panoramic views of the location and the sheer overwhelming bulk of the 220-ton bronze effigy are effectively conveyed thanks to the film's skilled cinematography.

David Mitchell's compelling début novel *Ghostwritten* (1999) has a chapter set entirely on Lantau Island and closes with a surreal and deftly written death scene at the Big Buddha. Corporate lawyer Neal Brose, who narrates this tale of money laundering, spectral visitation and impulsive escape from typical Hong Kong overwork stress, wanders across Lantau having deliberately missed his commuter ferry from Discovery Bay to Central. "There are so many cities in every single city," he observes as he suddenly becomes aware of the gulf separating the old inscrutable Lantau of the villages from the melting-pot artificiality of modern commuter town, Discovery Bay. His encounter with the Buddha is the defining and illuminating moment for the troubled expatriate: "Lord Buddha's lips were full and proud. Always on the verge of words but never quite speaking. His lidded eyes, hooding a secret the world needs."

Southern Lantau, with its long unspoiled coastline, is one of the most picturesque and peaceful locations in the whole of Hong Kong. Country Park trails and wooded hills end in attractive coastline and beaches, including Hong Kong's longest and most beautiful beach, Cheung Sha. The sunset on the south-west side of Lantau is not to be missed. Nor is the old fishing village of Tai O further west, famed for its salt pans and dried seafood market. Its stilted houses built on either side of the creek and four seventeenth-century temples to god of war Kwan Tai, city god Hung Shing, goddess of the sea Tin Hau and Sung princes' protector, Hau Wong make the village highly distinctive.

The remains of two Qing Dynasty forts, one at Fan Lau Kok and one near Tung Chung (complete with nineteenth-century gun battery), are all that survive of Lantau's military garrisons. Modern Tung Chung has been transformed into a bustling new town much like Tseung Kwan O or Sha Tin as a result of the North Lantau development, especially of Chek Lap Kok. The planned super-bridge linking West Lantau with Macau and Zuhai on the other side of the Pearl River Delta, still under discussion, is yet another bold leap of the imagination that epitomizes the optimism of the Hong Kong spirit, underlining its importance as the gateway to south China.

Cheung Chau

The small but vibrant island of Cheung Chau is situated off the south-east coast of Lantau. Ferries from Central come here regularly, and the island is one of the most popular weekend destinations, especially in early May at the time of the Cheung Chau Bun Festival. The name means simply "Long Island", but another name given to it is "Dumb-bell Island" because of its short, narrow strip in the middle, shaped like a hand-grip connecting two chunky weight-like extremities. Cheung Chau was a notorious pirate base in the eighteenth and nineteenth centuries, and that incorrigible pirate king Cheung Po-tsai not only set up a base here, but is reputed to have buried his treasure in one of the caves on the rocky south-west coast. During the 1920s the picturesque parts of the island were reserved, rather like the Peak, for Europeans only. As with the Peak, this obnoxiously racist exclusion ordinance was repealed after the Second World War.

Cheung Chau's active fishing port retains a traditional character and is well preserved. Fresh fish and vegetables, all island produce, are

on sale on its bustling waterfront. The island has a unique quality in Hong Kong in that it has a double waterfront, the two bays on the east and west sides forming a natural isthmus. The ferry pier is on the busier western side and is only a short walk from one of the Cheung Chau's attractions, the Bak Dai Temple (sometimes known as the "Temple of Jade Vacuity") built in 1783. Approaching this impressively sited temple from a broad flight of steps and passing the stone lion guards, one enters one of the most aesthetically pleasing of all Hong Kong's temples. The pride of the temple is an enormous iron sword reputedly dating back over a thousand years to the Sung Dynasty and found on Cheung Chau by a fisherman. This trophy, which is thought to bring good luck to fishermen, is kept in a glass case.

Bak Dai, the god of the north, has the responsibility of preventing droughts and floods by controlling the rain. He seems to have done his job properly since the island has the reputation of being harmonious and prosperous in spite of its hybrid population made up of Tanka boat people, Hoklo (from Fujian province) and Cantonese people. Perhaps that is why every May the annual *ta tsiu* (celebration and purgation) thanksgiving for Bak Dai is so exuberant. The god himself is even consulted on the question of the most auspicious date, although his choice is remarkably consistent and does not seem to stray beyond the first week of May. The festival involves an impressive parade in which children are dressed up to represent the gods Bak Dai, Kwun Yam, Tin Hau and Kwan Tai and are held aloft on the moving floats thanks to barely visible steel rods that keep them secure. The parade is called the *Piu Sik* or "floating colours" parade because the bright costumes float through the air in the manner beloved of traditional Chinese stories and also martial arts epics.

After the parade is the competition that gives the celebration its slightly misleading English name of "the Bun Festival". Three towers of buns (Chinese *bau*, or flour buns) containing thousands of buns on each are erected next to the Bak Dai Temple and young people scramble up to the top in a frenzied bid to collect the most. When one of the towers collapsed in 1978 causing serious injuries the event was banned, but in the last few years it has been revived with improved safety measures.

Cheung Chau's most famous daughter of modern times is Olympic athlete Lee Lai-shan (or San-san, as she was affectionately dubbed). She won the gold medal for windsurfing at the Olympic Games in Atlanta in 1996, and remains for the time being Hong Kong's only Olympic medallist. The winds around Cheung Chau provided particularly favourable conditions for the sport, which has increased greatly in popularity in Hong Kong in the wake of San-san's remarkable success story.

Filmmaker Evans Chan, who lived and studied in Hong Kong before migrating to the US, made his first film, the1991 *To Live(e)* about a young Hong Kong couple living on Cheung Chau. The film is inspired by the political events surrounding Hong Kong in the lead-up to the 1997 handover and the severe loss of confidence in the Territory following the Tiananmen Square massacre. It also refers to Western condemnation of Hong Kong's change of policy on the port-of-first-call policy permitting Vietnamese economic refugees to land. As female protagonist Rubie points out in one of her first frank letters to UN representative Liv Ullman, who has criticized Hong Kong people's heartlessness, the Western response to Hong Kong was hypocritical: "It remains a mystery to me that even though both China and Vietnam practice communist rule, why is it acceptable to Western governments in particular, to send refugees back to China but not Vietnam? Is it because Vietnam is still being punished for beating America in a war that ended 15 years ago?" The film is rather evocatively entitled in Chinese *Letters from a Floating World*, recalling the various literary descriptions of Hong Kong as a "floating city". It also links with Chan's other protagonist, Rubie's partner, John, who is struck by the close analogy between Hong Kong and Marco Polo's depiction of the city of Aglaura in Italo Calvino's imaginative fiction *Invisible Cities*.

Lamma Island

Lamma Island is the third biggest of the islands after Lantau and Hong Kong Island. Its name in Cantonese, Nam Nga Dou, means "south fork island" and refers to its position south-west of Hong Kong and its twin prong shape. Although the island never had a big population, it became very popular in the 1980s and 1990s as a haven for temporary Hong Kong residents whose rent was not subsidized by a corporate employer. This phenomenon was especially apparent when rents were sky-high in the feverish days before the 1998 Asian economic slump. The alternative, almost hippy, ambience of the island makes it utterly distinctive among Hong Kong's already cosmopolitan communities. Outlying island life is slow by comparison with the frenetic pace of Kowloon and the business districts of Hong Kong. On Lamma this effect is amplified by the relaxed approach of the non-indigenous, more temporary residents.

Lamma has two main focal points, both served by ferry from the Outlying Island Ferry Pier behind the IFC complex in Central. One ferry goes to Sok Kwu Wan, situated at the eastern prong of the island facing Aberdeen and noted for its plethora of waterfront seafood restaurants. The main attraction here is the fresh daily catch of the local fishermen. Evening junk trips to So Kwu Wan from Central pier rarely involve exploration further than the waterfront restaurants. The other community, what may be loosely described as Lamma's centre point, is at Yung Shue Wan at the western tip. This is livelier than So Kwu Wan because it is more residential in nature. There is a well-developed community spirit in Yung Shue Wan, blending the local and the non-local more ideally than the corresponding cosmopolitan development on Lantau, Discovery Bay. Not only are there no motorized vehicles on Lamma Island, but, crucially, there is no high-rise development on the island at all, thereby affording residents and visitors alike an uninterrupted view of Lamma's hills, sandy beaches and the surrounding sea. Close to Yung Shue Wan is a cave that was reputedly the hide-out of Cheung Po-tsai, named after the man who is arguably one of Hong Kong's first celebrities. A more recent Hong Kong celebrity, the charismatic film-star of *A Better Tomorrow* and many other films, Chow Yun-fat, was actually born on Lamma Island, but as yet there are no geographical features bearing his name.

One of the best-known imaginative representations of Lamma, and indeed any of the islands, is Stanley Kwan's prescient 1999 film *The Island Tales*, often rated in the top ten Hong Kong films of recent times. It is set on a fictionalized "Mayfly Island" but clearly recognizable as Lamma in the voice-over description. At the opening of the film the sleepy island has become energized by activity and soon we realize the reason for the cluster of police launches in the harbour. It is announced that an epidemic has broken out on the island, and it is therefore being quarantined and sealed off with immediate effect. This Hong Kong-Japanese co-production, which authentically mixes English, Cantonese and Japanese, anticipated the alarming effects of the SARS and bird-flu outbreaks in Hong Kong in the early years of the new millennium.

Po Toi San: Honourable Schoolboy, Perfidious Albion
My own imaginative introduction to Hong Kong many years ago was John Le Carré's espionage novel, *The Honourable Schoolboy*, so it is perhaps fitting that I should close with a reference to it. The thrilling finale to this novel of betrayal and conspiracy takes place on Po Toi San, south of Repulse Bay and rather isolated, in that it is closer to China mainland islands in the South China Sea than to the main cluster of Hong Kong's islands. The penultimate chapter of the novel sees Le Carré's sympathetic protagonist Jerry Westerby taking a hired boat to Po Toi Island in order to warn wealthy Hong Kong businessman Drake Ko that his (Westerby's) MI6 masters and their supposed partners from the CIA are planning to kidnap Ko's long-lost brother Nelson, a double agent for China and the Soviet Union. Westerby has worked out that the latter will arrive secretly by fishing boat at Po Toi amid the

distraction of the noisy and colourful Tin Hau festival celebrations on the island. Westerby's impression evokes a timeless quality about outlying island life, particularly those islands less touched by modernity, such as Po Toi:

Ahead of them, perhaps a mile, lay the mouth of Po To's main bay, and behind it, the low brown ghosts of China's islands. Soon they could make out a whole untidy fleet of junks and cruise boats jamming the bay, as the first jingle of drums and cymbals and uncoordinated chanting floated to them across the water. On the hill behind lay the shanty village, its tin roofs twinkling, and on its small headland stood one solid building, the temple of Tin Hau, with a bamboo scaffold lashed round it in a rudimentary grandstand, and a large crowd with a pall of smoke hanging over it and dabs of gold between.

The endgame of *The Honourable Schoolboy* exemplifies the perfidy and power politics at the dark heart of a world run by the omnipotent and unscrupulous. Fortunately, apart from some apparent Foreign Office interference in last governor Chris Patten's reforms, the transition from British rule to Chinese sovereignty seems to have been conducted in an atmosphere of good faith, defying the gloomier prognostications for Hong Kong's future. Hong Kong may be "the leaf on the pond's edge", according to poet Leung Ping-kwan (*From the Bluest Part of the Harbour*), "a border legend, a plotless detail in the weeds of history", but even Hong Kong, the metaphorical leaf on the edge of the pond, can influence the centre. China seems, to a certain extent, to be rebuilding itself along Hong Kong lines. "Under water, leaves grow together, new leaves furl in the heart. Beneath the winds' quarrels, a hidden song needs other listening."

MY CITY

This is a city
where a village boy could become a movie star of Hollywood
    renown,
where film stars demonstrated against nude photos of an actress
    taken against her will.
The death of an artist could draw thousands to the streets,
a white rose each in torrents of rain.

This is your city
where men are charmed by women intelligent and supple, skin
moisturized by humidity most months of the year. One married
    a Danish prince,
others are wooed with diamonds by neon waters and some still
    single fly
weekends to play golf.

This is our city
where vegetable sellers, taxi drivers, people in their seventies feel
    proud
a Hong Kong girl dreamt their dream, brought home Olympic
    gold surfing the winds
and waters off Cheung Chau, an island even smaller
than Hong Kong.

This is the city
which alerted the world to the deadly virus
named Sars, the city of researchers, working round the clock
    with scientists
in eight other countries, breaking its genetic code
in just three weeks.

This is a city
of people who donate money for flood victims in China.
Personal tragedies in newspapers attract immediate support
from strangers. A city where young people volunteer to clean
old people's homes
and orphans are not left alone.

This is your city
where most young men do not get drunk on Friday nights. Most
teenagers do not do drugs, few swear at their teachers and
most parents, however poor, still make sacrifices
for their children.

This is our city
with more mobile phones per square foot than anywhere else.
People do not tire of communication, with their friends,
families, colleagues,
stock brokers, estate agents, slimming consultants, fortune
tellers,
yoga trainers, image makers.

This is the city
with an award-winning airport
and glass castles where willowy shadows work long hours and
the night
begins at nine in designer style,
sparkling with wine.

This is a city
of Chinese silk, Belgian chocolates, French wine, German cars,
Swiss watches. Scottish mountains in fog give way to
Mediterranean sun and laughter. Foreigners come for a year
or two, attend concerts, watch fireworks by the harbour,
stay a lifetime.

This is your city
with measures against corruption ranking high.
Politicians attack each other only in words. Bombs are not
found on the underground and no one is imprisoned for
what they say as the whole world watches.

This is our city
where spies abound, masquerading as journalists,
photographers,
researchers, art dealers, bartenders, restaurant owners, events
organizers,
innocuous schoolteachers, honourable schoolboys and what else
I do not know.

This is the city
with a history
unforetold.

This is Hong Kong –
my city
of poetry.

Agnes Lam
20 April 2003
Hong Kong in spite of SARS (severe acute respiratory
syndrome)

Further Reading

All books published in Hong Kong unless otherwise stated

Abbas, Ackbar, *Hong Kong: Culture and the Politics of Disappearance.* Hong Kong University Press, 1997.

Auden, W. H. and Isherwood, Christopher, *Journey to a War.* London: Faber and Faber, 1939. Revised 1973.

Baker, Hugh, *Hong Kong Images: People and Animals.* Hong Kong University Press, 1990.

Barrett, Dean, *Hangman's Rock.* New York: Village East Books, 1999.

Beatty, Ann; with Ken Keobke, *A Walk along Hollywood Road.* Hippocampus Press, 1998.

Bickley, Gillian, *Moving House and Other Poems from Hong Kong.* Proverse. 2005.

Bickley, Gillian, *The Golden Needle: The Biography of Frederick Stewart.* David Lam Centre, Hong Kong Baptist University, 1997.

Bickley, Verner, *Searching for Frederick.* Asia 2000, 2001.

Booth, Martin, *Gweilo.* London: Bantam, 2004.

Chan Sui Jeung, *Traditional Chinese Festivals and Local Celebrations.* Wan Li Book Co., 2001.

Cheng Po-hung, *A Century of Hong Kong Island Roads and Streets.* Joint Publishing Company, 2003.

Cheng Po-hung and Toong Po-ming, *A Century of Kowloon Roads and Streets.* Joint Publishing Company, 2003.

Cheng Po-hung, *A Century of New Territories Roads and Streets.* Joint Publishing Company, 2003.

Cheung, Juanita and Yeoh, Andrew, *Hong Kong: A Guide to Recent Architecture.* Ellipsis-Konemann, 1998.

Cheung, Martha (ed.), *Hong Kong Collage: Contemporary Stories and Writing.* Oxford: Oxford University Press, 1998.

Clarke, David, *Hong Kong Art.* Hong Kong University Press, 2001.

Clavell, James, *Tai-Pan.* London: Hodder and Stoughton, 1975.

Clavell, James, *Noble House.* London: Hodder and Stoughton, 1981.

Coates, Austin, *Myself a Mandarin.* New York: Frederick Muller Ltd., 1968.

Endacott, G. B., *A Biographical Sketch-book of Early Hong Kong.* Singapore: Eastern Universities Press, 1962.

Edwards, Jack, *Banzai, You Bastards*. London: Souvenir, 1991.

Feign, Larry, *The World of Lily Wong*. Hambalan Press, 1995.

Gao Xingjian, trans. Mabel Lee, *One Man's Bible*. London: Flamingo, 2002.

Hacker, Arthur, *The Hong Kong Visitor's Book*. Odyssey Publications, 1997.

Hacker, Arthur, *Arthur Hacker's Wan Chai: A Social History from the Qin Dynasty to 1997*. Odyssey Publications, 1997.

Han Suyin, *A Many-Splendoured Thing*. London: Sheridan Books, 1995. (Originally published 1952 by Jonathan Cape.)

Hase, Patrick and Sinn, Elizabeth, *Beyond the Metropolis: Villages in Hong Kong*. Joint Publishing Co., 1995.

Hayes, James, *The Great Difference—The New Territories and its People, 1898-2004*. Hong Kong University Press, 2005.

Hong Kong. Pacific Century Publishers Ltd, 2003.

Hong Kong Writers' Circle, *Sweat and the City—Stories and Poems from the Hong Kong Workplace*. Hong Kong Writers' Circle, 2006.

Huang, Tsung-yi, Michelle, *Walking Between Slums and Skyscrapers—Illusions of Open Space in Hong Kong, Tokyo and Shanghai*. Hong Kong University Press, 2004.

Ingham, Mike and Xu Xi, *City Stage: Hong Kong Playwriting in English*. Hong Kong University Press, 2005.

Jefferies, Alan, *The Crocodile who Wanted to be Famous*. Sixth Finger Press, 2004.

Johnson, Elizabeth, *Recording a Rich Heritage: Research on Hong Kong's "New Territories"*. Hong Kong Heritage Museum, 2000.

Lam, Agnes, *Water, Wood, Pure Splendour*. Asia 2000, 2001.

Lanchester, John, *Fragrant Harbour*. London: Faber and Faber, 2002.

Lang, Graeme and Ragvald, Lars, *The Rise of a Refugee God: Hong Kong's Wong Tai Sin*. Oxford University Press, 1993.

Law Kar and Bren, Frank, *Hong Kong Cinema*. Maryland: Scarecrow Press, 2004.

Le Carré, John, *The Honourable Schoolboy*. London: Hodder and Stoughton, 1977.

Leung Ping-kwan, *Travelling with a Bitter Melon*. Asia 2000, 2002.

Lim, Patricia, *Discovering Hong Kong's Cultural Heritage: Hong Kong and Kowloon*. Oxford: Oxford University Press, 2002.

Lim, Patricia, *Discovering Hong Kong's Cultural Heritage: The New Territories*. Oxford: Oxford University Press, 1997.

Liu Yichang, *The Cockroach and Other Stories*. Renditions, 1995.

Lindsey, Oliver and John R. Harris, *The Battle for Hong Kong, 1941-5*. Hong Kong University Press, 2005.

Logan, Bey, *Hong Kong Action Cinema*. London: Titan Books, 1995.

Lo Kwai-Cheung, *Chinese Face-Off—the Transnational Popular Culture of Hong Kong*. Hong Kong University Press, 2005.

Mason, Richard, *The World of Suzie Wong*. Pegasus Books, 1994.

Maugham, W. Somerset, *The Painted Veil*. London: Vintage, 2001. (First published in 1925 by Heinemann.)

McKirdy, David, *Accidental Occidental poems*. Hong Kong: Chameleon Press, 2005.

Mitchell, David, *Ghostwritten*. London: Hodder and Stoughton, 1999.

Mo, Timothy, *An Insular Possession*. London: Picador, 1987.

Mo, Timothy, *The Monkey King*. London: Abacus, 1978.

Morris, Jan, *Hong Kong*. New York: Vintage, 1997. (2nd edition)

Moss, Peter, *Hong Kong—Another City, Another Stage*. FormAsia, 2002.

New, Christopher, *A Change of Flag*. Asia 2000, 2001.

New Christopher, *The Chinese Box*. Asia 2000, 2000.

Outloud. *An Anthology of Poetry from Outloud Readings, Hong Kong*. XtraLoud Press, 2002.

Parkin, Andrew (ed.), *From the Bluest Part of the Harbour*. New York: Oxford University Press, 1995.

Parkin, Andrew and Wong, Laurence, *Hong Kong Poems*. Vancouver: Ronsdale Press, 1997.

Parsons, Tony, *One For My Baby*. London: HarperCollins, 2001.

Patten, Christopher, *East and West*. London: Pan, 2002

Pullinger, Jackie; with Andrew Quicke, *Chasing the Dragon*. London: Hodder and Stoughton, 1980. Reprinted 2001.

Roberts, Lorraine, *Sights and Secrets: Sketches and Paintings of Hong Kong*. Blacksmith Books, 2003.

Roberts, Lorraine, *Sketches of SoHo*. Blacksmith Books, 2005.

Row, Jessm, *The Train to Lo Wu and Other Stories*. Los Angeles: The Dial Press, 2005.

Sekou, Lasana M., *37Poems*. Saint Martin: House of Nehesi Publishers, 2005.

Siu Kwok Kin and Sham Sze, *Heritage Trails in Urban Hong Kong*. Wan Li Book Co., 2001.

Slavick, Madeleine-Marie, *Delicate Access*. Sixth Finger Press, 2004.

Snow, Philip, *The Fall of Hong Kong: Britain, China and the Japanese Occupation*. New Haven, CT: Yale University Press, 2003.

Stokes, Edward, *Hedda Morrison's Hong Kong—Photographs and Impressions, 1946-7.* Hong Kong University Press, 2005.

Theroux, Paul, *Kowloon Tong.* London: Penguin, 1998.

Tsang, Steve, *A Modern History of Hong Kong.* Hong Kong University Press, 2004.

Tu, Elsie, *An Autobiography.* Longman, 1983.

Tu, Andrew & Elsie, *Shouting at the Mountain.* Chameleon Press, 2004.

Vittachi, Nuri, *The Ultimate"Only in Hong Kong" Collection.* Chameleon Press, 2000.

Vittachi, Nuri, *The Feng Shui Detective.* Chameleon Press, 2000.

Vittachi, Nuri, *Asian Values.* ODP. 1996.

Welsh, Frank, *A History of Hong Kong.* London: HarperCollins, 1997 (reprinted).

White, Barbara-Sue, *Hong Kong: Somewhere Between Heaven and Earth.* Oxford University Press, 1996.

Wong, David T. K., *The Evergreen Tea House: A Hong Kong Novel.* Salisbury: Muse Publishing, 2003.

Wong, Jennifer. *Summer Cicadas poems.* Hong Kong: Chamelion Press, 2006.

Wordie, Jason, *Streets—Exploring Hong Kong Island.* Hong Kong University Press, 2002

Writer's Circle, *Haunting Tales of Hong Kong.* Writers' Circle, 2005.

Xi Xi, trans. Eva Hung, *Marvels of a Floating City.* Renditions, 1997.

Xi Xi, trans. Eva Hung, *My City: A hongkong story.* Renditions, 1993.

Xu Xi, *History's Fiction.* Chameleon Press, 2001.

Xu Xi, *Hong Kong Rose.* Hong Kong: Chameleon Press, 2003.

Xu Xi, *The Unwalled City.* Chameleon Press, 2001.

Xu Xi and Ingham, Mike (eds.), *City Voices: Hong Kong Writing in English, 1945 to the Present.* Hong Kong University Press, 2002.

Yeung, Hark Wai Man and Fong So, *Our Elders.* Fong and Yeung Studio, 2000.

Young, Gavin, *Beyond the Lion Rock—The Story of Cathay Pacific Airways.* London: Penguin, 1988.

FURTHER VIEWING

Fist of Fury. Dir. Lo Wei, 1972. (Bruce Lee Siu-lung)

Way of the Dragon (a.k.a. *Return of the Dragon*). Dir. Bruce Lee Siu-Lung, 1972.

Enter the Dragon. Dir. Robert Clouse, 1973. (Bruce Lee Siu-lung)

Police Story 1, 2 and *New Police Story*. (Jackie Chan). 1984/85/2004.

A Better Tomorrow 1, 2 and *3*. Dir. John Woo (Chow Yun-fat), 1986/87/89.

A Bullet in the Head. Dir. John Woo, 1990.

Rouge. Dir. Stanley Kwan, 1987.

Island Tales. Dir. Stanley Kwan, 1991.

Days of Being Wild. Dir. Wong Kar-wai, 1990.

Chungking Express. Dir. Wong Kar-wai, 1994.

In the Mood for Love. Dir. Wong Kar-wai, 2001.

2046. Dir. Wong Kar-wai, 2004.

To Liv(e). Dir. Evans Chan.Yiu-shing, 1991.

Journey to Beijing. Dir. Evans Chan Yiu-shing, 1997.

The Life and Times of Ng Chung-ying. 2002.

Hong Kong, 1941. Dir. Po Tsieh-leong. 1984.

Love in a Fallen City. Dir. Ann Hui, 1984.

Ordinary Heroes. Dir. Ann Hui, 1999.

The House of 72 Tenants. Dir. Cho Yuen, 1972.

The World of Suzie Wong. Dir. Richard Quine, 1960.

Love is a Many Splendored Thing. Dir. Henry King, 1955.

My Name Aint Suzie. Dir. Angie Chen, 1986.

City of Glass. Dirs. Cheung Yuen-ting and Alex Law, 1998.

He's the Woman, She's the Man. Dir. Peter Chan, 1994.

The Story of Kennedy Town. Dir. Ng Ma, 1993.

Made in Hong Kong. Dir. Fruit Chan

Hollywood, Hong Kong. Dir. Fruit Chan

One Nite in Mong kok. Dir. Derek Yee, 2003.

Infernal Affairs. Dirs. Andrew Lau and Alan Mak, 2003.

The Mission. Dir. Johnny To Kei-fung, 1999.

PTU. Dir. Johnny To Kei-fung, 2003.

Election 1 and *Election 2*, Dir. Johnny To Kei-fung, 2005/06.

My Life as McDull. Dir. Brian Tse (writer Alice Mak), 2001.

McDull—Prince de la Bun. Dir. Brian Tse (writer Alice Mak), 2003.

July (documentary about 1 July 2003 protest march). Dir. Tammy Cheung.

The Chinese Box. Dir. Wayne Wang, 1997.

i-City [animation] 9. Hong Kong Arts Centre (DVD). Asia Video Publishing Co., 2005.

Below the Lion Rock. Television Drama Series. RTHK recordings. (VCD and DVD)

Index of Literary & Historical Names

Index of Places & Landmarks

HONG KONG is the epitome of the modern city and a crossroads between eastern and western cultures. Today the city is most famously characterized by its breathtaking skyscraper skyline, dominating its "fragrant" harbor. The hundred-year-old Star Ferry, which continues to ply the seven-minute route between Hong Kong Island and the Kowloon Peninsula, enhances the nocturnal magic of this unique maritime city, composed of China's southernmost peninsula and an archipelago of more than two hundred islands.

Hong Kong has always been something of an anomaly, and an outpost of empire, whether British or Chinese. Once described as a "barren island," the former fishing community has been transformed by its own economic miracle into one of Asia's World Cities, taking in its stride the territory's 1997 return to Chinese sovereignty. Beneath the surface of Hong Kong's clichéd self-image as Pearl of the Orient and Shopping Paradise, Michael Ingham reveals a city rich in history, myth, and cultural diversity.

■ City of Occupation and Immigration: The Buddhists; the Sung emperor and the Mongols; the northern Chinese; the British; other expatriates; the triads; sailors of all descriptions; the Japanese army; the Filipino "maids"; the rugby fans.

■ City of Glass, Bamboo, and Fung Shui: Temples and markets; walled village and city; skyscrapers and hotels; buildings and values—ancient and modern.

■ City of Cultural Hybridity: Sun Yat-seng and Sir Catchick Paul Chater; Chinese opera and cinema; classical music and Canto-pop; Bruce Lee and Chris Patten; Suzie Wong and Wong Kar-wai; Timothy Mo and Mickey Mouse.

Michael Ingham teaches at Lingnan University, Hong Kong, and is a founding member of the local Theatre Action drama group.

Cover photographs: Getty Images
Cover design by Tracy Baldwin

OXFORD
UNIVERSITY PRESS
www.oup.com

ISBN 978-0-19-531497-7

90000

9 780195 314977